A LEADER'S GUIDE TO
MATHEMATICS CURRICULUM TOPIC STUDY

A LEADER'S GUIDE TO MATHEMATICS CURRICULUM TOPIC STUDY

PAGE KEELEY
SUSAN MUNDRY
CHERYL ROSE TOBEY
CATHERINE E. CARROLL

CORWIN
A SAGE Company

WestEd.

Maine
MATHEMATICS
and SCIENCE Alliance

A JOINT PUBLICATION

CORWIN
A SAGE Company

FOR INFORMATION:

Corwin
SAGE Publications, Inc.
2455 Teller Road
Thousand Oaks, California 91320
E-mail: order@sagepub.com

SAGE Publications Ltd.
1 Oliver's Yard
55 City Road
London EC1Y 1SP
United Kingdom

SAGE Publications India Pvt. Ltd.
B 1/I 1 Mohan Cooperative Industrial Area
Mathura Road, New Delhi 110 044
India

SAGE Publications Asia-Pacific Pte. Ltd.
3 Church Street
#10-04 Samsung Hub
Singapore 049483

Acquisitions Editor: Dan Alpert
Associate Editor: Megan Bedell
Editorial Assistant: Sarah Bartlett
Project Editor: Veronica Stapleton
Copy Editor: Amy Rosenstein
Typesetter: Hurix Systems Pvt Ltd.
Proofreader: Scott Oney
Indexer: Sheila Bodell
Cover Designer: Michael Dubowe
Permissions Editor: Karen Ehrmann

This material is supported with funding from the National Science Foundation under a Teacher Professional Continuum, Category III, Grant no. ESI-0353315 "Curriculum Topic Study: A Systematic Approach to Utilizing National Standards and Cognitive Research," awarded to Page Keeley, PI, at the Maine Mathematics and Science Alliance. Any opinions, findings, conclusions, or recommendations expressed in this material are those of the authors and do not necessarily reflect the views of the National Science Foundation.

Library of Congress Cataloging-in-Publication Data

Keeley, Page.

A leader's guide to mathematics curriculum topic study / Page Keeley ... [et al.].

p. cm.

A Joint Publication with WestEd and the Maine Mathematics and Science Alliance

Includes bibliographical references and index.

ISBN 978-1-4129-9260-2 (paper w/CD)

1. Curriculum planning. 2. Curriculum enrichment. 3. Mathematics—Study and teaching. I. Title.

QA11.2.K437 2012
510.71–dc23

2011049014

12 13 14 15 16 10 9 8 7 6 5 4 3 2 1

Contents

Preface

OVERVIEW OF THE CTS PROJECT

Curriculum Topic Study (CTS) is a National Science Foundation–funded project that developed a process, guidelines, and materials for K–12 educators to deepen their understanding of the important science and mathematics topics they teach. CTS builds a bridge between state and national standards, research on students' ideas in science and mathematics, and opportunities for students to learn science and mathematics through improved teacher practice. Principal investigator Page Keeley, of the Maine Mathematics and Science Alliance, directed the project, in collaboration with coprincipal investigator Susan Mundry, from WestEd.

The CTS process, tools, and materials engage educators in a systematic and scholarly method of using national and state standards documents and research summaries on student learning to study a curricular topic; analyze findings from the study; and apply the new knowledge gained about content, curriculum, instruction, and assessment to teaching and this book, learning. Rather than providing the answers, CTS promotes inquiry among educators by guiding them in discovering new ideas about teaching and learning connected to the curricular topics they teach.

The four books resulting from the project include the following: *Science Curriculum Topic Study: Bridging the Gap Between Standards and Practice* (Keeley, 2005), *Mathematics Curriculum Topic Study: Bridging the Gap Between Standards and Practice* (Keeley & Rose, 2006), *A Leader's Guide to Science Curriculum Topic Study* (Mundry, Keeley, & Landel, 2010), and this book, *A Leader's Guide to Mathematics Curriculum Topic Study* (Keeley, Mundry, Rose Tobey, & Carroll, 2012). In addition to the four books, there is a website that provides updates on the project and supplementary materials to support CTS. The URL for the website is www.curriculumtopicstudy.org.

THE KNOWLEDGE BASE THAT INFORMED CTS

There has never been a greater need for students to learn and excel in mathematics. Our future society will increasingly be dependent on the STEM disciplines of science, mathematics, engineering, and technology. Experienced teachers with strong backgrounds in STEM subject matter and extensive pedagogical content knowledge may be our very best hope for supporting student learning and interest in mathematics. Pedagogical content knowledge (PCK) is the specialized knowledge about teaching and learning that helps teachers understand what makes the learning of specific topics easy or difficult for students and develop strategies for representing and formulating subject matter to make it accessible to learners (Shulman, 1986). Teachers with the background knowledge in subject matter content and specialized knowledge of teaching mathematics tend to produce higher achievement outcomes among their students (Darling-Hammond, 2000; Goldhaber & Brewer, 2000; Monk, 1994). Research on professional development programs in science and mathematics shows greater positive effects on student learning from programs that focus on building teachers' content knowledge and on understanding of how students learn subject matter (Brown, Smith, & Stein, 1996; Cohen & Hill, 2000; Kennedy, 1999; Weiss, Pasley, Smith, Banilower, & Heck, 2003; Wiley & Yoon, 1995). That is why effective teacher professional development in mathematics must not only address the content teachers need to know in order to successfully teach developmentally and conceptually appropriate ideas and skills at their grade level; it must also be designed to help teachers understand how to best identify, organize, and teach important content.

PURPOSE OF THIS BOOK

In 2006, the CTS parent book, *Mathematics Curriculum Topic Study: Bridging the Gap Between Standards and Practice* (Keeley & Rose, 2006), was published. It provides the introduction, process, and material teachers need to conduct a curriculum topic study. The purpose of the present volume, *A Leader's Guide to Mathematics Curriculum Topic Study,* is to support leaders in facilitating the CTS process and applications. It offers designs and suggestions for using CTS in a variety of professional development configurations to improve K–12 mathematics teachers' content knowledge and various aspects of their curricular, instructional, and assessment work.

Connection to Standards, Including the Common Core

Furthermore, this guide is designed to strengthen the ways national standards and research on learning are embedded within effective professional development strategies. This *Leader's Guide* is designed to provide leaders with a standards- and research-based "tool box" filled with a variety of content-specific professional development designs, tools, and resources that will strengthen professional development and help educators become more effective teachers of mathematics. It provides the flexibility to incorporate revised and new standards such as the *Common Core State Standards for Mathematics* (NGA Center & CCSSO, 2010) or the National Council of Teachers of Mathematics (NCTM) *Focal Points* (NCTM, 2006) into the existing CTS guides published in 2006 before these more recent standards were released.

Audiences

The primary audiences for this book include the many professionals who lead or support teacher professional development and preservice education in mathematics in Grades K–16. These include national, regional, and local mathematics professional developers; mathematics teacher leaders; coaches and teachers on special assignment; facilitators of professional learning communities; state and local mathematics specialists and supervisors; project partners from school-university partnerships, including mathematicians and mathematics education faculty in schools of arts and sciences and education; and faculty and student teacher supervisors in teacher education programs. All of these primary audiences can use this resource book to enhance their own teaching and provide courses, workshops, institutes, and other professional development experiences for current and future mathematics teachers.

Secondary audiences include principals, district curriculum and assessment coordinators, and curriculum materials designers and assessment developers who can use the book as a resource to strengthen the mathematics programs in their schools, improve the effectiveness of their committee work, and increase teachers' understanding of the research on mathematics teaching and the most important mathematics concepts they need to teach in K–12 to improve learning results.

The Need for CTS in Professional Development

The CTS approach to professional development that is the subject of this book is designed to enhance teachers' understanding of the mathematics content that is most important for all students to learn and how to improve students' opportunities to learn the content through effective curriculum, instruction, and assessment. CTS provides mathematics educators with processes, tools, and resources to link content standards and the research on learning to classroom practice. Classroom practice includes teachers' content knowledge, the curriculum or instructional materials they use, instructional contexts and strategies, and uses of assessment. CTS provides a powerful yet simple way for mathematics educators to engage in professional development that will help them do the following:

- Enhance their adult mathematics literacy;
- Explore implications for effective instruction;
- Identify the key ideas and skills students need to progress through their K–12 learning;
- Use research on students' learning in mathematics to inform teaching;
- Recognize connections within and across topics in mathematics as well as connections to science topics; and
- Be better consumers of their state standards, district curriculum, and instructional materials.

CTS is a valuable resource for leaders and designers of teacher learning in a variety of settings ranging from one-day to multiday workshops, to weeklong institutes, to semester preservice and graduate courses, to professional learning communities (PLCs) that meet regularly over a year or more. Over the past decade or so, professional development in mathematics has been undergoing a transformation from primarily "one size fits all" workshops and immersion experiences to more ongoing, subject and need-focused programs, often situated in teachers' real work, such as through examining student work, reviewing and selecting instructional materials, viewing and discussing video demonstration lessons, developing common lessons and assessments, and coaching and mentoring (Loucks-Horsley, Hewson, Love, & Stiles, 2010; Sparks, 2002).

These new forms of professional development have come about as the field has gained a deeper understanding of how people learn and begun to seek ways to embed teacher learning in their real work. However, a major challenge to making these forms of professional development work is ensuring that the teachers and facilitators have tools to focus this work on the appropriate K–12 content and how to teach and assess it effectively. For example, we have seen many groups coming together to examine student work with insufficient content knowledge, a lack of knowledge about students' ideas that provides a lens for identifying misconceptions and common errors, and inconsistent interpretations of the meaning and intent of the learning goal being assessed. Furthermore, the protocols needed to support teachers to learn from their professional development experience and make productive decisions about using what they learn in the classroom were often missing or ineffective.

This *Leader's Guide* was developed to bring the standards- and research-based content-specific knowledge of teaching and learning mathematics into the center of the many "new" more building-based or job-embedded professional development strategies, such as looking at student work or PLCs. It provides guidelines and structure for facilitators to engage teachers in evidence-based dialogue, supported by standards and research on learning. For example, a facilitator's use of CTS can enhance a group's collegial learning in contexts such as looking at student work, by first engaging the teachers in answering key questions such as the following:

- What should the students in this grade be expected to know about this topic?
- What common misunderstandings do students of this age-group tend to have?
- What prior knowledge is necessary to support the understanding of this topic?
- Is there content you are unsure about that you would like to learn more about in order to interpret student responses?

This information provides teachers with a stronger foundation for looking at their students' work and connecting it to key ideas in the standards and the research on how students think about the key ideas. Furthermore, it strengthens facilitators' ability to lead a group through the process by enhancing their knowledge.

Bridging the Gap

The CTS project set out to increase the use and application of national standards and research in the classroom and in professional development for teachers. The major national standards publications that guided the development of state standards and curriculum from 1989 through 2007 and much of the present are *Science for All Americans* (American Association for the Advancement of Science [AAAS], 1989), *Benchmarks for Science Literacy* (AAAS, 1993), including published summaries of research on learning in Chapter 15; *Principles and Standards for School Mathematics* (NCTM, 2000); and *Atlas of Science Literacy*, Volumes 1 and 2 (AAAS, 2001–2007)—along with *Research Companion* (NCTM, 2003). Collectively these resources provide educators with a rich professional knowledge base on the key ideas and skills needed for mathematical literacy, commonly held ideas students bring to their learning, contexts and implications for instruction, conceptual difficulties and developmental implications for learning, and the coherent growth of learning from kindergarten to high school graduation. These publications have been available to teachers since the start of standards-based reform in the mid-1990s. Yet, through the hundreds of CTS workshops the authors have given and observed, the majority of teachers who are first introduced to CTS indicate they have never used these seminal resources.

In addition, this *Leader's Guide* includes suggestions for flexibly adding the *Common Core State Standards for Mathematics* or the NCTM *Focal Points* to the CTS process. These recent standards documents came out after the CTS parent book was published. However, CTS is such a flexible process that can accommodate updates to standards and new research that it is very easy to assimilate new reform documents into the CTS process. In other words, CTS is never obsolete! Every introductory CTS workshop we piloted began with an overview of the national standards and research publications listed above accompanied by a show of hands when the following questions were asked: "How many of you have heard of or own this book and use it? How many of you have heard of or own this book but have never used it? How many of you are hearing about and seeing this book for the first time?" Most surprising are the number of hands that still go up when the last question is asked. We may assume that the same response will be given to the *Common Core* and the *Focal Points.* This lack of use of the professional publications that form the backbone of standards- and research-based teaching and learning is further amplified in studies such as the National Research Council's 2002 report, *Investigating the Influence of Standards.* A conclusion of this report was that although they have been out for almost a decade, standards have not made a significant impact where it matters most, in the classroom.

Furthermore, new teachers are now entering the profession who were elementary school students at the time standards were first introduced. Career changers are also entering the profession as new teachers. They missed the 1990s' wave of learning about standards while they were working in noneducation fields. During the 1990s and early part of the 21st century, today's experienced teachers were introduced to standards and the basic principles of standards-based reform. For more than a decade, they have been immersed in a flurry of activities such as alignment of curriculum, backwards planning for standards-based lessons, and development of aligned assessments. Although the attention to standards has subsided somewhat as teachers developed familiarity and acceptance of standards, we still need to acknowledge that new teachers, both young and career changers, entering teaching today did not experience the introduction to standards that our experienced teachers did. With the new *Common Core,* this flurry of activity will continue. Today standards are almost taken for granted. However, that does not mean that experienced teachers are using them effectively. In addition, the research has not been easily accessed by teachers outside of a university setting. Clearly, although we have made progress in the last few years, we still have many more years ahead of us to reach the level of implementation where all teachers are effectively focusing on standards and using research to inform their teaching.

Translating the standards and research into practical use in the classroom is a continuing challenge for mathematics education reform. The materials developed by the CTS project are designed to support educators to meet this challenge. The developers of CTS realized that teachers needed both a reason to use the national standards and research on learning as well as an efficient process for working with them. Facilitators of teacher learning needed realistic designs and suggestions for how to engage teachers in new forms of professional development that lead them to identify and examine the various considerations that support science literacy learning for all students. CTS was developed to help teachers and professional developers methodically incorporate the standards and research into their work.

CTS began with identifying 92 key curricular topics in the standards and thoroughly vetting the common standards and research documents to identify the readings that could be used by teachers and professional developers to explore and study these key topics. Tools for applying the study results were developed, followed by designs for professional development that would embed CTS into a variety of teacher learning contexts.

Implications for Professional Development

Finding time to stay abreast of the standards and research is difficult. A teacher's day is already jam-packed, and many legitimately ask, "Where can we find the time we need to learn all this?" The answer lies in making better use of existing professional development time and in engaging in learning about and using the standards and research in the regular school day. The authors believe every professional development experience, whether it is a content institute, an overview to new curriculum materials, a teacher-directed study group, grade-level team meetings to examine student work, or others, is a ripe opportunity to use CTS. The current trend to providing more substantive and ongoing professional development and forming learning communities is transforming what and how teachers learn, yet it is essential that these new forms of professional development focus on important content and how to teach it (Feger & Arruda, 2008; Hord & Sommers, 2008; Loucks-Horsley, Hewson, Love, & Stiles, 2010; Wei, Darling-Hammond, Andree, Richardson, & Orphanos, 2009).

The CTS process provides the resources that link the theoretical knowledge that comes from a careful examination of standards and research to the situations teachers face in their schools and classrooms. It is this situated use of CTS that supports such a wide variety of strategies for teacher learning.

Studies have also shown that the types of professional development closely linked to improved student learning provide opportunities for teachers to engage in professional dialogue and critical reflection (Birman, Desimone, Garet, & Porter, 2000; Cohen & Hill, 1998; Weiss et al., 1999). Increasingly, professional development is focused on breaking down the isolation of teaching and building a professional culture in schools characterized by groups of teachers examining student results and thinking, reflecting on practice, discussing research and what works, and developing teacher leadership (Schmoker, 2004). The advantage of teachers working collaboratively and learning from their own practice is that teaching practice, aligned with clear and explicit student learning goals, becomes the centerpiece of the professional development. Teachers examine and/or critique actual artifacts of teaching and learning, such as lessons, student work, and cases of teaching and learning. CTS can provide the focus and direction collaborative groups need to advance their learning. Teachers in these groups learn to engage in authentic dialogue about the specific teaching and learning ideas in the standards and how these ideas compare with their own curriculum, instruction, and assessment. They analyze research on children's ideas and compare those to their own students' ideas. They look for ways to incorporate the research into their own curriculum and reflect on how to use this knowledge to enhance learning. For science teacher collaboration to be successful, it needs a strong content focus and well-developed skills for dialogue and reflection. CTS provides those critical elements.

CTS Impact on Teachers and Teacher Educators

This *Leader's Guide* is designed to enhance teachers' and professional developers' knowledge and performance (e.g., strengthen content knowledge and support the design of content-rich professional development). In mathematics, teachers and professional developers are particularly challenged because even if they are knowledgeable in one mathematics grade level, they may not know much about other grade levels they are working with—CTS meets the diverse needs of a wide range of teachers and leaders in mathematics (e.g., the high school teacher leader who is working with elementary teachers on instructional strategies for first graders, or the university mathematician codeveloping a middle school curriculum).

In working with teachers around the country, the CTS developers have documented the substantial impact the process has had on what teachers understand about mathematics learning and how they approach their curriculum, instruction, and assessment. In the evaluation surveys and interviews, teachers who use CTS have reported that they

- deepen their understanding of the mathematics content they need to teach K–12 curricular topics effectively;
- can better translate mathematics content for adult learning (such as through university courses) to content appropriate for K–12 settings;
- can identify and clarify core knowledge and skills in mathematics, including broad integrated themes, big ideas, concepts, skills and procedures, specific ideas, terminology, facts, and formulas embedded in the content standards and curricular objectives;
- improve coherency of mathematical ideas as they develop over multiple grade levels;
- make effective use of the research base on student learning to identify potential learning difficulties, developmental considerations, and misconceptions or common errors associated with a mathematics curricular topic;
- apply effective content-specific pedagogical strategies and identify useful contexts for teaching mathematical ideas as they relate to a particular topic;
- improve their ability to make connections within and across mathematics topics;
- improve their ability to integrate mathematics with science topics; and
- engage in substantive evidence-based discourse with their colleagues about goals for student learning, modifications needed in instructional materials, and methods for enhancing student understanding.

Mathematics leaders (teacher leaders, university faculty, instructional coaches and mentors, professional developers, and mathematics specialists) also benefit personally from using CTS. Leaders have commented that they have been able to increase the focus of the professional development on content and PCK and achieve greater results. For example, as part of engaging teachers in a mathematics lesson, some professional developers now have teachers do a CTS on the topic of the lesson before they experience the lesson. This both enhances teachers' understanding of the important content and builds awareness of common preconceptions, errors, and overgeneralizations students might bring to their learning. By embedding CTS into their content institutes, mathematicians and scientists increase the opportunity for teachers to translate their content-learning experiences into developmentally and conceptually appropriate content and activities for the grade level they teach. This bridge between adult learning, often the "science and mathematics of scientists and mathematicians," and K–12 student learning, or "school science and mathematics," has been missing from many of the professional content learning experiences designed for teachers by experts in a scientific or mathematical field. These experts know their content well but are unfamiliar with PCK and K–12 learning. CTS is the tool that leaders can use to help teachers situate their adult learning experiences in the classrooms or other contexts in which they teach.

Leaders have also commented on the versatility of the materials and how they have been able to use them in a variety of situations, including one-on-one coaching, PLCs, small informal teacher meetings, and large content institutes. Although the materials may be used differently depending on where a teacher is on the teacher professional continuum, CTS adds value to every level of teaching from preservice to novice teachers to experienced teachers to teacher leaders and to those who leave the teaching profession to support teachers. The process and the quality of the materials are helping all types of leaders in mathematics education strengthen their work with teachers by focusing more precisely on standards and the research on students' ideas in mathematics. In addition, when used along with mathematics leaders, it strengthens the connections and collaboration among the STEM disciplines.

Ultimately the impact of CTS is demonstrated through the improved learning of students taught by teachers who regularly use the process to inform their teaching. These students benefit from higher levels of engagement because of teachers' understanding of how to make content accessible to all students. They also benefit from increased coherence in the use of curriculum materials and design of instruction as their teachers use CTS to identify gaps in the curriculum, select appropriate representations, strengthen the connections among concepts, and use a variety of formative assessment techniques to elicit students' ideas and monitor learning throughout the course of instruction.

ORGANIZATION OF THIS BOOK

The *Leader's Guide* is organized into seven chapters. Chapter 1 provides the overall rationale for CTS, addresses the question "Why should educators use CTS?," and introduces leaders to the language of CTS. Chapter 2 provides the leader with an understanding of what the CTS process is and discusses how it supports the development of mathematical literacy. Chapter 3 is written especially for professional developers planning to use CTS in their work with teachers. It summarizes key information about research on effective professional development for mathematics teachers and provides the overall tips and strategies for using CTS in professional development. Chapter 4 includes the designs to lead introductory sessions for CTS. If you are just getting started with CTS, you can use these designs to help your participants experience CTS by doing partial or full-guided topic studies on several topics that will acquaint them with the process as well as the resources. Chapter 5 provides the designs and guidelines for leading full topic studies on particular topics (e.g., fractions), guidelines for designing your own full topic study, and suggestions for combining topics. Chapter 6 leads you through ways to use the applications of CTS in a content, curricular, instructional, or assessment context. Finally, Chapter 7 discusses examples of how to embed CTS in ongoing professional development strategies, such as how to use CTS within lesson study groups or collaborative inquiry into examining students' thinking. The CD-ROM contained in the back of the book provides masters for all handouts and PowerPoint presentations to accompany the introductory material in Chapters 1 through 3 as well as the designs and suggestions in Chapters 4 through 7. In addition, we encourage you to check out the CTS website at www.curriculumtopicstudy .org for updates to this *Leader's Guide* and materials shared by CTS users.

Acknowledgments

This CTS *Leader's Guide* was informed by the work of many dedicated professionals from across the nation who are working to improve the quality of mathematics education for all students. The Maine, New Hampshire, and Vermont teacher leaders participating in Maine's Governor's Academy and the Northern New England Co-Mentoring Network, and the staff at the Maine Mathematics and Science Alliance were the CTS pioneers, trying out the earliest versions of the CTS process and applying it to their roles as teacher leaders, mentors in their districts, and professional developers. They generously gave of their time and suggestions for improving the process and embedding it into ongoing professional development.

Our many national field testers and pilot sites contributed significant suggestions for the development and revisions of the tools and designs included in this *Leader's Guide*. Our pilot and field testers included mathematics specialists, university faculty from colleges of arts and sciences and education, Mathematics and Science Partnership Project Directors, Fellows from WestEd's National Academy for Science and Mathematics Education Leadership, regional professional development providers, state and district mathematics coordinators and specialists, and professional developers. They generously took time to try out our designs, provide us with feedback, and gather and provide workshop comments from their participants. The authors wish to thank all of the hundreds of mathematics facilitators and workshop participants who generously agreed to provide us with valuable feedback.

We also wish to thank our project design team who gave their time and expertise to advise us and guide the development process. Special thanks go to Cathy Carroll and Karen Cerwin from WestEd; Joëlle Clark, Northern Arizona University; Francis Eberle, National Science Teachers Association; Jeanne Harmon, Center for Strengthening the Teaching Profession; Mark Kaufman, Retired Director of the TERC Eisenhower Regional Alliance; Fred Gross, Education Development Center; Nancy Kellogg, Science Consultant, Boulder, Colorado; Pam Pelletier, Boston Public Schools and Adjunct Instructor, Harvard University; and Joyce Tugel, Maine Mathematics and Science Alliance. We also wish to thank our evaluator, Bill Nave, for the insights he shared with us that informed development of this project and helped us understand the impact CTS has on teacher learning.

We thank all the authors and organizations that developed the resource books used for the CTS process. Without the vision and ideas you put into these resources, the CTS process would not exist. These include the following: Dr. James Allen Paulos of *Beyond Numeracy*; the American Association of Science and Project 2061, *Science for All Americans*, *Benchmarks for Science Literacy*, and *Atlas of Science Literacy*,

Volumes 1 and 2; and the National Council of Teachers of Mathematics, *Principles and Standards for School Mathematics* and *Research Companion.*

We are grateful to the National Science Foundation for funding this project. We especially wish to thank our program officer, Dr. Michael Haney, for his support and encouragement.

Our very special thanks go to our colleagues at WestEd and the Maine Mathematics and Science Alliance who have provided input, examples, and materials for this book. Our deep appreciation also goes to Laurie Mitchell, CTS administrative assistant at the Maine Mathematics and Science Alliance, whose organizational skills were invaluable in assembling materials for the national review and helping assemble the CD-ROM.

Our deep gratitude to Dan Alpert, our acquisitions editor at Corwin, who never gave up on us, despite delays, delays, and more delays because of our busy schedules and juggling of several simultaneous manuscripts. Thank you for your patience and perseverance!

We especially give our thanks to our wonderful family members who give us tons of support and put up with our long hours of work on weekends and holidays and love us anyway.

We wish to acknowledge the pilot testers, field testers, and reviewers of the materials in this book:

Caroline Arline
MATHS MSP Project, ME

Jean May Brett
Louisiana Department of Education, LA

Kathy DiRanna
WestEd K–12 Alliance, CA

Matthew Freedman and Nancy Bunt
Allegheny Math & Science Collaborative, PA

Stephanie Hall
LEARN, CT

Karen Heinz
Rowan University, NJ

Kelly Kenney
Hickman Mills School District, MO

Christie McDougal and Mary Knuck
Arizona Department of Education, AZ

Theresa Moody and Wil Van der Veen
Raritan Valley Community College, NJ

Darlene Ryan
Chapel Hill, NC

Donna Sorila and Eileen Spinney
Fitchburg Public Schools, MA

Meghan Southworth
Maine Mathematics and Science Alliance, ME

Billie Sparks
Wisconsin Academy of Staff Development, WI

Kim Zeidler
University of Kentucky Math & Science Partnership, KY

About the Authors

Page Keeley is the principal investigator, project director, and developer of the CTS project. Page is the senior science program director at the Maine Mathematics and Science Alliance (MMSA; www.mmsa .org). Page designs and oversees several projects for the MMSA, consults with school districts and organizations throughout the United States, is a frequent speaker at national and state conferences, and serves on several national advisory boards. She was the principal investigator/project director on two other NSF-funded projects—the *Northern New England Co-Mentoring Network* (www.nnecn.org) and *PRISMS-Phenomena and Representations for Instruction in Middle School Science*, a National Science Digital Library project in partnership with the American Association for the Advancement of Science (AAAS) Project 2061. Page is also the director of the Maine Governor's Academy for Science and Mathematics Education Leadership.

In addition to the four CTS books, Page is also the primary author of more than eight publications on formative assessment in science and mathematics featured on the website www.uncoveringstudentideas.org. She is a fellow of the first cohort group of the National Academy for Science Education Leadership. Prior to joining the MMSA in 1996, Page taught high school biology and general chemistry and middle school science and mathematics in Maine for 15 years. She served as National Science Teachers Association (NSTA) District II director from 1997–2000, served on the NSTA Executive Board from 1997–1998, and was the 2008–2009 president of the National Science Teachers Association. She received the Presidential Award for Excellence in Secondary Science Teaching in 1992, the Milken Foundation National Educator Award in 1993, and the AT&T Maine Governor's Fellow for Technology in 1994.

Prior to teaching, she worked as a research assistant at the Jackson Laboratory of Mammalian Genetics in Bar Harbor, Maine. In 2010, she received the Susan Loucks-Horsley Award from the National Staff Development Council for her leadership in science and mathematics professional development and change. She is the science education delegation leader for the People to People Citizen Ambassador Professional Programs and led the South Africa delegation in 2009, China in 2010, and India in 2011. She received her B.S. in life sciences from the University of New Hampshire and her M.Ed. in science education from the University of Maine.

Susan Mundry is a coprincipal investigator for the CTS project and is a coauthor of the science and mathematics CTS *Leader's Guides*. Susan is the deputy director of Learning Innovations at WestEd (www .wested.org) and associate director of WestEd's Math, Science & Technology Programs, where she leads projects focused on improving educational practice and oversees the research and evaluation projects at WestEd. Susan is codirector of a research study examining the distribution of highly qualified teachers in New York and Maine for the Northeast and Islands Regional Educational Laboratory and is the coproject director for the Intel Mathematics Initiative. She is the codirector of the National Academy for Science and Mathematics Education Leadership, a leadership academy designed to enhance the knowledge, skills, and strategies of leaders in science and mathematics education reform. Building on this work, she provides technical assistance to several large urban school districts engaged in enhancing leadership and improving mathematics and science programs.

Susan coauthored the NSF-funded toolkit, *Teachers as Learners*, a videotape collection of eighteen professional development programs, a guidebook, and website activities that illustrate diverse strategies for teacher learning in science and mathematics. She was also a coprincipal investigator of an NSF project developing a simulation game for effective professional development and codeveloped *The Change Game* (*Making Change for School Improvement*), a simulation game that enhances leaders' abilities to lead change efforts in schools and districts. She has conducted several research studies on attributes of effective professional development, including serving on the national evaluation team for the study of the Eisenhower Professional Development Program led by the American Institutes for Research, where she worked on the development of national survey instruments and the protocols for case studies. She is coauthor of the best-selling book *Designing Professional Development for Teachers of Science and Mathematics* (third edition 2009), *Leading Every Day: 124 Actions for Effective Leadership* (2002, 2006), which was named the National Staff Development Council 2003 Book of the Year, and *The Data Coach's Guide to Improving Learning for All Students* (2008).

Cheryl Rose Tobey is a coprincipal investigator for the mathematics section of the CTS project and coauthor of *Mathematics Curriculum Topic Study: Bridging the Gap Between Standards and Practice* (2006). Cheryl was formerly the Mathematics program director at the Maine Mathematics and Science Alliance, where she served as the principal investigator and project director of two Title IIa State Mathematics and Science Partnership projects. Cheryl was also the coprincipal investigator and project director for MMSA's NSF-funded Local Systemic Change Initiative, Broadening Educational Access to Mathematics in Maine (BEAMM). She currently works for the Education Development Center (EDC), where she is the implementation director for the Education Pathways to Mathematics Achievement Study and a mathematics specialist for the NSF-funded Formative Assessment in the Mathematics Classroom: Engaging Teachers and Students (FACETS) and Differentiated Professional Development: Building Mathematics Knowledge for Teaching Struggling Students (DPD) projects. She also serves as a project director for an Institute for Educational Science (IES) project, Eliciting Mathematics Misconceptions (EM2).

Cheryl's work is primarily in the areas of school leadership, school-based program support, materials development, mathematics professional development, formative assessment and research study implementation. Cheryl was a fellow in Cohort 4 of the National Academy for Science and Mathematics Education Leadership and is the primary author of the *Uncovering Student Thinking: 25 Formative Assessment Probes* series, which uses the development process described in this volume, *A Leader's Guide to Mathematics Curriculum Topic Study*. Before joining MMSA in 2001, Cheryl was a high school and middle school mathematics teacher in Washington State and Maine for 10 years. She received her B.S. in mathematics education from the University of Maine at Farmington and her M.Ed. at City University, Seattle, in Curriculum and Instruction.

 **Catherine E. Carroll** is a contributing author of the *Leader's Guide to Mathematics Curriculum Topic Study.* She is a senior research associate and project director in WestEd's Science, Technology, Engineering, and Mathematics Program, engaged in several mathematics education projects. Cathy is coprincipal investigator for the NSF-funded Researching Mathematics Leader Learning project, conducting research on how leaders develop and enhance their skills as mathematics professional developers to support teachers in deepening their mathematics knowledge for teaching. She coauthored *Learning to Lead Mathematics Professional Development (LLMPD),* a video-based case curriculum designed to develop leaders' facilitation skills, content knowledge, and pedagogy, enabling them to design and implement effective, high-quality mathematics professional development, and coordinates leadership development services related to the *LLMPD* materials. She also coauthored WestEd's *Making Mathematics Accessible to English Learners: A Guidebook for Teachers* (2009) and coordinates related workshop opportunities. Cathy served as the mathematics content specialist for Teachers as Learners: A Multimedia Kit for Professional Development in Science and Mathematics, a collaborative project of WestEd, WGBH, and the Boston Museum of Science. She also served on design teams for the Arizona Middle School Mathematics & Science Initiative as well as the Advisory Board for the Mathematics for All Project, a collaboration of Bank Street College and the Education Development Center. Previously, Cathy was director of the Mathematics Renaissance Leadership Alliance, a mathematics leadership initiative funded by the California Department of Education to work with district-based leadership cadres in developing teacher leadership and administrative support for quality mathematics programs. Earlier she served as associate director for Mathematics Renaissance K–12 and, prior to that, as regional director for the Middle Grades Mathematics Renaissance, a component of California's State Systemic Initiative. Cathy has nearly twenty years of experience as a middle school mathematics teacher. She is recognized nationally for her expertise in mathematics leadership and professional development, consulting with districts and projects across the country to design and facilitate leadership seminars. She received the 2008 Susan Loucks-Horsley Professional Development Award from the National Staff Development Council.

Introduction to the *Leader's Guide*

This book, *A Leader's Guide to Mathematics Curriculum Topic Study,* is the natural companion to the parent book, *Mathematics Curriculum Topic Study: Bridging the Gap Between Standards and Practice* (Keeley & Rose, 2006). The curriculum topic study (CTS) parent book provides an introduction to the process of CTS; the resources used to engage in CTS; various ways to use CTS to support content knowledge, curriculum, instruction, and assessment; and the 92 CTS study guides that contain the prevetted readings used in CTS. It has become an essential resource used by mathematics educators to improve their practice. This Leader's Guide offers practical suggestions for using the parent book, including tools, designs, and additional resources for incorporating CTS into the work mathematics leaders do to support teacher learning. This *Leader's Guide* was developed to assist teacher educators and leaders, such as preservice faculty, mathematicians who provide content support to teachers, mathematics specialists, instructional coaches, teacher leaders, and professional development providers, in developing the professional knowledge base mathematics teachers need to be effective in the classroom. It provides tested strategies for introducing the CTS process that builds preservice and inservice teachers' knowledge of the research on learning mathematics and the national standards, focal points, and benchmarks that are the bedrock for ensuring quality teaching and mathematical literacy for all. Furthermore, it supports forms of teacher learning in collegial groups and professional learning communities (PLCs) that are guided by a common knowledge base as teachers work together to plan lessons, examine student work, develop assessments, select curriculum, and go about the daily business of educating our nation's youth.

ADVICE FOR USING THIS *LEADER'S GUIDE*

Users of this *Leader's Guide* may wonder how they should begin using this book. You may be asking, *Where do I start? In what order do I use it? What else do I need to effectively use this book?* There is no single answer to these questions. It depends on your familiarity with

CTS and your purpose for using it. We do encourage all leaders who use this *Leader's Guide* to have a copy of the parent book as well as the resources listed in Table 1.1. Often, throughout this guide, we will be referring you to sections and pages in the parent book, and it will help you to have it to consult.

Table 1.1   Essential Resources for Leaders of CTS

CTS Resources	Available Through
Mathematics Curriculum Topic Study (Keeley & Rose, 2006)	Corwin (http://www.corwin.com)
Beyond Numeracy (Paulos, 1992)	Major bookstores and online booksellers
Science for All Americans (AAAS, 1989)	Oxford University Press (http://www.us.oup.com/us/) Major online booksellers Available to read online at http://www.project2061.org/publications/sfaa/default.htm
Benchmarks Online (AAAS, 1993–2009)	Oxford University Press (http://www.us.oup.com/us/) Major online booksellers Available to read online at (includes new and revised benchmarks) (http://www.project2061.org/publications/bsl/default.htm)
Principles and Standards for School Mathematics (NCTM, 2000)	Major online booksellers NCTM (http://nctm.org) Available to read online for NCTM members
Research Companion to Principles and Standards for School Mathematics (NCTM, 2003)	Major online booksellers NCTM (http://nctm.org)
Atlas of Science Literacy Volumes 1 and 2 (AAAS, 2001–2007)	Major online booksellers NSTA Press (http://www.nsta.org/store/) All maps are available online at http://strandmaps.nsdl.org
Common Core State Standards for Mathematics (NGA Center & CCSSO, 2010)	Common Core State Standards Initiative (CCSSI) (http://corestandards.org)

Note: Although not in the original CTS guides, the Common Core State Standards can be added by the facilitator to Section III in the 2006 CTS guides.

Before you begin using this *Leader's Guide*, it is important to become familiar with the parent book, CTS resources, and experience a CTS. If you have never conducted a CTS on your own, pull out your parent book. From it, select one of the 92 CTS topics of interest to you, and follow the process described in Chapter 3 of that book, "Engaging in Curriculum Topic Study." Wear two hats as you conduct your own CTS: (1) As a learner, reflect on what knowledge you gained as you did the CTS, and (2) as a leader of professional development, consider what you need to do to facilitate this type of learning with others. Compare what learners do with what a facilitator would do throughout the process on pages 49–50 of the parent book to get a sense of what the teachers you work with will be doing and what you will be doing as a CTS facilitator.

CTS is a versatile professional development tool with multiple uses and purposes. We do not prescribe a linear, step-by-step process for using CTS in your work. Where you start, the sequence you use, the designs you select, the tools you use, and the supplementary resources you include will be as varied as the diverse types of leaders who are using CTS. Each of the chapters in this book will begin by describing what is in the chapter and how leaders might use it. Although step-by-step scripts are provided for many of the CTS designs, we encourage you to adapt the materials to the needs of your audience and to your own facilitation style.

Before implementing the designs, tools, and suggestions in this book, it is important to have a deep understanding of how CTS enhances professional development, the different purposes it achieves for teacher learning, the variety of ways to embed it into your own teacher learning contexts, and the language used throughout CTS and this book. This groundwork should be done first if you plan to regularly use CTS in your work. This chapter addresses the question "Why Use CTS?" It will provide you with the rationale for using CTS and lay the groundwork for you to use the material provided in the subsequent chapters.

UNDERLYING BELIEFS

As suggested in the Preface to this book, the education field has undergone a tremendous transformation in beliefs about what constitutes effective learning for both children and adults and what it takes to be a quality teacher. There is a growing recognition of the complexity of teaching and the vast array of knowledge a teacher must possess to meet the needs of a wide range of students. We know more now than ever before about procedural and conceptual learning in mathematics, and we are learning more all the time. As the education field, and in fact our entire culture, becomes one that is knowledge-using and knowledge-producing, teachers are increasingly using and contributing to the education knowledge base. These developments have provoked two strong underlying beliefs that undergird the CTS work. These are as follows:

1. Teachers, like other professionals, must possess and continue to build their own *specialized knowledge base*. For teachers, this consists of content knowledge and knowledge about teaching in a specific content area, including an understanding of how children of a certain age learn, called pedagogical content knowledge (PCK). Teachers continue throughout their careers to develop and actively use their specialized knowledge base to guide their educational practice.

2. Teachers, like other professionals, should be engaged in *collegial professional learning communities* that are guided by strategic and enduring goals and focused on enhanced learning and ongoing improvement. These communities should be knowledge-using and knowledge-producing and be guided by two very basic ideas: Use the knowledge generated from standards and research to provide evidence and justification for your ideas, and learn from the expertise of others shared through peer-reviewed literature, conference presentations, and the wisdom of thoughtful practitioners.

Each of these beliefs has changed how we think about the content and purpose for professional development for mathematics teachers and has had a major impact on how teachers are engaged in professional learning. CTS supports teachers to build their specialized teaching knowledge and participate in productive collegial communities focused squarely on putting research and standards to work in the classroom. Throughout this book, you will see examples of how teachers can use CTS to enhance their content and pedagogical knowledge in collegial, collaborative learning environments. You will see how teachers use knowledge gained from CTS as well as contribute new knowledge about teaching and learning in their own unique contexts through professional development strategies described in Chapter 7 such as study groups (or PLCs), case discussions, and video demonstration lessons.

THE NEED FOR A COMMON PROFESSIONAL KNOWLEDGE BASE

Over the last few decades, the education field has learned more about what it takes to develop qualified teachers in mathematics and the knowledge, skills, and mind-sets that support teaching and learning in this discipline. New ideas have been shaped and influenced by the growing research base that provides educators with insights into how students develop their understanding of specific ideas in mathematics and how mathematical misunderstandings may impede learning if they are not surfaced and taken into account when designing instruction. There is greater awareness and use of recommended practices such as establishing a clear and coherent curriculum, focusing on an explicit set of standards-based learning goals, using instructional strategies that support and deepen student learning of key mathematical ideas, and embedding standards- and research-based assessments throughout instruction that inform teaching and provide information on the extent to which students are achieving a learning goal. Increasingly educators are asked by administrators and others to justify requests for new programs or practices with objective evidence of success. Stakeholders want to know what works and are looking to professional educators to identify and explain effective practices that can lead to increased student achievement.

These developments have given way to new ideas about teacher professional development. We know that mathematics teaching involves much more than procedures, hands-on activities, and use of manipulatives, teaching tips, and general pedagogical techniques. Professional teachers must possess both content and PCK, the specialized knowledge of content and how children learn it. This knowledge enables teachers to focus on important learning goals and provide developmentally appropriate and coherent instruction and assessments. Quality professional development programs are increasingly focused on enhancing teachers' understanding of mathematical content and how to teach it. Teachers are learning to review and revise their instructional materials and methods to better reflect alignment with standards and research on learning and are taking collective responsibility for knowing not only their content, but also how children think about mathematical ideas and what types of experiences, examples, and representations can best support learning.

One of the characteristics of professional teachers is their belief in the importance of acquiring their own professional libraries or having access to professional resources to regularly inform their teaching and expand their knowledge base. Knowledge of effective mathematics teaching does not end after graduation from a teacher preparation program or graduate program. Teachers are constantly seeking the wisdom and knowledge shared by researchers and expert practitioners that help them grow and develop as professional mathematics teachers. There is a plethora of professional literature to support mathematics teacher learning. However, the vast collection of literature can be narrowed down to six major publications that best support standards- and research-based teaching and learning across all the areas of mathematics, grade levels, and teacher expertise. These are the common and collective resources identified by the CTS project that can be used with the 92 mathematics curriculum topics identified in the parent CTS book. These professional resources should be in the library of every mathematics teacher and teacher educator, whether they are part of their own collection or shared within a school or organization. These resources are listed in Table 1.1 and provide a common knowledge base that all teachers can refer to and use. The fact that these books were authored by highly respected scientists, mathematicians, researchers, and mathematics educators and some, such as the national standards documents, went through an extensive national review process that involved consensus from the mathematics education community at large makes them credible and relevant to all mathematics educators striving to develop shared understandings of content, teaching, and learning. Having access to these books is like having an expert at your fingertips 24/7! In addition, we have added the link to the *Common Core State Standards for Mathematics* to Table 1.1 (NGA Center & CCSSO, 2010). When the CTS parent book was published in 2006, these standards were not available. Hence, they are not included in the CTS study guides. However, facilitators can choose to add these to the guides when working with a group to conduct a topic study. More information about including the *Common Core State Standards for Mathematics* is included in Chapters 2, 4, and 5.

CTS MAKES THE KNOWLEDGE BASE ACCESSIBLE

As described in the Preface, many teachers, and even some teacher educators, have never used or even heard of some of these resources, even though most have been out for more than a decade. As the use of CTS grows, these resources are becoming better known and more frequently used in the mathematics education community. As a facilitator, one of the changes you will see firsthand as you use CTS with teachers is the renewed emphasis and embrace of the national standards and research literature, even though states have their own standards.

Prior to CTS, getting to know and use national standards and research on learning posed several difficulties. The focus on state standards shifted teachers' attention away from the more detailed source documents on which many of these state standards were based. As we discussed in the Preface, we found that many teachers had no knowledge of publications like *Science for All Americans* (American Association for the Advancement of Science [AAAS], 1989) and the *Research Companion to Principles and Standards for School Mathematics* (National Council for Teachers of Mathematics [NCTM], 2003). Some had heard of the NCTM *Principles and Standards for School Mathematics* (NCTM, 2000) and the *Benchmarks for Science Literacy* (AAAS, 1993, 2009) but had never opened a copy or even realized that these publications contained much more than a list of what students were expected to know and be able to do in mathematics. They didn't know enough about the publications to know how useful they could be in informing teaching and learning. Furthermore, we now have the *Common Core State Standards for Mathematics* (NGA Center & CCSSO, 2010), which was not available when CTS was first published in 2006.

For others, the standards and research publications were available, but a process for using them was missing. Some teachers found navigating through the publications to be difficult and unwieldy. They consulted the standards documents, sifting through the hundreds of pages of text to find what was relevant to their curriculum, their students, or their teaching and often struggled and became frustrated because the answers they were seeking were so hard to find. They did not know how to use the essays or why the learning goals were written a certain way. They struggled with figuring out how to sequence and connect standards coherently. Many never realized there was a chapter in the back of the *Benchmarks for Science Literacy* that contained summaries of mathematics research connected to the chapters describing what all students should know. They didn't realize how *Science for All Americans* is the seminal, enduring document that lays out a vision for the standards documents, including an eloquent description of the mathematics all adults should know and be able to use to be considered a mathematically literate person.

For those who persevered, their efforts paid off in gaining clarity about the standards and how they relate to teaching and learning, but it took a substantial time commitment and their searches often ended when they identified learning goals for their particular grade span. As advocated by Project 2061 of the AAAS, all teachers need a broad and deep understanding of all science, mathematics, and technology topics, what we commonly refer to today as the STEM disciplines. They should know what every 12th-grade graduate is expected to know and the level of schooling in which students are expected to learn certain ideas in mathematics. They should understand not only the learning goals at each grade span, but also the research suggesting what is difficult or easy for students to learn, the contexts and strategies that support learning, the connections within and across mathematics topics, and how a coherent understanding grows over the K–12 sequence. But how do teachers develop this knowledge? Where can they find the tools and the time? CTS provides the means and the organized process to help education professionals use these professional publications efficiently and effectively. Most important, it has gotten the books off the shelf and into the hands of teachers so they could use them. The CTS project identified 92 relevant curriculum topics and prescreened and identified all the readings from the resource books that would contribute to a teacher's understanding of the professional knowledge described above. These readings are combined in a study guide and facilitated through a process that engages teachers in a deep and thoughtful study of teaching and learning connected to a curricular topic they teach.

In our experience introducing CTS to teachers, familiarity with and access to the CTS resources tended to be more on the side of the standards documents than the research. Teachers seemed to have less familiarity with and access to the research base on student learning. We know from cognitive research that students often have strong preconceptions and develop their own rules and generalizations about mathematical ideas that may support or interfere with their learning (Bransford, Brown, & Cocking, 2000; Donovan & Bransford, 2005). Being aware of student difficulties and the sources of those difficulties, and designing instruction to diminish them, are important steps in achieving the goal of mathematical understanding (Yetkin, 2003). For example, some students hold the common misconceptions that multiplication makes things bigger or that the larger the denominator is, the larger the fraction (Rose, Arline, & Minton, 2007). Each of these ideas is encompassed either explicitly or implicitly in the state standards teachers and students are held accountable for achieving. By using CTS, teachers can identify key ideas in their standards and then refer to research summaries to know what may make the learning difficult or comprehensible to students. They can use this information to plan instruction at their own grade level or comprehensively across grade levels. They now have a way to access and link the research to K–12 student learning goals.

BUILDING PROFESSIONAL COMMUNITY

The other underlying belief that is changing teacher professional development for the better is the growing commitment to building PLCs among teachers. After more than a century of schools that operated like multiple one-room schoolhouses under one roof, the idea of a PLC and teamwork in schools is finally taking hold. In the recent past, teachers across the hall or just next door may have been struggling with the same questions and problems with no reason or way to collaborate to find solutions. Increasingly, teaching is being deprivatized by the growing number of PLCs in schools that examine practice and results on a regular basis and pursue solutions to the problem of poor student performance. However, like other innovations, building a PLC does not happen by magic, and there are many pitfalls that must be addressed. In our work, we have focused on putting the "professional" into the PLC. We have asked, "What are the tools teachers need to make sure they reflect the knowledge of the profession in their learning communities?" Our conclusions are that PLCs must be research-based and standards-driven to be "professional." Historically, isolation among teachers led to very little sharing of what works among educators. Recent technologies and new organizational structures are helping to change that. Yet teachers' days are still highly structured and scheduled, and they need efficient and effective ways to work together and put their professional knowledge to work. Through CTS, once teachers learn the process, they can quickly and efficiently explore the readings on any given mathematics topic to address questions of practice and inform deliberations and decisions for their own teaching and to share with others in their PLCs. Whether they are involved in a formal PLC that meets to examine results and pinpoint areas for improved student learning or a grade-level team monitoring how new curriculum materials are working, the CTS process will support and enhance these collegial groups of teachers to use the research and the standards to inform their work. Through the use of CTS we have seen the conversations in these groups shift from the autobiographical stories that emanate from "What are you doing in your classroom?" to scholarly discussions that pertain to all teachers, such as, "What do the national standards and research say, and how might we apply that in our classrooms to support implementation of our state standards?" Examinations of curricular or instructional strategies are enriched because teachers base their analyses on whether the materials and strategies reflect important and challenging key ideas and research on how children learn as opposed to focusing only on their own opinions or biases, or on the materials' style, layout, or reading level.

As schools and school districts support new organizational arrangements that reduce hierarchy and promote collaboration, CTS can help at every juncture. As Ann Jolly, a former middle school teacher and an Alabama Teacher of the Year, reports, "PLC's involve teams of teachers in working together to study, learn, and support one another as they make changes in classroom practice. This process is collaborative rather than isolated. Ongoing learning and support continue throughout the school year. This professional development occurs at the school site and focuses on needs of the specific students in that school. Teachers work as interdependent colleagues, and a culture of collaboration and collective responsibility takes root. When teachers work together in PLCs to implement new teaching practices, over 90% of teachers do so successfully. Teamwork and collaboration work!" (Jolly, 2007, para. 8).

PLCs are usually organized as collaborative teacher groups focused on learning and achieving desired results. Eaker, DuFour, and Burnette (2002) suggest that PLCs systematically address four key learning questions:

1. What do we want students to learn?

2. How will we know if they have learned it?

3. What does student learning data reveal?

4. What are we going to do if students are not learning?

Too often, however, these collaborative groups lack a systematic focus on disciplinary content and drawing upon the knowledge base on learning mathematics to adequately address these questions. Table 1.2 shows how the CTS process and specific sections of the study guides in the CTS parent book can be used to address these questions. Beginning with the first question, CTS can guide the school community to ensure that the mathematics learning objectives the group chooses are enduring and that important ideas reflected in the national standards are clarified so that key ideas and procedures are clear and explicit and supported developmentally and conceptually by research. In addressing the second and third questions, CTS can also help the community use assessments that probe for understanding by using the CTS process to develop and use ongoing formative assessments that link key ideas in the standards to common misconceptions and misunderstandings, and reveal whether students have similar ideas to those identified in the research. Teachers examine students' results on assessments that reveal their thinking to decide what is needed next. The fourth question may be answered by examining the K–12 articulation of learning goals to determine whether gaps exist that may pose barriers to learning, analyzing curriculum materials to see the extent to which they promote learning of the key ideas, identifying instructional contexts that have proven effective in supporting learning, or even by examining teachers' own content knowledge to determine whether they are making the right connections. Table 1.2 shows how the different sections of the CTS process can support key questions for PLCs. (For a refresher on the six different sections of a CTS guide and the resources that are used with the sections, turn to page 21 in the parent CTS book or refer to Handout A1.5 in the Chapter 4 folder of the CD-ROM for this guide.)

Table 1.2 Key Questions for Professional Learning Communities and How CTS Can Help

Key Question	PLC Use of CTS
What do we want students to learn about a particular mathematics topic?	• CTS Sections III, V, and VI: Identify the learning goals that align with the topic; unpack the concepts, ideas, or skills within the learning goals for the topic. • CTS Section V: Identify the connections among related concepts; examine how key ideas build. • CTS Section I: Examine the culmination of K–12 mathematics literacy ideas for enduring understanding and use into adulthood.
How will we know if they have learned it?	• CTS Section IV: Identify common difficulties and misconceptions that may be revealed through instruction and assessment. • CTS Sections III, IV, and VI: Develop and use formative assessments and culminating performance tasks to check for understanding before, throughout, and at the end of instruction.

Key Question	PLC Use of CTS
What does the student learning data reveal?	• CTS Section III: Identify the extent to which students' ideas match the key ideas in the standards. • CTS Sections II and IV: Identify common difficulties, errors, and misconceptions that impede learning.
What are we going to do if they do not learn?	• CTS Section II: Examine instructional contexts and suggestions to determine if curricular or instructional changes are needed. • CTS Sections II and IV: Examine ways to address student difficulties and misconceptions. • CTS Section V: Examine the K–12 articulation of learning goals to see if there are gaps that need to be filled; look for ways to make stronger connections among a coherent set of learning goals.

OBSERVATIONS AND VOICES FROM THE FIELD

The results of using CTS have been impressive. As one teacher leader who used CTS said, "The process is an essential tool to bridge the gap between research and standards-based practice in teaching mathematics." A mentor teacher reported that CTS is especially useful in situations where mentors work with novice teachers and that the novice teachers are not the only beneficiaries. She described how mentors also show tremendous growth in skills and understandings when they use CTS as part of an induction program for beginning teachers.

Many users have commented on the ease and versatility of the CTS materials. For example, one participant said, "The [materials] allowed for a directed view of where to look in the CTS guides for the information we needed." Another pointed out that "developing our own [assessment] probes helped to give insight into what it takes to develop a good formative assessment item that can uncover the misconceptions our students have."

One of the greatest results we have seen comes from the teacher "ah-ha" moments. For example, one leader reported this insight: "Our participants left the workshop with an awareness of how the CTS process can enrich their current teaching practices. Several of the teachers commented that they had never used any of these source books prior to their CTS introduction. From now on they will become an integral resource for their district planning."

As another teacher commented: "I will use this to preview the most important mathematics to teach."

Teachers have also pointed out that the most valuable aspect of CTS for them is the review and discussion of misconceptions and misunderstandings described in the research on learning. As one teacher said, "It's a 'wake-up call' to all teachers that instruction strategies/techniques that address misconceptions and common errors are keys to learning."

One professional developer we worked with summed up the value of CTS this way: "CTS is a systematic procedure anyone can use; it provides synthesized information on specific topics and thus saves time in looking for answers; it helps users work from a common understanding of a particular topic to answer a specific question; and it helps users develop the habits of good research strategies."

After experiencing CTS, leaders of professional development for mathematics teachers immediately saw the significance of using CTS to enrich and invigorate teacher learning programs. Many professional developers in mathematics are not experts in every mathematics topic area or grade level. Some with excellent backgrounds in one grade level, such as high school mathematics, may be responsible for designing teacher learning programs in the middle or elementary grades. They need an easily accessible process for gaining a clear vision of the important mathematics across the K–12 system and how to make the mathematics content accessible to all students. CTS provides such a tool.

PROFESSIONAL DEVELOPMENT DESIGNS ARE ENHANCED THROUGH CTS

Professional development for mathematics teachers comes in a variety of forms and structures ranging from half-day workshops to weeklong institutes, to ongoing collaborative structures like PLCs. Regardless of the type or length of the professional development experience, CTS increases the focus on the content by connecting it to the key ideas in the standards and the research on learning. This increased focus ultimately translates into improved student achievement. For example, leaders who are instructional coaches should routinely do a CTS on the topics they are addressing in their coaching. Sometimes these leaders use this information for their own planning, but more often they incorporate it into the work they do with teachers, such as collaboratively planning and providing feedback on a lesson. In Chapter 7, you will find examples of professional development where the leader uses CTS with teachers in the context of particular professional development strategies. CTS is so valuable for leaders that we believe that no professional development leader should plan content-focused workshops, sessions on looking at student work, or any mathematics professional development without first doing a CTS on the topics they will address in their professional development session. This book contains the tools and resources to support them not only to do that, but also to build in rich CTS experiences for the teachers they work with to improve mathematics education.

CTS is a versatile resource designed to address multiple needs, audiences, and contexts. Likewise, this *Leader's Guide* addresses the multifaceted nature of professional learning and the different types of leaders who may design and support teacher learning using CTS. To give you a sense of the versatility of CTS when it is used within different contexts, the following are just a few examples of the various ways leaders use CTS. They also show how the CTS underlying beliefs of building specialized knowledge of mathematics teaching and learning as well as supporting collaborative group learning are manifested through these examples.

CTS USE BY COLLABORATIVE SCHOOL TEAMS

Improving student learning is at the heart of what teachers do. When teachers encounter students having learning difficulties, one reaction has been to simply reteach the content in the same or a slightly different way. Another approach is to gather data to find out what the students are having difficulty understanding and if other teachers at the same grade level are experiencing similar results. In this second approach, CTS resources help to pinpoint how to make the content more accessible to students. Improving opportunities for students to learn mathematics content by first examining teachers' own content knowledge, analyzing key ideas they want their students to learn, identifying instructional contexts that can enhance learning, becoming aware of the research on students' ideas in mathematics and how they impact learning, and understanding how learning progresses from one idea to the next in a coherent sequence of ideas improves both the quality of teaching and subsequently the depth and endurance of learning.

For example, a middle school team might observe that their students seem to perform poorly on assessment items on the state test that involve measurement. The teachers wonder what they can do to improve students' abilities to use different measurement systems. Although their students have had opportunities to use measurement skills in both science and mathematics, the students always score low on the measurement section, especially when it involves metric systems of measurement. The team decides to use the Linear Measurement Module (see Chapter 5) to investigate the topic. During the CTS, they clarify the specific measurement concepts and skills students are expected to know and be able to do. Furthermore, the team was interested in delving deeper into the research, which pointed out that students often know how to take measurements but do not know when to measure or what to measure.

Overall, the CTS helped the team understand why their instruction was not working for their students and what they needed to do so that their students could achieve the targeted learning goals. As a group, they revisited their curriculum and instructional materials and strengthened the measurement components. The conversation shifted in the team from an activity focus to a learning focus, guided by the common knowledge base they now had as a team as a result of doing the CTS together.

CTS USE IN PRESERVICE TEACHER EDUCATION

Preservice teachers in mathematics education courses benefit tremendously from using CTS at the beginning of their careers. Not only does it establish a habit of practice that will be useful to them throughout all the stages of their career, but it also helps them link their preservice experience to the current emphasis in many schools on standards and research-informed instruction. For example, most preservice teachers are asked to design at least one lesson as part of their methods course requirements. CTS provides the information they need up front to ensure their lesson appropriately addresses important key ideas in mathematics and anticipates the commonly held ideas students might bring to their learning. CTS creates the awareness needed for preservice teachers to design effective lessons that address standards and are informed by research on learning. In the process, many preservice teachers, particularly those who have limited mathematics backgrounds, find they are gaining new knowledge about content, teaching, and learning and realize areas where they would like to continue their mathematics content learning. It also brings a deep appreciation early on in their careers of the need to have and use a professional library of resources that will help them teach in a system that increasingly focuses on accountability to standards and instructional decisions based on research.

CTS ENHANCES MATHEMATICS EDUCATION LEADERSHIP

CTS has many benefits for people in mathematics education leadership roles such as school and district administrators, teacher leaders, and coaches. In our CTS work, we encourage all leaders working in these roles to use CTS to increase their familiarity with mathematics standards and learning research and how they are used to inform curriculum, instruction, and assessment. Depending on one's role, these leaders may need more in-depth understanding of the key ideas in the learning goals and the commonly held ideas noted in the research on learning in any particular grade spans.

District Mathematics Coordinators

For example, district mathematics coordinators are often responsible for curriculum adoption and development committees, overseeing and supporting coaches, arranging and approving professional development in mathematics, making classroom observations, requesting resources and manipulative materials and related tasks that require them to have a very broad and deep understanding of K–12 mathematics. Very often they may be specialists in one particular area of mathematics education (e.g., high school mathematics) but may not have firsthand knowledge about what learning strategies are effective for teaching basic geometry concepts in Grade 4 or the common difficulties students have when learning about fractions. They can benefit from basic numeracy topics engaging in full curriculum topic studies on topics that are the focus of new curriculum to inform the selection of professional development programs and to make a research-based case for using certain instructional strategies or materials. Every mathematics coordinator should own a copy of the CTS book and the accompanying resource books listed in Table 1.1. They should actively share these books with the people they work with to encourage others to use CTS to inform teaching actions and decisions.

District Mathematics and Science Coordinators

Some smaller districts combine coordination responsibilities for both science and mathematics. These Mathematics and Science Coordinators benefit from using both the mathematics CTS book and the parallel science version—*Science Curriculum Topic Study: Bridging the Gap Between Standards and Practice* (Keeley, 2005). Figure 1.5 in the CTS parent book shows how several of the resources used in mathematics CTS are also used in science CTS. In addition, there are several topics that overlap such as the Graphs and Graphing or the Mathematical Modeling CTS guides used in science and the Graphic Representation or the Modeling CTS guides used in mathematics. Engaging teachers in a study of similar cross-disciplinary topics helps coordinators facilitate the integration of common topics across the mathematics and science curriculum as well as foster a STEM approach to teaching and learning.

Table 1.3 Common CTS Resources in Science and Mathematics

CTS Resources	Comments
Mathematics Curriculum Topic Study (Keeley & Rose, 2006) and *Science Curriculum Topic Study* (Keeley, 2005)	These parent books are designed to parallel each other.
Science for All Americans (AAAS, 1989)	Describes the level of literacy all adults should have in science and mathematics after completing a K–12 education.

CTS Resources	Comments
Benchmarks for Science Literacy (AAAS, 1993) or *Benchmarks Online* (AAAS, 2009—includes new and revised benchmarks)	Describes explicit learning goals, descriptions of effective teaching and instructional contexts, and summaries of the research on learning.
Atlas of Science Literacy, Volumes 1 and 2 (AAAS, 2001–2007)	Visually illustrates a progression of understanding from K–12 and shows connections within a topic and across topics.

Principals

Programs that train principals can also use CTS to help prospective school administrators develop an understanding of what they should look for when teachers are teaching certain mathematics topics. For example, one principal said he was wondering why a teacher he observed had been asking her students questions about content that was not directly addressed in the lesson being taught, and he noted it in the evaluation as a concern. After the lesson, he asked the teacher about it. She shared with him that she had a hunch that students were missing some of the prior knowledge needed to understand the topic of probability that she was teaching. She pulled out the map on Probability from the *Atlas of Science Literacy* (AAAS, 2000) and showed the principal the concepts and specific ideas that students are expected to develop at each grade level and pointed out the areas she was probing students about to see if they had the prior knowledge that served as a precursor to the ideas she was trying to develop in her lesson. She showed him the CTS study guide that indicated which *Atlas* map to use to examine the topic she was teaching. The principal developed a greater appreciation for what this teacher was doing to assess prior knowledge and quickly saw how using CTS himself would inform his classroom observations. Although principals do not have to know every bit of information on the 92 mathematics topics included in Mathematics CTS, it is important for them to experience CTS enough so that they know its purpose and can suggest teachers use it as they are planning lessons, developing assessments, and reviewing the essential content students should learn. In addition, administrators should encourage teachers to use CTS to justify decisions they make regarding teaching and learning.

Teacher Leaders and Instructional Coaches

Teacher leaders and coaches are other key leadership groups that can strengthen and enhance their leadership capacity through CTS. Teacher leaders and coaches are often chosen because they stand out among peers and are successful with their own students. When they begin to work with a variety of teachers they are challenged to know the goals for mathematics learning across many grade levels and they must be a resource for teachers who may be teaching topics at a grade level the coach or teacher leader is not familiar with firsthand. CTS helps in both areas. When leaders use CTS themselves, they can quickly and efficiently review the standards and research to inform what they do to support their teachers. They can also introduce CTS tools to the teachers they work with so they have access to the information they need anytime. It is like having a virtual expert on call anytime the coach, mentor, or teacher leader is not readily available to provide assistance.

The Language of CTS

Like any new tool or resource, CTS comes with its own language, specialized terminology, and operational definitions. For the purpose of clarity, Table 1.4 lists words and terms frequently used throughout this *Leader's Guide*. Descriptions of how this terminology is used in the context of CTS as well as operational definitions for words that may have different meanings in other contexts is provided for leaders to ensure consistency when using CTS in your professional development contexts. In addition, this chart is provided as Handout 1.1 in the Chapter 1 folder on the CD-ROM if you choose to share it with teachers, adapt it, or add your own additional terminology that you use in your CTS professional development.

Table 1.4 CTS Specialized Terminology

CTS Terms	*Clarification*
Common misunderstandings	A pervasive notion about a mathematics concept that has been studied in groups of students with results published in the research literature and is very likely to be held by students outside of the study.
Common Core State Standards	A robust set of standards developed by the Common Core State Standards Initiative and accepted by 40+ states that describe core ideas in mathematics crucial for success in college and careers.
Concept	A mental construct used to conceptualize a mathematical idea (e.g., similarity, mean, ratio, linearity, etc.).
Conceptual knowledge	Knowledge of mathematical ideas and their interconnections that enables one to understand mathematics and solve problems.
Content knowledge	Knowledge of disciplinary subject matter (e.g., geometric ideas, measures of central tendency, proportionality, functionality, etc.).
CTS	An acronym that stands for curriculum topic study.
Grain size	How broad or specific a topic is (e.g., Geometric Shapes is a large grain size topic whereas Triangles is a smaller grain size topic).
Integrated topic	Cross-cutting topics in mathematics that help provide coherence to the mathematics curriculum and are threaded through multiple content areas (e.g., proportionality cuts across measurement, geometry, number and operation, algebra, and probability).
Key idea	An important idea unpacked from a learning goal. Sometimes there are several key ideas embedded in one learning goal.
Leader's Guide	A shorthand way of referring to this book, *A Leader's Guide to Mathematics Curriculum Topic Study*.
Learning goal	A teaching and learning target that specifically describes what students should know or be able to do. In the NCTM *Principles and Standards*, these are referred to as "Expectations."

CTS Terms	Clarification
Misconception	A catch-all term for ideas students have that are not entirely mathematically correct (e.g., partial understandings, overgeneralizations, misunderstandings, common errors).
National standards	Both the *Benchmarks for Science Literacy* and the *Principles and Standards for School Mathematics*.
Overgeneralizations	A type of common misunderstanding developed when an algorithm, rule, or shortcut is extended to another context in an inappropriate way.
Parent book	A shorthand way of referring to the resource *Mathematics Curriculum Topic Study: Bridging the Gap Between Standards and Practice* (Keeley & Rose, 2006).
PCK	An acronym that stands for pedagogical content knowledge. This is the specialized knowledge about mathematics teaching and learning that teachers need to understand in order to make content accessible to students.
Preconception	An idea formed, often early on, before students formally encounter the content. Preconceptions can form outside of school or during previous curricular contexts.
Procedural knowledge	Knowing algorithms, representations, and mathematical facts and when to use them to solve problems.
Procedure	A standard process for solving a class of mathematical problems.
Professional learning community	A group of team members who regularly collaborate toward continued improvement in meeting student learning needs through a shared vision and focus on curriculum, instruction, and assessment.
Research	Although there are many kinds of research in education, in CTS this refers specifically to cognitive research (research on learning).
Science literacy	The understandings and ways of thinking that are essential for all citizens in a world shaped by science and technology. Included in science literacy are understandings related to the nature of mathematics, mathematical ideas, and mathematical skills (AAAS, 1989).
Sophistication	Refers to the complexity of an idea at a given grade level. For example, the 3-5 symbolic representation idea "mathematical ideas can be represented symbolically" is at a lower level of sophistication than the 6-8 idea relating symbolical equations to describe the relationship between two quantities.
Standards	Common goals established nationally, statewide, or locally that are widely accepted by the mathematics education community and provide a focus for teaching and learning.

(Continued)

Table 1.4 (Continued)

CTS Terms	Clarification
Study guide	Refers to one of the 92 CTS study guides.
Teacher educator	Anyone who facilitates teacher learning such as preservice faculty, mathematicians working with teachers, staff developers, coaches, and so on.
Topic	A conceptual organizer or category for related learning goals that can be taught in a variety of contexts (e.g., Geometric Shapes is a CTS topic, but Tangrams is a context in which manipulatives are used to teach about geometric shapes).
Topic study	A shorthand way of referring to a curriculum topic study.

Chapters 1 and 2 in the parent book, *Mathematics Curriculum Topic Study* (Keeley & Rose, 2006), introduce the user to CTS and the tools and collective resources used with the process. In Chapter 2 of this *Leader's Guide*, we will expand upon these two chapters by describing what leaders need to know in order to introduce CTS effectively in their work with mathematics educators.

2

Introduction to CTS for Leaders

The purpose of this chapter is to provide the curriculum topic study (CTS) leader with basic background on CTS and guidance about using the CTS parent book, *Mathematics Curriculum Topic Study: Bridging the Gap Between Standards and Practice* (Keeley & Rose, 2006) to prepare to lead CTS sessions. The chapter reviews what CTS is and what it is not. It provides an overview to the resource books that are used with CTS, defines what is meant by mathematical literacy, and demonstrates the value of knowing and using standards and research to guide practice. In this *Leader's Guide*, the authors provide substantial background and guidance on using CTS based on our experiences, but we think of new ways to apply CTS often. We therefore encourage CTS users to visit our website www.curriculumtopicstudy.org regularly for new updated ideas and suggestions and to use the "contact the CTS project" option on our website to share ideas and materials you have developed using CTS.

WHAT IS CTS?

CTS is a rigorous, methodical study process designed to help mathematics educators deeply examine a common curricular topic. The CTS process utilizes a common set of books that include standards and cognitive research resources, 92 different mathematics topic study guides, and a variety of tools and processes to systematically examine a curricular topic. In addition to the mathematics CTS described in this *Leader's Guide*, there is also a science version of CTS. CTS is best described as

- A *process* that incorporates a systematic study of standards and research.
- A set of *tools* and collective *resources* for improving curriculum, instruction, and assessment.
- An intellectually engaging, collaborative *professional development* experience where teachers come together to develop a common knowledge base about teaching and student learning.

17

The CTS approach was adapted from the American Association for the Advancement of Science's (AAAS) Project 2061 study of a benchmark. This detailed study procedure involved clarifying the meaning and intent of a benchmark learning goal from the *Benchmarks for Science Literacy* (AAAS, 1993, 2009) using several tools from Project 2061's collection of science literacy resources. (Note: Project 2061's use of the term "science literacy" includes science, mathematics, design, and technology—what are commonly referred to as STEM fields.) The premise behind this study procedure is that in order for educators to help students achieve the learning described in a benchmark, they must first understand what the benchmark statement intends students to be able to know or do. Taken at face value, a benchmark statement, a standard, a performance objective, or any learning goal, regardless of the language we use to label it, can be easily misinterpreted as to its meaning, the boundaries that describe how far to take a concept, experiences and teaching approaches that contribute to learning the key ideas and skills, and the level of sophistication expected by the learning goal. Educators who have experienced the Project 2061 systematic study procedure note a significant difference in their understanding of a learning goal after completing a benchmark study.

Although studying a single learning goal is important and worthwhile, the CTS project developed a procedure similar to Project 2061's study of a benchmark to examine teaching and learning at the larger grain size of a curricular topic, eventually drilling down to specific learning goals. Since many teachers target multiple learning goals within a curricular unit or cluster of lessons, similar tools and resources for studying a curricular unit are needed. Although standards may differ from state to state and instructional materials may include different curricular objectives, curricular topics are similar in schools across states as well as how they are organized in instructional materials. CTS expands the resources for a topic study beyond the Project 2061 tools to also include the National Council of Teachers of Mathematics (NCTM) *Principles and Standards for School Mathematics* (NCTM, 2000) as well as an adult mathematics trade book, *Beyond Numeracy* (Paulos, 1992), and a compendium of research on teaching and learning mathematics in a *Research Companion to Principles and Standards for School Mathematics* (NCTM, 2003). In addition, there is a website, www.curriculumtopicstudy.org, that provides optional suggestions for supplementary readings and materials that are topic specific. With the adoption of the Common Core State Standards for Mathematics in 2010, we have also included this resource in the materials provided in this *Leader's Guide*. The CTS resources are listed in Table 2.1 and discussed further in this chapter.

Table 2.1   CTS Mathematics Resources

- *Science for All Americans* (AAAS, 1989)
- *Beyond Numeracy* (Paulos, 1992)
- *Benchmarks for Science Literacy* (AAAS, 1993, 2009)
- *Principles and Standards for School Mathematics* (NCTM, 2000)
- *Research Companion to Principles and Standards for School Mathematics* (NCTM, 2003)
- *Atlas of Science Literacy, Vols. 1–2* (AAAS, 2001–2007)
- *Common Core State Standards for Mathematics* (NGA Center & CCSSO, 2010)
- State standards or frameworks and curriculum guides
- Optional: Additional supplementary resources (videos, journal articles, websites, trade books)

We recommend that professional developers and leaders of CTS become thoroughly familiar with what CTS is and the underlying knowledge and research base that supports it. Take the time to read Chapter 1, "Introduction to Curriculum Topic Study," in the CTS parent book. It will give you the background you need to be prepared to answer questions about what CTS is, what CTS means by a "curricular topic," how CTS addresses content and pedagogy at the topic level, and what CTS can do to deepen mathematics teachers' understanding of content, teaching, and learning.

WHAT CTS IS NOT

Although it is important to know what CTS is, it is also important to know what CTS is not. CTS helps educators seek solutions or answers to problems or questions related to standards-based content, curriculum, instruction, or assessment, but it does not provide the solution. CTS provides the analytic lens and tools needed to make sense of these problems or questions and help educators think through what they need to understand better in order to be effective teachers (e.g., how their students learn, curriculum alignment, and state standards interpretation). CTS also does not provide the answers unique to their own contexts. Instead, it engages educators in a process that helps them uncover what they need to know and helps them think about how to apply that knowledge to their own situations. The tool draws on and enriches professional dialogue among teachers as they use their professional knowledge to apply their CTS discoveries to their own situation. The following describes limitations to be aware of when using CTS:

- CTS is not the complete remedy for weak content knowledge (CTS is used to enhance and support content learning and to raise awareness of content that teachers need to learn).
- CTS is not a collection of teaching activities (CTS describes considerations one must take into account when planning or selecting teaching activities and contexts).
- CTS is not a description of "how to's" (CTS helps you think through effective teaching based on knowledge of learning goals and how students learn, but does not prescribe a particular pedagogical approach).
- CTS is not a quick fix (CTS takes serious, dedicated time to read, analyze, and reflect on teaching and learning).
- CTS is not the end-all for professional development (CTS can help teachers identify the need for additional professional learning experiences).

CTS AND MATHEMATICAL LITERACY

When educators use CTS, they develop a deeper understanding of mathematical literacy and the implications for curriculum, instruction, and assessment. When leading a CTS session, it is important to share with educators what we mean by *mathematical literacy*. The Program for International Student Assessment (PISA) defines mathematical literacy as "the capacity to identify, understand and engage in mathematics, and to make well-founded judgments about the role that mathematics plays in an individual's current and future private life, occupational life, social life with peers and relatives, and life as a constructive, concerned and reflective citizen" (Organization for Economic Cooperation and Development, 2003). Furthermore, the NCTM *Principles and Standards for School Mathematics* describe how in a changing world, those who understand and can do mathematics will have significantly enhanced opportunities and options for changing their futures. The need to understand and use mathematics as an educated adult includes the following (NCTM, 2000, pp. 4–5):

- *Mathematics for life*—Since the underpinnings of everyday life are increasingly mathematical and technological, knowing mathematics can be personally satisfying and empowering.
- *Mathematics as a part of cultural heritage*—Because mathematics is one of the greatest cultural and intellectual achievements of humankind, everyone should develop an appreciation of that achievement.
- *Mathematics for the workplace*—The level of mathematical thinking and problem solving in the workplace has increased dramatically.
- *Mathematics for the scientific and technical community*—Although all careers require a foundation of mathematics knowledge, those who pursue work as mathematicians, scientists, statisticians, and engineers require deep knowledge of mathematics.

When educators use CTS, they are identifying the mathematical knowledge, procedures, and skills that *every* student is expected to know and use, regardless of whether he or she will go on to pursue higher education in mathematics or become a mathematician. Because the K–12 content of CTS is rooted in the standards, CTS describes the threshold of mathematics teaching and learning, not the ceiling. It does not describe the mathematics needed for advanced coursework or the standards or the concepts and procedures that exceed mathematical literacy at a given grade level nor does it spell out all the mathematics taught in the K–12 curriculum. It focuses on the knowledge, procedures, and skills described in the standards that every student must attain in order to progress to the next stage of increasingly sophisticated ideas or understand the important connections between concepts. To learn more about adult and K–12 science and mathematical literacy, CTS leaders are encouraged to read the introduction to *Science for All Americans (SFAA)*, the "About Benchmarks" section in the front of the *Benchmarks for Science Literacy*, and Chapter 1, "Vision for School Mathematics," in the NCTM *Principles and Standards for School Mathematics (PSSM)*.

The *PSSM* lists six principles for school mathematics (NCTM, 2000). A careful examination of these principles will show how CTS easily fits into and supports these comprehensive principles as shown by the examples in Table 2.2.

Table 2.2 CTS and the *PSSM* (Noncontent Standards)

PSSM *Principles* (NCTM, 2000)	*Description of* PSSM *Principle*	*Example of How CTS Supports the Principle*
Equity	Excellence in mathematics education requires equity—high expectations and support for all students.	CTS helps teachers identify the mathematics all students must have access to and opportunities to effectively learn the content.

PSSM *Principles* (NCTM, 2000)	*Description of* PSSM *Principle*	*Example of How CTS Supports the Principle*
Curriculum	A curriculum is more than a collection of activities: it must be coherent, focused on important mathematics, and well articulated across grades.	CTS provides a variety of tools and processes to help teachers analyze, select, and articulate their curriculum.
Teaching	Effective mathematics teaching requires understanding what students know and need to learn and then challenging and supporting them to learn it well.	CTS helps teachers examine content-specific instructional implications that inform effective teaching. Examining the research on learning informs assessment strategies that can be used to elicit preconceptions.
Learning	Students must learn mathematics with understanding, actively building new knowledge from experience and prior knowledge.	CTS connects teachers to learning research that helps them understand what makes the learning of specific concepts difficult. Teachers link the findings from research to their own instructional contexts and knowledge of their students.
Assessment	Assessment should support the learning of important mathematics and furnish useful information to both teachers and students.	CTS provides a process to develop diagnostic assessments that explicitly link key ideas to common misconceptions for formative purposes.
Technology	Technology is essential in teaching and learning mathematics; it influences the mathematics that is taught and enhances students' learning.	CTS helps teachers focus technology use on learning mathematics so that the emphasis is on the content, not the technology itself.

Facilitators of CTS will benefit from becoming familiar with all of the sections of the *SFAA, Benchmarks for Science Literacy,* and *PSSM* when questions about mathematics education or issues that are related to CTS but not specifically addressed in the CTS process arise. A knowledgeable facilitator can make the link between the broader teaching and learning recommendations in *SFAA, Benchmarks for Science Literacy,* and *PSSM* and the specific recommendations that are revealed through the study of a specific curricular topic. As we point out in Chapter 1, there is a professional knowledge base that all of us working in mathematics education should know and be able to apply. These resources are the foundation of that knowledge.

COMMON CORE STATE STANDARDS FOR MATHEMATICS AND NCTM FOCAL POINTS

In 2010, 3 years after the publication of the CTS parent book, the Common Core State Standards Initiative (CCSSI) collaborated with states to develop common core standards in English language arts and mathematics. These common standards are being adopted by multiple states for the purpose of providing shared expectations for student learning and reducing the mile-wide, inch-deep approach to teaching and learning.

In 2006 NCTM published *Curriculum Focal Points for Prekindergarten Through Grade 8 Mathematics: A Quest for Coherence* as a companion to the *PSSM* (NCTM, 2006). The *Focal Points* include learning goals derived from the *PSSM* but instead of grade-level spans (K–2, 3–5, 6–8), they describe the most important mathematics concepts, skills, and procedures for each grade level K–8. Since its release, many states and school districts have used *Focal Points* to revise their standards and curriculum.

Naturally the question arises, "How do the *Common Core State Standards in Mathematics (CCSSM)* differ from the NCTM-developed *Focal Points* and how do these fit with CTS? A comparison conducted by Achieve (2010) showed that the two documents are similar in terms of rigor. They generally describe the same content, although some content occurs earlier in the *CCSSM*. They are also similar in terms of coherence and focus but differ in levels of specificity. One major difference is purpose—the *CCSSM* lay out a vision for college mathematics readiness whereas the NCTM *Focal Points* (as well as *Benchmarks for Science Literacy* and NCTM's *Principles and Standards for School Mathematics*) focus primarily on mathematics literacy for all regardless of whether students go on to take more advanced mathematics in college.

As far as implications for CTS, the content is similar in both documents. However, CTS users might want to be aware of some of the changes when doing a CTS. The website http://www.achieve.org/CCSSandFocalPoints provides a useful content comparison between the *CCSSM* and the NCTM *Focal Points*. In addition, Handouts 2.1 and 2.2 on the CD-ROM are Crosswalks to the *CCSSM* and NCTM *Focal Points* linking sections of these documents with selected readings on a CTS study guide.

KEY POINTS ABOUT STANDARDS AND RESEARCH ON LEARNING

CTS is described as a "standards- and research-based" study of a curricular topic. In order to understand what this means, beliefs about standards and research need to be addressed in order to make the best use of the CTS process and resources. These beliefs have surfaced during the CTS project's work with many educators and represent some of the misconceptions that still linger since the introduction of standards. In addition, many teachers have entered the teaching profession poststandards movement and may not be as aware of what standards really are and how they can be used as their colleagues who experienced the wave of standards-based reform. CTS session leaders may wish to precede the introductory CTS sessions with an opportunity to surface and discuss participants' beliefs about standards and research. Handout 2.3: Ten Common Beliefs about Standards and Research on Learning, found on the CD-ROM in the Chapter 2 folder, can be used prior to engaging in CTS to surface teachers' beliefs and initiate dialogue about standards and research prior to learning about the specific resources used in the CTS process. You might use this as a kickoff discussion or prior to beginning your CTS work. If you are working with a group of teachers over months or years you can help them revisit their beliefs from time to time and reflect on how they are changing.

Key points to make about standards and research that can be surfaced and discussed using Handout 2.1 during any of the CTS sessions include the following:

- *Standards are for all students.* Mathematics standards describe the important skills and knowledge that all students should be expected to learn, regardless of their academic placement. This does not mean that students who struggle with learning cannot start with simpler concepts and gradually work their way to achieving a standard. Whether students are in honor classes or needing remedial services, the standards are written for all students. Although there are circumstances that may make it difficult for some students to achieve particular standards, it is important that they have every opportunity to learn the ideas and skills in the standards.

- *Standards are the threshold, not the ceiling.* A common myth about standards is that they "dumb down" content and do not allow students to learn more advanced ideas. The standards examined when using CTS Study Guide Sections III, V, or VI are not intended to limit students' knowledge. They describe what *all* students are expected to know in order to be mathematically literate (as well as college ready if supplementing CTS with the *CCSSM*). They are the threshold for building mathematical literacy. However, that does not mean students can't go further. Depending on the readiness of students and the context for learning, students can engage in learning beyond the standards—if they have demonstrated they have met the standards that are prerequisite to building more sophisticated knowledge.

- *Standards are not intended to limit what is taught.* Standards provide clear direction and focus for teaching and learning. Although teachers must focus on helping students achieve the standards, this does not mean that other topics of mathematical interest cannot be taught. There is limited time in the curriculum to teach all the important mathematical ideas, so teachers must ensure that standards are being met. However, other ideas in mathematics can sometimes be integrated with the standards, or special topics of interest can be taught as long as they do not replace students' opportunity to learn the ideas essential to achieving mathematical literacy.

- *National standards can and should be used with state standards.* Many educators believe that state standards replace national standards and that there is no use for the latter when they are being held accountable to state standards. National standards (*Benchmarks* and *PSSM*) are just as useful today as they were when they were released before states crafted their own standards and can be used along with the NCTM *Focal Points* and the *CCSSM*. Using state and national standards should not be an either/or decision, for several reasons. First, instructional materials are not explicitly developed for a particular set of state standards, and their alignments to state standards are at best topical. Materials are developed to align with the national standards and often to the standards used in large states that have a formal textbook adoption process. Understanding the connection to the national standards and their relation to state standards can strengthen the alignment and use of instructional materials. Second, there is wide inconsistency across state standards in coherence, interpretation, and specificity. Using national standards to interpret the meaning and intent of a state standard improves interpretation within a state as well as promoting consistency from one state to another. This is particularly important as our society has become increasingly mobile and students may attend school in more than one state. However, as more states move toward adopting the

CCSSM, there will be shared expectations across states as well as opportunities for common assessments and curriculum.

- *Standards are not a curriculum.* Standards inform curriculum but by themselves, they are not the curriculum. Curriculum is the way content is organized for teaching and learning. Content standards are the learning goals that are targeted by the curriculum. Often textbooks or other instructional materials have been aligned to the standards, but one must keep in mind that alignment is sometimes shallow at most. Teachers must still have opportunities to examine standards and organize learning goals in ways that are developmentally and conceptually sound.

- *Standards can be repeated in the curriculum.* Repeatedly teaching the same content, especially after students have learned the content, is counterproductive. In mathematics, students often revisit the same concepts and skills over and over again in successive grades even after they have learned them. A former president of NCTM once remarked that he started off the school year with a new topic. The students, used to the redundancy of the curriculum, remarked, "Why are you teaching us this? We never learned this before!" However, research on learning indicates that some concepts must be encountered several times in different contexts and at different levels of complexity before students can attain an enduring understanding. This differs from redundancy where students are learning the same material, in the same way, in the same context over and over.

- *Rigor does not mean difficult.* Some educators believe that standards undermine efforts to provide a rigorous and challenging curriculum. Rigor is a term often misused. Rigor does not mean difficult or refer to quantity of content. Rigor implies active, challenging, deep, intellectual learning. If students are deeply immersed in thinking about and applying intellectually challenging content, then they are engaged in rigorous learning. Too often students are taught advanced topics that they lack the necessary prerequisites to learn for the sake of "rigor."

- *Standards do not prescribe a pedagogical approach.* Standards describe the goals for learning. Some of these goals are best achieved through open-ended problem solving or use of manipulatives while others may be learned through other more direct approaches. There is no one method of instruction prescribed in the standards.

- *Knowledge, procedures, and skill standards are not intended to be taught separately.* Standards are not designed to be a "checklist" curriculum, with each standard taught separately from the others. This approach not only makes it seem as if there are too many standards to cover but also leads to disjointed learning and a curriculum that lacks coherence. Many standards can and should be taught as a cluster of interrelated ideas, procedures, and skills connected in a coherent way. This includes clusters of knowledge standards as well as clusters of procedural and skills standards, all of which contribute to mathematical practices.

- *Cognitive research informs teaching and learning but does not prescribe it.* Research is very helpful in informing educators about difficulties students are likely to encounter, commonly held ideas they may have, and the developmental appropriateness of content and context. However, students are unique individuals and their readiness depends on several factors including their prior knowledge and experiences, the quality of the school's curriculum, the skill of the teacher, and other factors. Because research may point out that some students struggle with a concept or procedure at a certain age, it does not necessarily mean one must not teach it. Teachers should use their best judgment about their own students and assess their readiness before teaching ideas that may be conceptually challenging to students. Research should be used to inform, not dictate what is taught.

USING CTS TO LEAD PROFESSIONAL LEARNING

CTS provides a methodical way to ensure that professional development is focused on the K–12 content and opportunities to learn necessary for mathematical literacy. It provides leaders with a standards- and research-based focus for their professional development designs and decisions. Whether leaders are involved at the school, district, or state level; working in a university; leading staff development; facilitating mathematics curriculum or assessment committees; or engaged in other types of mathematics education reform efforts that require knowledgeable and skilled leadership, CTS is a tool that brings increased content alignment, coherency, and consistency to leaders' work.

Leaders of teacher learning come from a variety of backgrounds, where they may have strengths in one area but not others. For example, university mathematicians working with teachers may have strong expertise in an area of mathematics, but little understanding of K–12 curriculum or developmental readiness of students at different grade levels. CTS helps them build a bridge from the university content they teach to what teachers need to take from that experience to shape curriculum and instruction at their specific grade levels. Teacher leaders may know the mathematics and instructional implications of their own grade level but lack knowledge of the other grade levels. A professional developer may be a masterful facilitator of adult learning but lack specific knowledge of content and common mathematical errors made by students. A high school teacher in one discipline, such as physics, may have little knowledge of teaching and learning when asked to teach a related discipline such as mathematics. A preservice educator may have particular expertise in instructional design and teaching methodologies but lack experience in using standards and cognitive research to inform these designs and methodologies. All of these are examples of how CTS can strengthen the professional development work that leaders do to improve teachers' practice.

CTS is a versatile tool that meets the diverse needs of a wide range of leaders in mathematics. Not only does it inform leaders and raise their level of knowledge; most important, it provides them with an intellectually stimulating process for developing a common core of content, teaching, and learning understanding within the various groups and types of teachers they work with from preservice to novice teachers to experienced veteran teachers to teacher leaders.

CTS RESOURCES AND TOOLS

The primary resource used for CTS is the parent book, *Mathematics Curriculum Topic Study: Bridging the Gap Between Standards and Practice* (Keeley & Rose, 2006). The parent book provides several tools for using CTS. The primary tool is the CTS study guide. In addition, there are several other tools described in Chapter 4 of the parent book that are used with the CTS study guides and study process. The CTS project also maintains a website at www.curriculumtopicstudy.org that provides additional material for CTS users and leaders of CTS. All of these resources and tools are described in the parent CTS book. In addition, this *Leader's Guide* includes additional information and specific designs and support materials for learning about and using the CTS process, resources, and tools. The following describes these resources and tools for those who are leading CTS.

The Parent CTS Book

In order to use this *Leader's Guide* to CTS, it is necessary for leaders to have the parent CTS book, *Mathematics Curriculum Topic Study: Bridging the Gap Between Standards and Practice* (Keeley & Rose, 2006). It contains the background material for teachers, a variety of tools, authentic vignettes of using CTS in a variety of contexts, and the 92 study guides that are at the heart of the CTS process. It is the book that CTS leaders will use with teachers. When the first edition of the parent book came out in 2006, the *Atlas of Science Literacy, Volume 2* was not yet published and therefore is not referenced in the study guides. If you are using the first edition (2006) of the parent book with this *Leader's Guide*, you can download a crosswalk between the CTS study guides and the new *Atlas* maps from the CTS website, www.curriculumtopicstudy.org, or print a copy of Handout 2.4: CTS Crosswalk to Atlas of Science Literacy from the Chapter 2 folder on the CD-ROM.

> **Facilitator Note**
>
> It is anticipated that there will be a second edition of the parent CTS book released sometime after 2012 that will update the study guides to include the *Atlas of Science Literacy, Volume 2* (AAAS, 2007) as well as include the recent Common Core State Standards in Mathematics. When the second edition of the parent book comes out, the CTS website will reflect the changes. Every effort will be made to make sure subsequent editions are matched to this *Leader's Guide*.

The Collective Set of CTS Resources

What makes CTS unique as a professional learning strategy is its systematic use of a collective set of professional resources that have been analyzed and vetted to match the content of the 92 curricular topics. The vetting process saves time for the busy teacher by selecting the readings and page numbers that are most relevant to studying a topic. These resources include the primary national standards resources—*Benchmarks for Science Literacy* (AAAS, 1993, 2009) and the *Principles and Standards for School Mathematics* (NCTM, 2000); two resources that describe adult mathematics literacy—*Science for All Americans* (AAAS, 1989) and an optional trade book, *Beyond Numeracy* (Paulos, 1992); two visual depictions of the K–12 growth of understanding and coherent sequences and connections of learning goals—*Atlas of Science Literacy, Volume 1* (AAAS, 2001) and *Atlas of Science Literacy, Volume 2* (AAAS, 2007); and three compendia of cognitive research summaries—*Benchmarks for Science Literacy*, Chapter 15 (AAAS, 1993), *Research Companion to Principles and Standards for School Mathematics* (NCTM, 2003), and the more recent research summaries in the *Atlas of Science Literacy, Volume 2* (AAAS, 2007).

This suite of CTS resources is described further in Chapter 2 of the parent resource, *Mathematics Curriculum Topic Study* (Keeley & Rose, 2006) on pages 27–30. Leaders of CTS are encouraged to take the time to become thoroughly familiar with these books by reading the descriptions of each resource and how it is used in Chapter 2 of the parent book. In addition, examine each book for its following elements:

- Layout and organization of content
- Introduction and overview of the resource
- Unique features that distinguish it from the other CTS resources
- Background material on science literacy or children's ideas

Of all the resources used for the CTS process, the *Atlas of Science Literacy* is probably the most complex to use and understand. It is essential for leaders to read the introduction to the *Atlas* as well as the supporting material that describes ways the maps are used, map keys, the nature of connections, and so on. The Project 2061 website at www .project2061.org includes useful information about the *Atlas* as well as an introductory PowerPoint explaining the resource. Take the time to become familiar with the *Atlas,* as there are many nuances that are not immediately obvious when using the maps. Another option for leaders is to attend an AAAS *Atlas* workshop. These are given at various locations around the country and are listed on the Project 2061 website.

Much of the research described in Chapter 15 of the *Benchmarks,* summaries in the *Atlas,* and the NCTM *Research Companion* was conducted a decade or more ago. However, much of this research on learning is still relevant today. The second volume of the *Atlas* contains research summaries from research that was available after the standards and *Atlas, Volume 1* were published. These summaries can be used to update the research base in CTS Section IV and will be referenced in the second edition of the CTS parent book.

Another question that may come up is how "dated" the standards resources are. At this time there is no scheduled effort to revise the *Benchmarks for Science Literacy;* however, the 2009 online version has revisions and additions that match the changes made in the *Atlas of Science Literacy.* These are indicated on the *Atlas Volume 2* maps by * (revised) or ** (new benchmark). You can also see a comparison between the original benchmarks and the updated benchmarks by visiting the Project 2061 website at www.project2061.org and accessing the online version of the *Benchmarks.* In addition, NCTM published the *Focal Points* in 2006 to break down *PSSM* standards into grade-level expectations K–8. These updates reflect necessary revisions after a decade of standards implementation but do not discard the original standards documents in favor of a new set of standards. This would be counterproductive to the hard work states, schools, and districts have done over many years of standards-based reform. Although we know a lot more about standards today than we did in the past, one can think of the standards documents as dynamic tools that are continually updated as needed without starting all over again and developing new sets of standards.

In 2010, an initiative spearheaded by the National Governor's Association developed *CCSSM.* These were not developed by NCTM but are similar in content in many respects to the NCTM standards. These common standards are being adopted by more than 40 states. The Crosswalks provided in Handouts 2.1 and 2.2 on the CD-ROM can be used to supplement CTS with sections from recent standards documents.

The CTS Study Guides

The heart of the CTS process is the CTS study guide. What makes these guides so useful to educators who have been using, or tried to use, national standards and research documents is that the relevant readings for particular mathematics topics have already been identified and vetted. For more information about the study guides and the six sections of each, review pages 22–23 in the CTS parent book and also refer to Handout A1.5: Anatomy of a Study Guide, which you can find on the CD-ROM in the Module A1 handouts folder for Chapter 4. One thing to be aware of is that each guide identifies the related readings. However, it is not always necessary to read all of the material listed in each guide. As the facilitator, there will be times when you will select certain readings and skip others. However, you will need to examine these carefully in order to ensure that important information needed for the purpose of your professional development session is not left out. The page numbers in each CTS guide reference the current editions of each resource book that are described in the CTS book. If you use a different edition in which the page numbers do not coincide with the guides, it should not pose a problem as each guide specifically lists the section titles and subtitles where the readings can be found. Likewise, for those resources that have online versions that are not numbered by pages, you can find the section for each reading by using the chapter or section titles.

It is important to note that there is overlap in the 92 study guides in terms of their grain size. The overlap is purposefully designed to allow the CTS user to study a topic using a broad sweep or a narrow one. For example, the topic "Geometric Shapes" or "Number Sense" is much broader than the topic of "Triangles" or "Decimals." Generally, the larger the grain size, the more sections there are to read and synthesize. Before designing a CTS session, leaders should carefully choose the appropriate grain size for their audience and the content of their professional development.

CTS Application Tools

Chapter 4 in the CTS parent book provides a description of some of the tools used with CTS such as tools for curriculum selection, K–12 scope and sequence articulation, hierarchy of content knowledge, instructional design, and assessment probes. Take the time to read the background on each of these applications and how CTS findings are applied in these various contexts. In Chapter 6 of this *Leader's Guide* are suggestions for integrating these application tools into your CTS professional development designs.

The CTS Website, www.curriculumtopicstudy.org

CTS is a dynamic resource that will continually be updated with new information, tools, and resources. Because new research on learning continues to be published, the CTS project maintains a searchable database with updated research findings linked to specific CTS guides. Although CTS uses a collection of common resources across all topics, the web lists topic-specific resources that can enhance the professional development experience such as videos of teaching and learning, assessment items, and content articles that can be used with specific topic guides. CTS leaders should check the website periodically for additional materials to supplement the parent CTS book as well as this *Leader's Guide*. Examples of ways to use the supplementary resources on the website with the CTS sections are shown in Table 2.3. When you visit the website, you have the option of emailing the supplemental resources to yourself or to colleagues, making them easy to access later for your own work.

Table 2.3   Examples of CTS Supplementary Website Resources and Their Use

CTS Study Guide Section	Examples of Supplement Type and Use
Section I: Identify Adult Content Knowledge	• Content trade books in mathematics—Provide information and visuals to support mathematics content learning. • Website—Provides content information specific to a topic. • Videos—Content experts explaining mathematics concepts.

CTS Study Guide Section	Examples of Supplement Type and Use
Section II: Consider Instructional Implications	• Instructional resource—Model lesson to illustrate effective instruction of a specific topic. • Journal article—Connecting research to practice in the classroom or information about specific teaching techniques. • DVD or Web Videos—Video footage of a teacher teaching a CTS topic.
Section III: Identify Concepts and Specific Ideas	• Mathematics education books—Provide specific information about the science standards such as "unpacking" a learning goal. • Website—Clarifications of learning goals.
Section IV: Examine Research on Student Learning	• Journal article or website—Link to recent research papers or articles about students' thinking in mathematics. • Assessment task—Example assessment probes designed to elicit research identified common errors and misconceptions.
Section V: Examine Coherency and Articulation	• *Atlas* strand maps—Links to specific online *Atlas* maps. • Websites—Links to strand map services such as the NSDL *Atlas of Science Literacy* online strand maps at http://strandmaps.nsdl.org/.

FROM GENERIC TOOLS TO CONTENT-SPECIFIC TOOLS

Leaders have a variety of excellent, general tools at their fingertips to improve and enhance teaching and learning. Many leaders incorporate these tools into their professional development. However, these tools are designed to be used by teachers of all disciplines. As a result, the unique features of mathematics as a discipline are often not explicitly addressed by many of these tools. It is assumed that mathematics educators can "fill in" their own content. However, in many cases, this perpetuates the notion of "practice as usual" if teachers have not been confronted with new ways of thinking about teaching and learning as it applies to specific content. CTS helps bring content specificity to many of the generic tools schools and professional developers are using to develop curriculum, instruction, and assessment, such as the following:

- *Understanding by Design* (Wiggins & McTighe, 2005)
- *Classroom Instruction That Works* (Marzano, Pickering, & Pollock, 2001)
- *Concept-Based Curriculum and Instruction* (Erickson, 1998)
- *Getting Results With Curriculum Mapping* (Jacobs, 2004)
- *Enhancing Professional Practice: A Framework for Teaching* (Danielson, 1996)
- *Professional Learning Communities at Work* (DuFour & Eaker, 1998)
- *Whole-Faculty Study Groups: Creating Student-Based Professional Development* (Murphy & Lick, 2001)

If you are using these tools with teachers in your professional setting, consider ways to use CTS to bring more content specificity to these tools. Many of the designs and suggestions provided in this *Leader's Guide* can be used with the generic tools. For example, when using *Understanding by Design* to design a performance task, it makes sense to conduct a curriculum topic study first in order to be well grounded in the research on learning and clarify what knowledge and skills are desirable according to the standards. Study groups often focus on implementing specific instructional strategies such as infusing reading and literacy strategies across the curriculum, including mathematics. The teachers could benefit from doing a CTS first to identify the important topics students could be writing and reading about and how to avoid introducing vocabulary that may confuse students or perpetuate misconceptions.

WHAT DO LEADERS NEED TO KNOW UP FRONT IN ORDER TO USE CTS OPTIMALLY?

As mentioned earlier, this *Leader's Guide* is intended to be used with *Mathematics Curriculum Topic Study: Bridging the Gap Between Standards and Practice* (Keeley & Rose, 2006). In order to lead others to use CTS effectively, leaders should first become thoroughly familiar with the parent CTS book. The following guiding questions based on material in the parent CTS book that is used with this *Leader's Guide* will prepare you to be an effective leader of the designs included in this book, or to design your own. In the spirit of constructivist learning, if you can answer each of these questions on your own, you will be well prepared to facilitate the designs in this book as well as develop your own and field any questions about CTS. Consider teaming up with a colleague from your school or organization who is using CTS and go through these questions together as a "study group." Thoroughly knowing the parent book this leader's guide is designed to support will enable you to be a knowledgeable, effective, and confident leader of CTS.

Questions for Chapter 1 of the CTS parent book:

- Can you describe what CTS is and what educators gain from it?
- Can you explain why standards and research are used in CTS?
- Why is CTS called a "systematic study process"?
- Why does CTS focus on topics? What does "topic" mean in CTS?
- Where did the CTS process originate? What informed development of CTS?
- How does CTS address teachers' needs at all levels of the professional continuum?

Questions for Chapter 2 of the CTS parent book:

- Can you describe the components of a CTS study guide and what the guide is used for?
- What are the resource books used in CTS?
- Why is CTS described as "having experts at your fingertips 24/7"?
- Can you describe why CTS is a versatile and flexible tool for teachers?

Questions for Chapter 3 of the CTS parent book:

- What are some examples of ways to process information from CTS readings?
- Where would you find Guiding Questions for each of the CTS Sections I–VI? How would you use these questions?

- What is the CTS learning cycle? How would you describe each of its components in terms of what the facilitator does?
- How is a student inquiry using a learning cycle similar to adult CTS inquiry using the CTS learning cycle?
- What does a CTS summary sheet look like and what is its purpose?

Questions for Chapter 4 of the CTS parent book:

- What are some ways to use CTS to improve content knowledge?
- What are some ways to use CTS in a curriculum context?
- What are some ways to use CTS in an instructional context?
- What are some ways to use CTS in an assessment context?

Questions for Chapter 5 of the CTS parent book:

- Which vignettes connect most to your work and the goals of teachers you are working with?
- How do the vignettes illustrate the use of CTS for curriculum, content learning, instruction, and assessment?
- Which vignettes address assessment and how do they illustrate the use of CTS?
- How do the vignettes illustrate how the different grades/levels engage in the CTS process?
- How can vignettes be used to help educators see the value in using CTS?

Questions for Chapter 6 of the CTS parent book:

- How are the CTS guides organized?
- How many guides are there in all?
- Besides the Numbers and Operations, Algebra, Geometry, Measurement, and Data Analysis categories, what other categories include CTS guides?
- How would you describe the differences in grain size of the guides?

Questions for Resources A and B (pp. 209–217) of the CTS book:

- What types of resources are found here?
- How might you use these resources?

Once you become thoroughly familiar with the parent CTS book and the various resources and tools it uses or contains, it is time to consider ways to design and facilitate effective learning using CTS. The next chapter connects CTS to the research on effective professional development and provides facilitation strategies for getting started, managing resources, choosing reading and processing strategies, accessing additional resources, and general tips to make your use of CTS successful. Subsequent chapters offer the specific designs for partial and full topic studies, applications that can be embedded in CTS, and designs and suggestions for embedding CTS within many different types of professional development strategies.

3

Considerations for Designing and Leading CTS

In this chapter, we review research-based principles on effective professional development and demonstrate how using the curriculum topic study (CTS) process as a resource for professional development planning and as a component of any professional development strategy can lead to more effective teacher learning programs. In later sections in this chapter, we describe the CTS learning cycle that is used for all CTS sessions and provide many facilitation strategies and tips that can be used to ensure your CTS sessions fully engage participants in active and thoughtful learning and reflection.

CTS AND THE PRINCIPLES OF EFFECTIVE PROFESSIONAL DEVELOPMENT

In the seminal work describing new ways of thinking about and designing professional development for science and mathematics teachers, Loucks-Horsley, Stiles, Mundry, Love, and Hewson (2010) suggested that professional development designers must pay attention to several key principles for quality teacher learning. In this chapter, we discuss how using CTS strengthens teacher learning programs by addressing many of these research-based principles and provides a strong rationale for how the CTS tools can lead to more effective teacher learning programs.

Education leaders, teacher educators, and professional developers in mathematics endeavor to create professional development programs that have the necessary ingredients and characteristics for success. In our work, we have found that programs designed with certain research-based principles for effective professional development first identified by Loucks-Horsley, Hewson, Love, and Stiles (1998) by synthesizing national standards from the National Research Council (NRC; 1996), National Council of Teachers of

Mathematics (NCTM; 2000), and the National Staff Development Council (2001) can serve as guideposts for the design of quality teacher development programs in mathematics. We have applied these principles directly to our designs for leading teachers through CTS and find that building the CTS strategy into any teacher development from preservice to inservice to teacher leadership development supports these programs to embody the important principles for effective professional development. When these principles are present in professional development, teachers have a greater chance of transforming their practice and enhancing student learning. The principles of effective professional development that we find most connected to the work of CTS are as follows:

1. The professional development design is based on a well-defined image of effective classroom learning and teaching and immerses teachers in developing a clear vision of standards- and research-based practice that ensures learning for all students.

2. The professional development experiences provide opportunities for teachers to build their mathematics content and pedagogical content knowledge (PCK) and examine practice to make direct connections to the classroom.

3. The professional development engages teachers as adult learners using effective means of gaining new knowledge and applying their insights to learning approaches they can use with their students.

4. Effective professional development builds a learning community based on collaboration that is focused on enhancing practice among mathematics teachers.

5. The professional development supports teachers to serve in leadership roles by developing their expertise in their subject matter and providing ample opportunities for them to share knowledge with their colleagues through many different leadership roles as mentors, coaches, facilitators, members of professional learning communities (PLCs) and study groups, and often just by opening their classroom doors to share practice (Loucks-Horsley et al., 2010).

In the next section, we discuss these five principles and provide examples of how CTS brings them to life in professional development initiatives.

Professional Development Is Driven by a Vision of Effective Teaching and Learning

What does it mean for professional development to be driven by a well-defined image of effective classroom teaching and learning, and how can CTS help you get there? As novelist Lewis Carroll once said, "If you don't know where you are going, any road will get you there." Unfortunately, since too often professional development is planned and carried out without a clear vision of where it is headed or what purpose it will accomplish, educators set off on any path. Using CTS, mathematics professional developers can better define where they are going and design the right learning paths to ensure their teachers will reach their learning destinations using navigation tools that will keep them from veering off on side trips, traveling unmarked roads and confusing highways, ending up in dead ends, and embarking on inefficient journeys that cover far more territory than needed.

Effective mathematics learning and teaching is described in six overall principles in the NCTM *Principles and Standards for School Mathematics* (NCTM, 2000). These call for all students to have an equitable opportunity to learn high-quality and important mathematics and for students to have "reasonable and appropriate accommodations … to promote access and attainment for all students" (p. 12). Effective mathematics learning also requires that students have a coherent, articulated curriculum that builds sophisticated understanding of mathematics over the grade levels. The third principle calls for teachers to be able to interpret where their students are with respect to mathematics knowledge and have a deep understanding of mathematics content themselves. In addition, the learning principle advocates for effective mathematics classrooms that provide students with opportunities to develop factual knowledge, procedural proficiency, and conceptual understanding in mathematics. In mathematics lessons, assessment is an integral component and informs the teacher and the students. Important ideas, not simply facts, in mathematics are assessed to show what is valued in mathematics knowledge. Finally, technology is used in mathematics classrooms to support and extend learning, including graphing tools, software, and simulations (NCTM, 2000).

Some of the first questions professional developers, teacher educators, and other leaders need to ask as they aim to provide teacher learning programs that are aligned to these principles are, *What do we want to see in the classroom? What would students be doing? What would teachers be doing?* Once they are clear about these, they are better prepared to decide, *What professional development will get us there?* But these questions are not always easy to answer. It is sometimes difficult to identify concepts and clarify the key ideas important for students to master as well as recognize the instructional implications that impact mastery of that content. Many teacher learning programs allow the instructional materials to dictate the answers to these questions. The problem with that, however, is that instructional materials are not always research- and standards-based. Textbooks and other materials may be written too broadly to appeal to many different standards. They may include activities that contextualize learning to the extent that students have difficulty transferring key ideas to other contexts.

To ensure that teacher education and professional development are based on a well-defined image of effective teaching and learning, we recommend that all teacher educators and professional developers consult the standards and research by engaging in targeted curriculum topic studies. As discussed in Chapter 2 of this *Leader's Guide*, CTS affords access to key information to inform the design of professional learning for teachers. Section I reveals the enduring understandings all adults, including teachers, should have about the topic; Section II uncovers suggestions for providing effective instruction on the topic and the student learning difficulties of which a teacher should be aware; Section III provides insights into the concepts and skills that make up the learning goals for the topic and helps clarify what is most important to teach; Section IV points out the common misunderstandings or difficulties students might have learning the topic and raises ideas about what might contribute to misunderstandings; Section V illustrates the progression of concept development from its most basic beginning in the early grades to a culminating, sophisticated mathematical idea in the later grades; and Section VI provides the opportunity to better understand how state and local standards, common core ideas, and curriculum align with national standards and research. This is critical information educators need to create professional development that is based on a well-defined image of effective teaching and learning.

For example, if you are planning professional development for middle and high school teachers focused on the topic of using data, you can turn to the study guides in the "Data Analysis" category and do a few topic studies on the most relevant topics to enhance your understanding of the content, curricular, and instructional considerations in that area of mathematics to inform your design. You might decide to pull out the CTS guide on "Line Graphs, Bar Graphs, and Histograms" and combine the study of that topic with the results of the study of "Summarizing Data." You could use the readings to identify and understand what is important for teachers to know to be well versed in Grades 7–12 content themselves and identify the learning implications for each grade level. Summarize your CTS findings to help you consider the key ideas to incorporate into your professional development design. Review your summary and use it to consider what materials and experiences make sense for the teachers or prospective teachers you work with and what experiences you can provide them that would best reflect the ideas described in the standards. You might focus your CTS work on either the specific grade levels of the teachers with whom you work or on all of Grades K–12 if your purpose is to work across grade levels or help teachers build a vision of how their grade level fits into the entire K–12 learning experience. Conducting a topic study on the content for your work with teachers as part of your design and planning process will lead to a more focused and effective program, driven by a vision of effective teaching and learning.

Professional Development Builds Content and Pedagogical Content Knowledge and Examines Practice

A primary purpose of professional development is for teachers to gain content and pedagogical content knowledge and reflect on their practice for the purpose of enhancing student learning. In recent years, there has been a growing research base pointing to the need for all teachers to have strong content and pedagogical content knowledge. Research studies that examined the relationship between teacher qualifications and background and student achievement in mathematics and science found certified high school math and science teachers (usually indicating coursework in both subject matter and education methods) had higher achieving students than teachers without certification in their subject area (Darling-Hammond, 2000; Goldhaber & Brewer, 2000; Monk, 1994). Several professional development programs that focus on building teachers' content and pedagogical content knowledge in science and mathematics show greater positive effects on student learning (Brown, Smith, & Stein, 1996; Cohen & Hill, 2000; Kennedy, 1999; Weiss, Pasley, Smith, Banilower, & Heck, 2003; Wiley & Yoon, 1995). Although many professional development programs focus on teaching content, Weiss and colleagues (2003) found it is necessary, but not sufficient, for teachers to have content knowledge:

> [Teachers] also must be skilled in helping students develop an understanding of the content, meaning that they need to know how students typically think about particular concepts, how to determine what a particular student or group of students thinks about those ideas, and how to help students deepen their understanding. (p. 28)

The CTS process clarifies the content necessary for mathematical literacy (i.e., what 12th-grade graduates should know and be able to use throughout their adulthood) and specifically, what students need to learn at a particular grade span. Engaging teachers in a CTS inquiry may lead them to discover that some of the activities they are using to teach certain topics are not aligned with the important content that students need to become mathematically literate or that they are not addressing concepts in enough depth or at a level of sophistication sufficient to promote real understanding. The CTS process also raises teachers' awareness of the content they need to understand better to teach more effectively.

Deepening pedagogical content knowledge is equally essential for effective teaching. This involves helping teachers learn

- what children of certain ages are capable of learning and doing;
- how to anticipate ideas that are likely to be difficult for students to learn and have strategies to help them;
- how to assess students' prior knowledge and help bridge the gap between where they are and where they need to go; and
- strategies for representing and formulating subject matter to make it comprehensible to different learners with varying styles, abilities, and interests (NRC, 2007; Shulman, 1986).

Furthermore, we know from the work of Bransford, Brown, and Cocking (2000) that expert teachers

- know the structure of knowledge in their disciplines,
- know the conceptual barriers that are likely to hinder learning, and
- have a well-organized knowledge of concepts and inquiry procedures and problem-solving strategies.

CTS, by virtue of its focus on the structure of mathematics content, research into students' conceptions, and pedagogical suggestions linked to key ideas and skills, supports teachers to develop this essential expertise. Because teacher knowledge and expertise have such a profound impact on student learning, processes that develop and strengthen teachers' knowledge and skills, such as CTS, are a sound investment toward improving professional development and ultimately student achievement in mathematics.

All professional development leaders are encouraged to do a CTS on the topics for their program so they can investigate the concepts and key ideas from the content that teachers should know (see Sections I and III of the CTS parent book), connections between ideas (see Section V), and instructional implications for teaching the content (see Section II).They can use what they learn to fine-tune their professional development designs and teacher education programs to focus directly on the key ideas that are found in the standards. With respect to enhancing pedagogical content knowledge, professional developers can turn to the readings in Section IV to explore the research on student learning for their topics. The research on learning reveals the commonly held ideas and misunderstandings students bring to their learning, and it is also likely that some teachers, especially those who do not have substantive preparation in mathematics, may hold similar ideas that need to be surfaced and challenged. Based on what professional developers glean from their topic studies, they may modify their plans to include activities that better reflect the suggestions for teaching the topic and build in formative assessments that help teachers identify and build on prior knowledge of the key ideas in the standards.

In addition to building content and pedagogical content knowledge, this principle calls for teachers to have opportunities to make direct connections to their teaching practice. Increasingly teachers are involved in teams and PLCs that afford the opportunity to examine practice for the purpose of increasing student learning. Early forays into collaborative work suffered from a lack of focus on the content and how to teach it (Loucks-Horsley et al., 2010). Groups lacked processes for drawing upon trusted mathematics resources and a strong knowledge base to guide their discussions. With few resources to guide them, teachers often relied solely on their own opinions or how things worked in their classrooms. Teachers gathered to examine student work and often used wonderful protocols, but needed help to make sound professional judgments about the quality of the content learning and to learn to look for evidence that students were learning important content, which involved knowing and being clear about the key ideas in a learning goal and the appropriate level of sophistication expected by it. They also needed to be aware of common errors and misconceptions that might surface during an examination of the student work. Examining student work often focused on what the students knew or did not know, but often failed to link the student results back to teacher practice and what they might do differently to improve students' opportunities to learn and demonstrate their learning. CTS directly supports teachers to deepen their content and pedagogical content knowledge and to use their new insights to examine practice in an accountable, collegial, and content-based way. Here is where engaging the teachers themselves in doing a CTS as part of their professional development really pays off. The authors have observed and participated in countless institutes, workshops, lesson studies, study groups, teachers' examinations of student work, coaching sessions, and other forms of professional development. What stands out for us is how using CTS to examine practice changes the conversation teachers have. Teachers move from talking in generalities to pointing out specific knowledge and skills discussed in the standards that they want their children to know and be able to use. They stop talking about what they do personally and start talking about what standards and research recommend.

When teachers use a standards- and research-based approach to examine student work, they focus more on what matters, the content students know, and the difficulties they may have in learning the content. This opens the door for rethinking lessons and intervening when students do not learn the content. Collaborative groups involved in examining student work, setting standards, and choosing and implementing curriculum have enriched their abilities to examine practice by using CTS first to develop a shared vision as to what to look for in student work or whether a lesson includes instructional strategies likely to address common errors and difficulties in mathematics or if curriculum reflects appropriate content for certain grade spans. Once teachers have CTS experience, they are able to discuss how the object of their CTS inquiry matches the standards and research. There is less talk about how things work in "my classroom," and more professional discourse based in evidence and standards that focus on all learners.

Although CTS is not a substitute for in-depth learning on content, it is a helpful tool for professional developers to use to focus what content they will immerse teachers in learning and an extremely helpful, versatile resource for teachers to use to discover what content and pedagogical content they need to know.

Professional Development Is Research-Based and Engages Teachers as Adult Learners in the Learning Approaches They Will Use With Their Students

This principle of effective professional development suggests that teachers need to have time to engage as adult learners in some of the same mathematics that they will teach their students. For example, like classroom instruction, the professional development should have some means of assessing prior knowledge and using what teachers already know to inform the professional development instruction. Instructors of teachers often use pre-tests to inform the course content. Teacher educators and professional developers can use CTS to develop assessments or assessment probes (see discussion and guidelines for doing this in Chapter 6, pp. 181–185>) or use existing assessment probes (e.g., Rose, Arline, & Minton, 2007) to surface teachers' existing ideas.

From there, you can design learning experiences for teachers that immerse the teachers in the content they need to learn. Teachers need the opportunity to experience the activities, mathematical inquiry, and tools they will use with their own students. Their learning is facilitated by guidance and probing questions from the professional development facilitator. The teachers are guided to explain their understanding and to revisit how that changes or adds to their own prior knowledge. Their experience is "bookended" by a reflection on their experience as adults and in their role as teachers. The facilitator helps teachers identify what they did as learners, what the facilitator did in terms of the lesson design, assessment of prior knowledge, use of probing questions, and providing feedback on whether the explanations teachers gave were correct. The teachers develop a view of how they would do these same steps with their own students and develop a plan to translate them to their own classroom.

Once again, CTS is a valuable tool for designing and immersing teachers in this type of learning. Conducting the readings in Section I of each study guide in the CTS parent book gives a picture of what the mathematically literate adult should know about the mathematics topic. Teacher educators can use this to begin to think about what teachers should know and understand and to develop or choose an assessment to measure prior knowledge. Focusing on the grade level of the materials being used, the professional developer would also want to review Sections II, III, and IV of the study guide. The findings from this review would help them to ask probing questions during the lesson and uncover persistent common errors or misconceptions. After teachers experience the topics as learners, they might be interested in doing a CTS themselves to explore what their students should know and understand and use that to plan their instruction. Effective professional developers need to design experiences for teachers that mirror what their students will learn, but that honor them as teachers and adults. CTS supports this by helping them get a view of both what they should know as mathematically literate adults and what goals they need to work toward for the grade level of their students.

Effective Professional Development Builds a Learning Community Among Mathematics Teachers

In recent years, we have learned more and more about what makes professional development have an impact on teachers' thinking and practice. Programs that provide opportunities for teachers to collaborate with their colleagues and other experts to improve their practice, take risks, and try out new ideas have a greater chance of having such an impact in the classroom where it counts. Hord (1997) and Hord and Sommers (2008) pointed out that there are five components of PLCs. These are as follows:

1. Shared beliefs, values, and vision

2. Shared and supportive leadership

3. Collective learning and its application

4. Supportive conditions

5. Shared personal practice

As introduced in Chapter 1, the importance of developing PLCs among teachers is an underlying belief that has guided the CTS work. PLCs by their very nature are bringing professional discourse into the regular school day. Teachers are committing to goals for student learning and reflecting and discussing how their actions will lead to those goals. The success of such groups demands that they use existing research and resources so they can "stand on the shoulders of giants," which is a primary goal of CTS, rather than continuously reinvent the wheel. The CTS resources and tools provide the help PLCs need to effectively conduct their work in a collaborative, content-focused setting.

CTS Develops Teacher Leaders

To support and sustain professional development, there needs to be a focus on building teacher leadership. Teacher leaders are encouraged to contribute to the profession in many ways, by shaping and providing professional development, mentoring and coaching, facilitating PLCs, developing and supporting ongoing improvements in their buildings, and leading others to use effective practice. In the Northern New England Co-Mentoring Network, an NSF-supported program that developed teacher leaders to serve as mentors and leaders of PLCs in schools in Maine, New Hampshire, and Vermont, teachers identified CTS as one of the essential tools in their leadership toolbox. (See the example in Chapter 7 of how CTS can be used to support mentor teacher leaders.) Whether they were guiding teachers to examine demonstration lessons, helping to select curriculum, planning teacher workshops, or mentoring a beginning teacher, the mentor teachers started by doing a CTS on the topic they were using. By using CTS and demonstrating the various ways CTS can be used in teachers' work, teachers became stronger leaders with a deep knowledge of the standards and research on learning. In their work with peer teachers, they shared their own opinions less; instead, they engaged others in examining the standards and research to inform and justify decisions. CTS is a tool that not only guides and informs leaders' work, but also provides them with a process to develop a common core of understanding within the various groups they work with and a shared language for discussing teaching and learning.

CTS LEARNING CYCLE

Leaders are encouraged to read and become familiar with the CTS learning cycle described on pages 38–48 in the Mathematics CTS parent book so that you will know and understand how participant learning evolves from one stage to the next. Figure 3.1 graphically shows the stages of a CTS Learning Cycle.

Many of the CTS designs included in Chapters 4 through 7 of this book are designed using the CTS learning cycle as shown in Figure 3.1 with specific strategies for each of the seven stages in the learning model, including engagement, elicitation, exploration, development, synthesis, application, and reflection. You may wish to vary these strategies to address the specific goals of your groups. Table 3.1 provides suggestions for facilitating each stage.

As you examine the full topic study design modules included in Chapter 5 of this *Leader's Guide*, notice how the stages of the learning cycle have been incorporated throughout the design. To print out a poster of the CTS Learning Cycle, see the file on the CD-ROM under Chapter 3. The icons in Table 3.1 are included to indicate the learning cycle stage that each of the module activities is designed to address.

Figure 3.1 The CTS Learning Cycle of Inquiry, Study, and Reflection

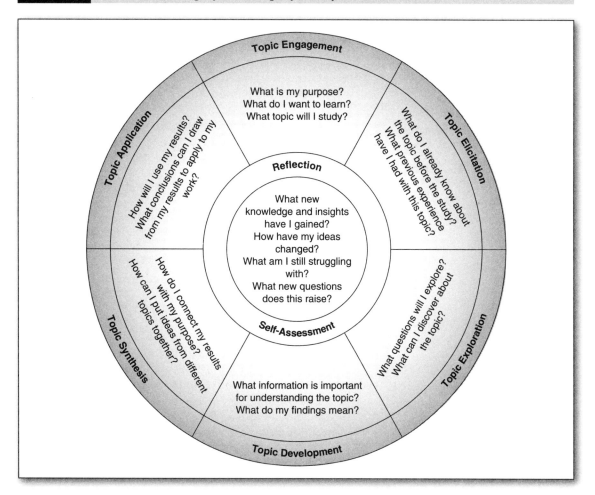

Table 3.1 CTS Learning Cycles and Suggestions for Facilitation

Stage in the CTS Learning Cycle	Icon	Suggestions for Facilitating Each Stage
TOPIC ENGAGEMENT: Establish a purpose for doing CTS; create interest in studying the topic.		• Use a hook showing student difficulty with a topic (e.g., video, student work, performance data). • Ask why the topic is important to K–12 mathematics. • Ask participants to record their personal goals for the session. (What do they hope to learn more about?)
TOPIC ELICITATION: Activate prior knowledge related to the topic (content, instructional considerations, learning goals, misconceptions, connections).		• Brainstorm ideas about the topic prior to doing CTS. • Use Frayer Model for terminology and operational definitions. • Provide 4-Square Template (CTS parent book p. 44). • Generate list of concepts that make up the topic. • Use assessment probes to predict student difficulties. • Generate beliefs about learning related to the topic. • Administer Pre-CTS questionnaire.

(Continued)

Table 3.1   (Continued)

Stage in the CTS Learning Cycle	Icon	Suggestions for Facilitating Each Stage
TOPIC EXPLORATION: Explore the topic by reading assigned sections of the text listed on the study guide with clear purpose.		• Choose grouping strategy and assign readings. • Review study guide sections with the group or create a reading assignment guide. • Provide time for individuals to read and process their assigned section. • Provide materials for recording information.
TOPIC DEVELOPMENT: Engage in group discussion to clarify and make meaning of the readings.		• Provide time for individuals in each small group to share and discuss each of the readings. • Select a large group debriefing strategy. • Raise and clarify major points with the large group. • Encourage groups to create a summary sheet of their findings. (This is usually done later, using the group's study results.)
TOPIC SYNTHESIS: Look across all sections of the CTS—combine CTS findings to support purpose for doing the CTS; combine findings when studying two or more topics.		• After each participant reports out on their reading section, have group discuss the overall significance of the study. • Encourage groups to share 3–5 major insights or key points gained from the CTS. • Compare and contrast "old" ideas with "new." • When two different topic studies are done simultaneously, combine similar and related findings from each topic.
TOPIC APPLICATION: Apply findings to a specific context related to participants' work.		• Choose a context application from the CTS parent book Chapter 6 to apply CTS results. • Revisit elicitation questions and respond by applying new information gained from the CTS.

FACILITATION TIPS AND STRATEGIES

As a professional learning strategy, CTS differs from other types of mathematics professional development, which often involve teachers in solving mathematics problems and examining student work and thinking in mathematics. Rather, CTS engages teachers in using text-based readings and having sense-making discussions supported by findings in the text. The process is directed at formulating questions about teaching and learning specific to a curricular topic, gathering data from text, analyzing the information, drawing conclusions from the information and having sense-making discussions, and communicating findings to others. In many ways, CTS also parallels the professional development design process in that a teaching or learning problem is identified, information is gathered from text readings to address the problem, the constraints of the classroom and context are considered, the findings from CTS are applied to propose a solution or develop a product (e.g., improve curriculum coherency, develop assessment probes that can be used to inform instruction, and enhance content knowledge), the applied results of CTS are evaluated for their impact on teaching and learning, and CTS results and products are communicated and shared with others.

A major difference between facilitating professional learning in a hands-on/problem-solving mathematics setting compared with facilitating learning in CTS is that the CTS leader must incorporate a variety of facilitation skills to guide teachers in managing the text materials and constructing new learning from the readings. Making the experience as rich as possible involves having a repertoire of facilitation tips and strategies to guide adult learners and manage group processes, including establishing productive norms for collaboration, reading, sense-making discussions, and teacher reflection. In this section, we share some of our tips and strategies for facilitating the type of learning that results from the CTS process of reading and discussing text. The first step facilitators must consider is how to acquire and manage the resource materials used for CTS.

ACQUIRING AND MANAGING MATERIALS

When designing professional development that incorporates CTS, facilitators must first acquire their own copies of the CTS parent book and all the CTS resources used to conduct a CTS. (See a complete list of resource books in Table 1.1, p. 2.) Second, facilitators must decide on how to provide access to the CTS resources when they use CTS in their professional development sessions. If the purpose of the professional development is to train teachers in the use of CTS with the expectation that they will continue to use it, then it is important to provide all teachers with their own copies of the CTS parent book. Whether or not you provide copies of the resource books depends on your budget, whether teachers have access to the resources in their schools or personally own copies, and the availability of an Internet connection during your sessions so that teachers with laptops can electronically access *Science for All Americans, Benchmarks for Science Literacy*, NCTM *Standards* or *Focal Points, Common Core State Standards for Mathematics*, or selected maps from the *Atlas of Science Literacy*. The following are a variety of options for acquiring and managing materials. Choose an option that best fits your audience and professional development context.

Options

- *Provide a set of resources to each participant.* This is obviously the most expensive and resource intensive approach. Professional developers who choose this option often fund this option with grant funds for participant materials. Several Math-Science Partnership (MSP) grants have included CTS in their professional development program and purchased materials for their participating teachers.
- *Provide a set of resources to each school team.* If participants attend your professional development as members of school teams and your funding source can support it, consider providing a set of materials to each team of up to five teachers from the same school. These materials can then continue to be used by the school team and their school colleagues for their CTS-related work.
- *Obtain and provide a session set of resources.* If you regularly use CTS in your work with teachers, consider acquiring your own set of materials to provide for use during your CTS professional development. For each group of six teachers, provide

  - One *Beyond Numeracy* (optional),
  - One *Science for All Americans,*
  - Two *Benchmarks for Science Literacy,*
  - Two NCTM *Principles and Standards of School Mathematics,*
  - One National Council of Teachers of Mathematics *Research Companion,* and
  - One copy of each volume of the *Atlas of Science Literacy.*

- *Obtain a partial session set and borrow or have participants bring their resources.* You may wish to purchase a few sets of resources and find an organization or school that can lend you additional session copies. You might also contact teachers in advance who may already have copies of some of the resources and ask them to bring them. Between your set, borrowed copies, and ones teachers own, you can gather enough copies for your audience to use.
- *Use paired readings.* If you have session copies but not enough for everyone in your audience, consider having teachers read the CTS sections in pairs. Choose one of the reading strategies discussed later in this chapter to have them process together as they read.
- *Alternate readings.* If all participants do not have their own books and there is a set of shared books provided on each table, alternate readings when you choose the option where every person reads all the sections. For example, while one person is reading *Science for All Americans,* have others at the table select a different book and section. Once that section reading is complete, the book is returned to the stack so someone else can use it when they finish with their book.
- *Provide handouts of the readings.* If resource book sets are not available, consider making copies of each of the readings and distributing the copies to groups. If you do this, be sure to put your full set of the resources on a "library display" so that teachers can look at the actual books during the breaks. Alternatively, if you have some session sets, but not enough to go around, or you have copies of some books but not others, you might combine providing copies of the actual books with copies of readings from the books.
- *Combine books with electronic access.* If you have a wireless Internet connection at your setting and some teachers bring their own laptop computers, provide access to the online versions of the resources to the teachers with laptops and provide the books to those who do not have laptops. If you are supplementing CTS with the *Common Core State Standards for Mathematics,* they are online.
- *Purchase used copies for sessions.* If your budget is limited, consider acquiring used copies of the books to make up your session sets. Amazon.com and other booksellers often sell used copies of each of these resources; you can assemble a set for a small percentage of the cost of buying all the books new.

> The CTS website (www.curriculumtopicstudy .org) provides links directly to the resources that are online.

One of the laments leaders frequently hear after introducing CTS to teachers is that they love the process but won't be able to use it after the session because their schools do not have the funds to buy the materials. From our experience, we have found that teachers who are excited about using CTS go back to their schools and share its value with their administrators. As a result, most of the teachers we have worked with have convinced their administrators to provide the resources for their continued professional development, a set for school-based PLCs or grade-level teams, or a school set to keep in their school's professional library. What they originally perceived as a roadblock to using CTS was overcome when their administrators saw the value of investing in these resources to build the capacity of their teachers to grow and collaborate as professionals for the purpose of improving student learning. One of our teachers remarked how her principal shifted from bringing in the "one shot wonder or motivational speaker" that cost the school $3,500 for one day to using those same funds to provide 18 sets of CTS materials for teachers to use. In addition, many of the teachers we have worked with have gone on to buy their own sets of materials to be part of their professional library that they will keep throughout their professional career. Many teachers recognize having a set of functional resources as part of the professionalism of teaching and recognize the value of investing in their own future (and they like that it is tax deductible). In summary, do not let remarks about not having the books discourage you after providing the professional development. You will be delighted to learn later when you see many of your participants again that this has not been an obstacle for their continued use of CTS.

DEVELOPING NORMS FOR COLLABORATIVE WORK

Collaborative teacher groups are guided by group norms that set parameters and expectations for how they will work together. In all of our professional development work, we have drawn upon the work of Garmston and Wellman (2008) to establish and set norms for collaboration and productive work. Their work has focused in part on ensuring that all members of a group develop the norms and skills to support collaborative work. They suggest groups adopt "seven norms of collaboration" that are driven by three conditions or commitments (Garmston & Wellman, p. 31):

1. Intention to support thinking, problem solving, and group development

2. Attention of the group members to attend fully to the other members

3. Linguistic skills of the listener or responder

The seven norms are universal and support all group development. They include the following:

1. *Pausing:* This includes four types of pauses: (1) when a question is asked to allow processing time; (2) when someone speaks, which allows others to hear what is being said before jumping into the conversation; (3) personal reflection time, when someone asks the group to give them a moment to think about a question or idea that has been raised; and (4) the collective pause, when the group stops and reflects or may write to collect their thoughts.

2. *Paraphrasing:* This norm ensures that the information shared has been understood. Garmston and Wellman suggest several "paraphrase stems" such as *you're suggesting . . .; you're proposing . . .; so what you are wondering is . . .;* and *so you are thinking that . . ."* (p. 33). Group members check for understanding before launching into discussions of their own interpretations.

3. *Putting inquiry at the center:* The basic idea of this norm is that group members "explore the perceptions, assumptions, and interpretations of others before advocating one's own ideas" (p. 34).

4. *Probing for specificity:* This norm helps guard against the miscommunication that can result when group members use vague terms, or use words like *best, worst, valuable, great,* and so forth without grounding them in clear criteria.

5. *Placing ideas on the table:* Effective groups signal when they are putting an idea on the table for consideration and when they are taking the idea off when it seems to have little support or is bogging down the group.

6. *Paying attention to self and others:* Everyone in the group needs to stay aware of how they are communicating with others and how their messages are being received. Group members consciously monitor their own verbal and nonverbal behavior and that of their group members.

7. *Presuming positive intentions:* Group members hold on to the idea that each member is a "committed professional who wants to solve a real problem" (p. 39).

Establishing these norms and supporting our groups to develop the skills needed to use them has been a major part of the success of CTS groups. In addition there are several norms that we have used that are specific to supporting the CTS work. We encourage you to start every CTS session by establishing your own norms, drawing from those above and the following norms specific to CTS work.

CTS GROUP NORMS

Honor Times

It will be very difficult to accomplish the goals of CTS if people are allowed to be off task or to use group time to take long "bird walks" sharing autobiographical stories, even when they are somewhat connected to the group task. Encourage your group to adopt a norm of honoring times and staying on task.

Cite the Evidence

This norm encourages all group members to share what they learned from the CTS readings without inserting their own opinions. Ask participants to stick to the facts and data from the readings, including citing the page and passage being cited. When it comes to CTS, we like the old line from TV's Jack Webb in *Dragnet*: "Just the facts, ma'am!"

Contribute to the Learning of Others

This norm reflects Garmston and Wellman's norm of paying attention to self and others. It reminds group members to be responsible for their own and their group members' learning by pausing, paraphrasing, and probing for specificity and making sure time is managed to allow everyone to contribute.

Share Resources

In most CTS sessions, people are sharing the many resource books used for the reading. Encourage everyone to complete their reading as quickly as possible and take notes they can refer to later during discussions, so they can make books available to others as soon as possible.

Check for Understanding

During the report out phase of most CTS sessions, it is essential for people to learn from what others have read. Encourage groups to manage their time to allow a few minutes for report out and then a pause to process and then clarify any confusing questions.

For information that is still unclear, encourage group members to jot a question on a sticky note and post it on a chart labeled the *CTS Content Questions* that is always posted during CTS sessions.

Maintain a Safe Learning Environment

The goal of all CTS sessions is learning. If teachers are fearful, they will be unable to reveal what they do not know, and this is counterproductive to the goals. Set the norm that it is safe to raise any question about something that is confusing or not understood. Make it safe by inviting everyone to post questions on the *CTS Content Questions* chart for those who do not want to ask a question publicly. Encourage small group members to ask each other for help with something they read that they do not understand. Since we often have a broad range of participants, from those who are new to teaching mathematics to those who may be math professors, it is important to establish that we are all responsible for one another's learning, and ask all participants to share their expertise with each other.

OPTIONS FOR ORGANIZING AND DISCUSSING READINGS

As the authors and field testers worked with CTS, we discovered the need to have structures and activities for participants to use to organize and discuss the readings in small or large groups. The following are recommended strategies we have used in our CTS sessions. Choose the strategy that best fits your audience and facilitation style. Facilitators can select any of these strategies to use in any of the facilitation designs included in Chapters 4 through 7.

Jigsaw Strategies

A commonly used reading strategy, a jigsaw builds on the idea that we learn best when we teach new material to others. It is also a way to cut back on the amount of reading one individual would have to do by having the readings distributed among a group, with each reading summarized and shared by the group member assigned to that reading. Participants are placed in cooperative learning groups of five to six people; group size is usually based on the number of CTS sections used, number of CTS resources used, or length or sections of a reading. The following are suggested ways to jigsaw the readings:

Option 1: Large Group Jigsaw With Expert Groups

In this option, sections are assigned by tables, counting off or passing out cards with the assigned reading. Each table group is an "expert" for their assigned reading or section of a CTS study guide. After the experts have read their section, they discuss their reading. For example, all the people who do the reading for CTS Section IA at a table discuss the IA section, or all the people who read Section II discuss their section. After expert groups have discussed the findings from their section, they summarize their results for the whole group on chart paper and briefly (1 minute or less) point out their major findings.

Option 2: Small Group Jigsaw With Expert Groups

In this option, each person in a small group is assigned to be the "expert" for a particular reading or section of a CTS study guide. Everyone in the group or at the table is assigned one of the topic guide readings. After the experts have read their section, they meet briefly with all the other "experts" in the room who read the same section for a discussion. For example, all the people who read Section IA meet and discuss their section, or all the people who read Section II meet and discuss their section. After expert groups have discussed the findings from their section, they return to their small groups and each expert takes a turn presenting a summary of the discussion to their own table group, resulting in all sections of the CTS readings summarized at each table group.

Option 3: Regular Small Group Jigsaw

This option is similar to the one above except experts do not meet in expert groups first. Each person in a small group volunteers to take a section to read, which they then summarize for the rest of their small group.

Option 4: Large Group Fishbowl Jigsaw

This option works best when you want to engage the whole group in processing the readings but need to parcel them out for the sake of time. Count off by numbers or pass out cards with the assigned reading. The readings will be spread out among the participants in the room. Bring each assigned reading group, or selected members of a group, up to the front of the room to sit in chairs as a panel, or in a circle in the center of the room, where everyone can see and hear them (in "the fishbowl"). Facilitate a discussion of the assigned reading to the group in the fishbowl while others listen and take notes. Provide time for those outside the fishbowl to ask questions, then switch to the next group, and so on.

Assigning Jigsaw Readings

There are a variety of ways to assign the jigsaw readings. The jigsaw breakdown you choose depends upon the number of resource books you have available (or you can make copies and use handouts) and the grade levels of your participants. Individuals can be assigned a section, or sections can be assigned to pairs. The latter is particularly helpful when using collaborative reading strategies (discussed later in this section) to extract meaning from the CTS assigned text sections. The following describes options for breaking down the jigsaw readings:

Assign by sections: IA, IB, IIA, IIB, IIIA, IIIB, IVA, IVB, V, and VIA or VIB (where appropriate) or I, II, III, IV, V, and VI (where appropriate). Review the readings before the session, and if the lengths of some readings are short, consider combining some sections.

Assign by book: Ask participants to read everything in one book, for example, all sections in NCTM *Standards* or *Science for All Americans.*

Assign by grade span: K–2, 3–5, 6–8, 9–12 assigned to read only their grade span sections of all of the following: IIA, IIB, IIIA, IIIB, and V. Everyone reads IA and, if *Beyond Numeracy* is used, include IB.

Other Strategies

In field-testing our designs, we found that some groups prefer jigsaws, and others prefer not to be restricted in their readings and discussions. Jigsaws can be overused. We recommend varying strategies if your professional development includes multiple opportunities to do CTS. Whether you choose to jigsaw or not depends on your audience and the topic chosen. The following are other strategies you can use to read and discuss CTS findings with others.

Option 5: Large Group Discussion, All Readings

This option works best when participants have access to all of the resource books or copies of the readings are provided so participants are able to do all or some of the readings in advance of the session. Each participant reads all the sections of the CTS study guide selected by the facilitator for a particular topic or module and makes notes that will be brought to the CTS session discussion. This option can also be used on-site without prereading if the time dedicated for reading during the session is considerably increased.

Option 6: Small Group Discussion, Assigned Expert

In this option, everyone has an opportunity to read and discuss any or all of the sections, depending on their pace and the number of books available. Prior to reading, the group assigns an "expert" for each selected reading. The "expert" starts with that reading in order to ensure that every selected section has been read by at least one person who can discuss it with the group, but the group members can read other sections as well if time allows. This option allows the group flexibility in reading what they are most interested in, provides an opportunity to sample the different books, and gives the participants a more complete picture of the different findings for each section. Many participants prefer this option.

CTS RECOMMENDED READING AND SUMMARIZING STRATEGIES

To ensure learning for participants, it is important to use structures and activities to process and summarize readings. The following are recommended reading and summarizing strategies. Facilitators can select any of these strategies to embed into any of the facilitation designs in Chapters 4 through 7 or their own designs for CTS professional development.

Say Something

This strategy was introduced to us by Bruce Wellman (adapted from Lipton & Wellman, 2004), who provided the facilitation skills training for both the Northern New England Co-Mentoring Network and the National Academy for Science and Mathematics Education Leadership, both of which worked with the CTS project to try out the CTS materials. It provides a structure for quick and ongoing processing of text materials.

Directions: Ask each member of your group to work with a partner. The pairs will individually read a section of text and stop when they get to a designated point. (The facilitator can designate the stopping points, e.g., every third paragraph or at the bottom of a page or ask the pairs to decide where they will stop.) When partners are ready, they start reading and then stop and "say something" to each other about what they just read; for example, you might ask them to say something about a significant idea or a connection to their work or something the passage made them think about. Remind them to keep the "something" they say short. Continue the process, stopping at several designated places to "say something" (such as at the end of a subsection or every few paragraphs) until they reach the end.

Question Stems

Providing a list of question stems for participants to use as they read focuses their reading and helps them make connections to their own context. Examples of question stems include the following:

- What are the key points made in this section?
- Give an example of how this section relates to your practice.
- What might you infer from reading this section?
- What evidence from this reading can be used to support our work?
- How does this compare with your prior knowledge?

Read, Write, Pair, Share

This strategy is similar to think-pair-share, but with the emphasis on the reading shaping the discussion. Participants read a section, record important ideas to share, pair up with a partner, and discuss the reading. You can combine this with the use of question stems to focus the sharing conversations.

Paired Reading

In this strategy, pairs of teachers help each other explore and make sense of the readings by reading the text aloud to each other, each taking turns, and summarizing the main ideas. The first partner reads a paragraph aloud, and the second partner summarizes the paragraph. Roles are reversed for the next paragraph. Continue alternating roles until the reading is completed. Once the entire reading is completed, both partners cooperatively summarize the main points of that section and identify any questions they have.

Problem Scenarios

This reading strategy provides motivation to read the text and helps teachers focus on the main ideas as they read. To use this strategy, a problem is posed for each CTS section. As teachers read the section, they record information that would address the person's problem. Examples of problem scenarios to use with each CTS reading section include the following:

Section I

Jenna doesn't have a mathematics background and is afraid she doesn't know enough about this topic to teach it. What does she need to know to be mathematically literate in this topic?

Section II

Jim's instruction just doesn't seem to be working with his students. What are some things he should consider when teaching this topic?

Section III

Ricia knows she should focus on the most important ideas when she is teaching this topic, but her state standards are too broad to know what the key ideas are. Furthermore, there is so much material in her textbook, she doesn't know what to focus on and what to leave out. How can you help Ricia focus on clear and meaningful learning goals?

Section IV

Andre is aware of the importance of considering students' prior knowledge. He knows there are common confusions and misunderstandings his students are likely to have but doesn't know what they might be. How can you help Andre become more aware of the misunderstandings his students might have related to this topic?

Section V

Florio's curriculum contains a list of learning goals he needs to teach this year. The curriculum provides no guidance on which ideas are connected and should be taught together, what precursor ideas should come first, and connections he can make to other areas of mathematics, technology, or science. How can you help him see the connections among important ideas in mathematics and how one idea can inform understanding of others?

Section VI

Anita uses her state's standards to guide her teaching but isn't always sure about what the standards intend as far as the experiences she should provide students, where to draw the boundaries in teaching content that may not be necessary or exceed the standards, and exactly what the key idea is in a standard. How can you help Anita clarify her state standards related to this topic?

You can use these scenarios or write your own. Post the scenarios or give each section group a card or sheet of paper with the problem they are addressing and space to record their response.

One-Word or One-Sentence Summary

In table groups, craft a one-word or one-sentence summary of the section you read (or you can use this as an end-of-the-day wrap-up). Each table chooses a spokesperson who is prepared to share the word or sentence and explain why the group chose it.

OSQ

As participants read a section, have them record and share the following:

*O*ne major new idea for me

*S*omething I already knew

*Q*uestions I have

Facilitators record the OSQs on flip charts as they are shared.

Focused Reading (Lipton & Wellman, 2004)

To use this strategy, introduce participants to three "focused reading" symbols.

1. √ —Got it. I know or understand this.

2. ! —This is really important or interesting.

3. ? —Something I do not understand

Post the three symbols above on a flip chart or PowerPoint and review them with participants. As participants go through their CTS readings, have them mark the text using these symbols (or use sticky notes). After reading in groups of three to four people, the participants review the items they marked with each of the symbols. They can start with the checks and review what they learned, then move to the points that were important, and finish with questions. Invite participants to help each other to clarify the places where they had questions if possible. If time permits, invite participants to share a few of the ideas they marked and address any that need clarification.

REPORTING OUT STRATEGIES

It is important for groups to have an opportunity to report out their CTS findings to others, both to reinforce their own learning and to share new insights with the whole group. This is also very useful for clarifying any ideas that are not correct. However, be aware that when one strategy is used too often or the reporting out takes too long, people may tune out. Participants' attention can wane if groups are not reminded to keep their reports brief and to the point. We often use a timer to keep report out to the designated time. It is also important for leaders to remember to encourage groups to speak from the CTS evidence, not their own personal opinions. The designs included in Chapters 4 and 5 show how various strategies can be used to report out CTS findings. Examples you can embed into any CTS design include the following:

Gallery Walks

In this strategy, groups record their CTS findings on chart paper in a form that others can understand (groups agree on main categories for what will be posted ahead of time). After all the charts have been posted, participants do a "gallery walk," visiting each poster and learning from what others did. During the gallery walk, you might encourage participants to jot down notes of things they want to remember or questions they might have for the groups.

Gallery Walk With Docents

This is a modified version of the gallery walk described above to be used with groups of thirty or fewer participants. After groups post their CTS findings charts around the room, the entire room stands and gathers around the first chart while a group member acts as a "docent," giving a brief report of the findings described on group's chart. When the report is finished, the whole group travels to the next chart and the process is repeated. This keeps people on their feet and attentive during the report out process.

Group Presentations

This typical form of reporting out involves small groups giving a brief presentation to the other groups on their CTS task. Encourage the group to focus on the major "ah-ha's" and "just the facts" they gained from studying their section(s).

Key Points

Each participant crafts four to five key points or take-away messages from their CTS findings. Each group member shares their key points with others at the table. When all the small groups are done, the leader asks each table to share just one key point from their table with the whole group.

Give Me Ten

After small groups have had time to discuss their findings and clarify understandings, the leader asks the whole group to list ten new things they learned from doing the CTS. The leader holds ten fingers up and counts down one at a time as each participant volunteers one learning. The leader wraps up after the tenth volunteer and provides a brief synthesis of the group's learning and adds any essential points that were not raised.

Partner Speaks

This strategy works well in small groups where CTS participants work primarily in pairs, rather than table groups. As pairs discuss their CTS findings, each person listens carefully to the partner and records key ideas and insights gained. After the discussion is finished, each person reports out a few of the key findings the partner shared. This strategy encourages active listening and allows all voices to be heard.

REFLECTION ON CTS

Reflection is a vital part of any CTS professional development design. The process of personal and group reflection allows CTS users to connect the theoretical basis of the standards and the research base on learning that contributes to a deeper understanding of a curricular topic. In the process of reflection, teachers think about what the CTS process means to them and how they and their students will benefit from it. The process of reflection promotes metacognition and helps teachers see how their beliefs, ideas, knowledge, and skills as a teacher may have changed as a result of CTS. The reflection process also surfaces issues that may need further attention or understandings that may need further development before teachers can apply them effectively. Group reflection provides an opportunity to see what others have learned and relate that to one's own learning. It also provides a formative assessment opportunity for the facilitator to gauge what participants gained from the CTS process. The following are some of the strategies we have used and field tested in CTS professional development designs. Any of these strategies can be embedded into the CTS designs that you use.

Bumper Sticker Statements

This engaging reflection strategy is used when participants are first introduced to CTS and are reflecting on the value of CTS tools and processes. Provide participants with sentence strips or 24-inch strips of paper (note: you can use a sheet of chart paper to make the strips). Ask them to work in groups to create bumper stickers that capture their views of CTS in short, catchy expressions they would want to share with other mathematics educators. When participants are done, ask each group to stand and read their bumper sticker and then post it on the wall for all to see.

PVF (Paired Verbal Fluency)

This technique is used as a partner reflection and involves partners taking turns in timed rounds, talking about their CTS findings (Lipton & Wellman, 2004). The activity only takes seven minutes yet the reflectors can surface quite a bit in this short time. Start by asking teachers to stand up and make eye contact with the first person they see and then move to stand with that person. Once all the pairs are matched, ask each partner to decide who will be partner A and who will be partner B (after they select partners announce that partner B will go first). Provide a discussion prompt such as "What was most valuable to you during this CTS session and what do you plan to do next?" Announce that when you give the signal, one partner will talk for exactly two minutes while the other partner listens actively but may not say a word while their partner is talking. After two minutes, announce "switch," and partners trade roles and repeat. At the next "switch," the first partner talks for one minute, followed by "switch" and the other partner talks for one minute. The last round is just thirty seconds each. Have them thank their partners, return to their seats, and ask for three to four people to share something they heard with the whole group.

Idea Exchange

Ask participants to reflect back on their experience and jot down three to five new ideas of things they will go back and use as a result of their CTS experience. Have participants get up and exchange one idea with five different people and then return to their seats. After everyone has shared, ask the whole group to share three to four ideas.

I Used to Think . . . But Now I Know . . .

On a PowerPoint slide or a handout, write the phrase "I used to think _____, but now I know _____" (Keeley, 2007; Keeley & Rose Tobey, 2011). Ask participants to fill in the blanks based on their CTS experience. When they are finished, ask all the people at a table to read their statements to their small group. When finished, ask for three to five examples to share with the large group. If the group is small (twenty or fewer participants), you can quickly go around the room and have each person read their statement.

Three-Two-One

Three-Two-One is a technique that scaffolds participants' reflections (Lipton & Wellman, 2004). It provides participants with an opportunity to reflect on their success in using CTS as well as recognize what was challenging for them. Participants are provided with a 3-2-1 handout and given time to fill it out. In pairs or small groups, participants share their responses. An example of three prompts to use with this technique is shown in Table 3.2.

Table 3.2 3-2-1 CTS Reflection

3-2-1

Three important ideas I will remember from CTS:

1.

2.

3.

Two things I am still struggling with or wondering about:

1.

2.

One thing that I will change in my practice:

1.

The [W]hole Picture

This strategy uses a metaphor to help participants reflect on CTS as a process for developing a complete "picture" of a curriculum topic. To prepare the materials for this strategy, take manila index folders and cut out a small hole or several holes (dime sized or smaller) in each folder. Place a picture from a magazine or other source inside the folder and glue it down. Make sure the part of the picture seen through the hole is representative of the picture but does not give it completely away. Put paper clips on the folder so participants won't open it. Pass out the folders to groups of two or three or table groups (depending on size of group) and have them look at the view through the hole. Have them share ideas as to what they think the picture inside is and why. After they have shared ideas, have them open the folder and compare their responses to what the actual picture is. Ask them, "How do these two different views of the picture represent the CTS process?" Ask for volunteers to share their ideas.

SUMMARIZING FINDINGS

Before or after participants leave a CTS session, they should be encouraged to develop a summary of their findings that can be archived or shared with others and that serves as a record of the information gained from doing a CTS. (Note: Many people like to have their laptops available so they have their summary typed and easily accessible.) Participants can also be encouraged to create their own summaries as they go back and use CTS in their work. The following describe some of the ways to have participants create summaries during the professional development session or after they go back to their own settings.

Poster Boards or Poster Sessions

CTS users can summarize and "present" their findings on posters that can be displayed in the schools, organizations, and other settings. Participants can work in groups or individually during a professional development institute to create a visual poster of their CTS summary. Alternatively, participants in an ongoing professional development program can be sent home with a trifold poster board to create a CTS summary poster of a topic of their choice to bring back and share at a later professional development setting. The posters provide a colorful, visual way to summarize and communicate CTS findings to other audiences. In the Chapter 3 folder in the CD-ROM at the back of this book are photographs of trifold posters created by teachers who used CTS. They shared the posters at professional meetings and at their schools, displaying them in the teachers' room and other public places for other teachers to view.

Summary Sheets

When there is time in a CTS session and computers are available, encourage participants to create a summary sheet of findings that can be saved and shared with their group. In addition, there are times when CTS facilitators might want to prepare summary sheets to either refer to during their CTS sessions or share with leaders they are working with who will be leading CTS sessions. There is no one format for developing a summary sheet. Three examples of summary sheets (fractions, proof and conjecture, and variables) are included in Chapter 3 on the CD-ROM at the back of this book. There is also an example of a K–12 summary on the CTS topic of *Integers* on pages 46–47 of the CTS parent book.

Digital Charts

The wall charts created by small groups during the CTS summarize the findings. Leaders can use a digital camera to photograph the charts and post them on a website or e-mail them electronically to participants who wish to have a record of the wall charts.

Take-Home Messages

Encourage participants to work in small groups to develop and write down five to six take-home messages that summarize their CTS experience and that they would want to remember when they leave the session. Have them record their take-home messages on chart paper and post them around the room. When groups are finished, have all participants walk about and note any additional take-home messages they want to add to their own lists.

STRATEGY FOR ADDRESSING THE ISSUE OF TIME AND DIFFICULTY

The facilitation tips and strategies described in this chapter should help you in managing materials, effectively forming groups, choosing processing strategies that promote learning, and facilitating learning during the different stages of a CTS professional development session. Before we get into the designs in Chapters 4 and 5 and the various professional development strategies CTS can be used with, we want to leave you with a strategy for addressing one of the common questions and concerns that comes up with CTS first-timers. This is the issue of time and difficulty of doing a CTS. Many teachers who have never previously experienced this type of in-depth, rigorous professional development that is not intended to be a one-time event are unsure about whether they would have the time or inclination to use CTS. Initially it may seem daunting to them and take inordinate amounts of time. One way of addressing this up front during an introductory CTS session is to use a strategy called "backwards spelling."

The strategy works as follows:

What

Take a word or phrase related to the CTS, the name of the CTS you will be using, or a general CTS word like *mathematics* and ask participants to spell it backwards (without looking at the word).

When

Use backwards spelling at the beginning of CTS, especially for first-timers, when you are describing the additional backwards design step of starting with a thorough study of the topic before making decisions about curriculum, instruction, and assessment.

Why

Backwards spelling is a good brain activator, and, in addition, it serves as a metaphor for explaining that teachers don't typically start with a study of the curriculum topic or learning goal, and how it might feel uncomfortable, time-consuming, difficult, or awkward at first.

How

Ask participants to spell the word *mathematics* backwards (without looking at the cover of their CTS book!). When everyone finishes, talk about how difficult that was and why and connect it to the first experience with the CTS process. Now ask them to spell it backwards five times in their head. Ask them if it got easier and why. Make the link to why repeated practice with CTS makes the process easier and faster, and how it allows you to come up with your own strategies for using it efficiently. It's OK to struggle through the beginning and feel like it is hard and takes a lot of time. Assure the group that like spelling backwards, it gets easier the more you use it. The proof is in the pudding. Having worked with hundreds of teachers who have been introduced to CTS, a majority of the teachers with whom we have kept in contact report that they use it seamlessly and with little effort as a regular part of their practice and professional development.

NEXT STEPS

Now that you have examined what leaders need to know and consider in order to effectively lead professional development in CTS or professional development that embeds CTS in a larger structure for teacher learning, it is time to examine a variety of CTS learning designs, starting with the introductory sections in the next chapter, and to choose ones, or design your own, to fit your professional development needs and contexts.

4

Tools, Resources, and Designs for Leading Introductory Sessions on CTS

This chapter provides three comprehensive modules for introductory curriculum topic study (CTS) sessions that serve to familiarize the new CTS user with the resource books, the CTS study guides, and the CTS study process. At the end of the chapter, we provide guidelines for developing your own modules based on those in the chapter with mathematics topics specific to your own work. There are three introductory modules we recommend for introducing CTS to new users, including the following:

Module A1—Introduction to CTS Using K–12 Snapshots. This module uses 15 "snapshots." Snapshots are questions or issues a teacher might raise, such as this one: "I will be teaching a unit on probability this year; what are the specific ideas students should learn at my grade level?" The question within each snapshot can be addressed using one section of a CTS study guide and usually by reading just one CTS resource book. When you introduce CTS through snapshots, your participants do not do a full curriculum topic study (i.e., they do not read all six sections of a CTS). Instead, the experience provides the new CTS user with an opportunity to engage in learning through some of the sections of a CTS study guide and a variety of different curricular topics, using a scaffold (a set of step-by-step instructions) to guide their investigation. This module is especially useful when you have a mixed group that may teach different topics and face different teaching and learning issues, and your goal is to introduce the CTS process and give the participants some practice using it to investigate a variety of questions about teaching and learning. Module A1 uses a K–12 snapshots activity that includes topics from all seven of the CTS topic categories listed on pages viii–ix in the parent CTS book. The CD-ROM contains additional snapshots that are content area specific (e.g., Numbers and Operations) or cut across all categories at the K–5 and 6–12 grade levels. Check the CTS website for additional examples of snapshots.

Module A2—Introduction to CTS Resource Scenarios: Modeling. A constructivist option for introducing and teaching the CTS process is to use resource scenarios. When you use resource scenarios, participants focus on a single topic and explore each of the CTS study guide sections for that topic, without first having to learn the structure and mechanics of using a CTS study guide. In essence, they construct their own knowledge of CTS and its resources by experiencing the CTS process first and then connect their experience to the tools and resources that are central to CTS. The resource scenarios raise particular questions about teaching or learning related to the mathematics topic and guide the user toward the designated reading for that topic from the CTS resources. An added feature of this option is that participants first consider their own prior knowledge of the topic and later develop an appreciation of how CTS can enhance their knowledge and practice by comparing their prior knowledge before doing a CTS with the knowledge they gained from CTS. After participants complete a resource scenario, the facilitator shows them the CTS study guide and makes the link between what they just did and how they can study any topic or answer their own questions that may be similar to ones in the scenarios they investigated by using the CTS study guides. After experiencing the process firsthand, participants see how different sections of a CTS study guide are used for different purposes and that there are different books and sections of the related readings that are linked to the purposes described on a CTS study guide. Module A2 uses a K–12 Resource Scenario on the topic "Modeling." The CD-ROM contains additional K–12 Resource Scenarios the facilitator may substitute in the session to address the grade levels, goals, and topics of interest of the participants, such as probability and Symbolic Representation.

Module A3—Full-Day Introduction to CTS Resource Scenarios and Snapshots. The two introductory sessions described above can be combined into one full-day introductory session, starting with the Resource Scenarios, and ending with snapshots as a way to gain more practice in using the CTS study guides and familiarity with the resources. Additional snapshots and resource scenarios included on the CD-ROM or CTS website can be substituted for either of the examples included in the module.

MAKE YOUR OWN CTS INTRODUCTORY SESSION

Modules A1, A2, and A3 provide sample topics and questions for the snapshots or resource scenarios. However, sometimes you may be working with an audience on a specific topic or category of topic ideas. Sometimes your audience will be grade-level specific. For example, you may be working with a group of middle school teachers who are coming together during a summer institute to learn more about teaching students how to work with data. You might decide to create your own set of snapshots that include CTS findings related only to the nine topics in the Data Analysis CTS category. Or you might have a mixed K–12 audience that is interested in learning about algebra topics across the grade levels, and you could decide to create a K–12 resource scenario on patterns and relationships. In these cases, you can adapt the modules in this chapter by using your own Snapshots or Resource Scenarios. The directions for developing your own snapshots and resource scenarios are found at the end of this chapter.

ESSENTIAL FACILITATOR PREPARATION

For each of the above introductory sessions, it is important for the facilitator to become familiar with the CTS findings from the module used to introduce CTS. Facilitator Notes that include the CTS findings are provided for the K–12 snapshots and resource scenarios in Modules A1, A2, and A3. Your familiarity with these findings will help you guide and focus the discussions and draw attention to key points that participants sometimes over-look or fail to mention in the discussion. If you choose the supplementary snapshots or resource scenarios from the CD-ROM, you are encouraged to develop your own facilita-tor notes before using them by reading all of the CTS resources related to your snapshots or resource scenarios and noting the important ideas that you hope teachers will gain and raise in the discussion, so you are ready to prompt them or raise them yourself if they are overlooked.

The next sections in this chapter provide the facilitation guides for the three CTS Introductory Modules (A1, A2, and A3). The handouts, facilitator resources, and PowerPoint presentations for each module are located on the CD-ROM in the Chapter 4 folder. Table 4.1 provides an at-a-glance summary of the Introductory Sessions.

Table 4.1   CTS Introductory Sessions at a Glance

Module	Time Needed	Grade Level	Content	When to Use
Module A1: Snapshots	2.5–3 hours	K–12	Examples from all seven of the CTS mathematics categories	Group is new to CTS; learn the CTS basics—what study guides are and how to use them and what resource books are used.
Module A2: Resource Scenarios	2.5 hours	K–12	Modeling	Group is new to CTS and wishes to learn how to conduct a full CTS. Learn the CTS sections and the purpose and resource books for each section.
Module A3: Combined Snapshots and Resource Scenarios	6 hours	K–12	All of the above	Same as A1 and A2 combined
Make Your Own CTS Introductory Session	Half day or full day	Your choice	Your choice	Same as A1, A2, or A3

Module A1

Introduction to CTS Using K–12 Snapshots, Facilitation Guide

BACKGROUND INFORMATION

Description of the Module

This module is a half-day introductory session to Mathematics CTS. It is best used when you have a group that is new to CTS and needs to learn the CTS basics, including what a study guide is, what the resource books are, and how they are used, and have some guided practice in using CTS to answer specific questions about teaching and learning. The K–12 snapshots are focused questions that can be answered fairly quickly by reading selected sections of a CTS guide without the need to do a full CTS. The snapshots give CTS newcomers a "taste" of the CTS books and process and prepare them to conduct a full CTS at another time.

Audience

This session is designed for preservice teachers, classroom teachers, and other educators who work with or across Grades K–12 mathematics education and who are interested in learning what CTS is and how it can be used in their work. It is used primarily to teach CTS to first-timers.

Purpose and Goals

This introductory module provides a way to introduce and practice using CTS within a variety of K–12 mathematics topic examples so that all participants can make a link to a topic and issue relevant to their teaching context. The goals of this module are to

- develop awareness of CTS as a tool that connects standards and research on learning to classroom practice;
- provide guided practice in using CTS; and
- consider a variety of ways to use CTS in curricular, instructional, assessment, and teacher development contexts.

Key Components

Key components of this introductory session include the following:

Time to Get Acquainted With CTS and Resource Books

Starting a full topic study can be overwhelming if teachers have not been introduced to the basics of using the mathematics CTS parent book and the resource books used with the CTS study guides. To support teachers in learning how to use CTS, this introductory session includes time for exploring the parent CTS book as well as the structure of a CTS study guide, and for becoming familiar with each CTS resource book and its purpose.

Scaffold

The multiple steps of CTS and the need to use different books for different purposes can be a lot to manage the first time through. To address this difficulty in managing multiple resources and sections of a CTS guide, this session features the use of a scaffold with step-by-step directions to guide novices through the process. After a few uses of the scaffold, teachers find they refer to it less and less as they learn the steps. Once they become familiar in the use of the CTS process, it becomes internalized and they no longer need the scaffold.

Reading and Group Processing Strategies

CTS always involves reading and interpreting text from the CTS resources. Strategies that help participants to process what they are reading with a partner or group are embedded in this introductory module, and other strategies for engaging participants in reading and processing are provided in Chapter 3 of this *Leader's Guide*. (Refer to these if you wish to substitute any of the ones suggested in this module.)

Application

For participants to apply what they learn and develop a commitment to using CTS, they need time to look at and discuss the different ways CTS can be applied to their own curriculum, instruction, assessment, and professional development and preservice or graduate education programs. This module provides time for participants to identify applications that are relevant to their own K–12 mathematics education work or preservice or graduate education context.

SESSION DESIGN

Time

Approximately 2.5 to 3.0 hours depending on the introduction to the CTS resources option chosen (includes a 10-minute break).

Agenda

Welcome and Overview (10 minutes)

- Welcome/Introductions (5 minutes)
- Goals and Overview of CTS (5 minutes)

Engagement—Preparing for CTS (50–65 minutes)

- Getting to Know the CTS Book and Guides (20 minutes)
- Getting to Know the CTS Resource Books (15–30 minutes, depending on the option selected)
- Introduction to CTS Scaffold (15 minutes)

Elicitation (10–15 minutes)

- Snapshots: Eliciting Prior Knowledge (10–15 minutes)

Exploration and Development (50 minutes—includes 10-minute break)

- Snapshots: Exploring and Practicing CTS (30 minutes plus 10-minute break)
- Key Learning and CTS Process Debrief (10 minutes)

Applications (10–15 minutes)

- Applications for Using CTS (5 minutes)
- Content, Curricular, Instructional, and Assessment Contexts (5 minutes)
- Optional: Vignettes (5 minutes)

Reflection (10 minutes)

- Think and Quick Write (5 minutes)
- Paired Verbal Fluency (PVF) Conversation (5 minutes)

Wrap-Up and Evaluation (5 minutes)

MATERIALS AND PREPARATION

Materials Needed by Facilitator

CTS Parent Book

Mathematics Curriculum Topic Study: Bridging the Gap Between Standards and Practice (Keeley & Rose, 2006)

Resource Books

One copy of each of the following resource books:

> **Facilitator Note**
>
> It is important for CTS facilitators to have both volumes of the *Atlas of Science Literacy*; but, for this module, only *Volume 1* is used. For a complete list of the mathematics topics that are addressed in each of the *Atlas* volumes, see the *Atlas of Science Literacy* Crosswalk—Handout 2.4 in the Chapter 2 folder of the CD-ROM.

- *Science for All Americans* (American Association for the Advancement of Science [AAAS], 1989)
- *Beyond Numeracy* (Paulos, 1992)
- *Benchmarks for Science Literacy* (AAAS, 1993, online version 2009)
- *Principles and Standards for School Mathematics* (National Council of Teachers of Mathematics [NCTM], 2000)
- *Research Companion to Principles and Standards for School Mathematics* (NCTM, 2003)
- *Atlas of Science Literacy*, Vol. 1 (AAAS, 2000)
- *Atlas of Science Literacy*, Vol. 2 (AAAS, 2007)

> **Facilitator Note**
>
> You may wish to use the *Common Core State Standards* for Mathematics or the NCTM *Focal Points* for the CTS Section III snapshots. CTS Topic Crosswalks to each of these documents are provided as Handouts 2.1 and 2.2 in the Chapter 2 folder on the CD-ROM.

CTS Module A1 PowerPoint Presentation

The Module A1 PowerPoint presentation is included on the CD-ROM. Review it and tailor it to your needs and audience as needed. Insert your date and location on Slide 1, add additional graphics as desired, and add your own contact information on the last slide. Select Resource Option 1 or 2 PowerPoint slides in the Chapter 4 PowerPoint folder on the CD-ROM that go with the option you chose to introduce the CTS Resources.

Supplies and Equipment

- Computer and LCD projector to show PowerPoint presentation
- Flip chart easel, pad, and markers
- Blank paper for note taking
- Sticky notes (small and large)
- Highlighter pens (optional)

Wall Charts

Print out signs of letters A through O from Facilitator Resource A1.9 in the Chapter 4 folder Module A1 handouts. Post these signs on a long wall or around the perimeter of the room where participants can see them (see Figure 4.1). Spread them out so that small groups of participants can gather in front of the signs.

Prepare and post an additional wall chart labeled CTS Reminders with these reminders:

When Doing a CTS

1. Record the *exact language* in Sections III and V.

2. Read only the text that is related to your specific inquiry.

3. Take notes and include the name of the book and page numbers.

4. Prepare and post another wall chart labeled *CTS Content Questions*.

Facilitator Resources

- Facilitator Resource A1.1: K–12 Snapshots Facilitator Summary Notes
- Facilitator Resource A1.9 Snapshot Signs

Materials Needed for Participants

Distribute CTS parent book and resource books as follows:

CTS Parent Book

Ideally each participant will receive a book; but if that is not possible, have at least one copy on each table.

CTS Resource Books

If sets of books are available, you will need one copy of each of the following for every four to five participants:

- *Science for All Americans* (AAAS, 1989)
- *Beyond Numeracy* (Paulos, 1992) (Optional)
- *Benchmarks for Science Literacy* (AAAS, 1993)
- *Principles and Standards for School Mathematics* (NCTM, 2000)
- *Research Companion to Principles and Standards for School Mathematics* (NCTM, 2003)
- *Atlas of Science Literacy*, Vol. 1 (AAAS, 2000)
- *Atlas of Science Literacy*, Vol. 2 (AAAS, 2007) (Optional—not used for this module)
- Optional: Copies of *Common Core Mathematics Standards* or *NCTM Focal Points*

> **Facilitator Note**
>
> If you do not have copies of the Mathematics CTS book for each participant, you will need to make copies of pages 27–30 and page 35 for each participant. If you do not have enough books for at least one per table, you will also need to prepare a table copy of the pages of CTS used during the "Application of CTS Activity" (see pp. 53–91 of the CTS parent book).

Facilitator Note

Several of these resources or sections of them are available online, and the CTS website provides the URLs and a direct link to the online resources, including the *Principles and Standards for School Mathematics* (must be an NCTM member to access the online version), *Benchmarks for Science Literacy, Science for All Americans*, and sample *Atlas* maps. If not enough resource books are available to provide a full set for every four to five people, you can create "Snapshot Folders" in which multiple copies of each of the individual snapshot readings are placed in folders labeled A–O in large letters on the front of the folder. These folders replace the books or supplement a limited supply of books. Four copies of each individual snapshot reading placed in each labeled folder work well for a group of up to twenty-five participants. You can add or decrease the number of copies, depending on the size of your group. If CTS books are not available for each participant, include copies of the appropriate CTS topic guide in each folder also.

For example, four packets of the readings for Snapshot A are placed inside a manila folder with a large "A" on the outside and four copies of the CTS guide, copied on different colored paper, are also placed inside the folder. These folders (A–O) are then placed in an area of the room where participants can take a reading and study guide out of the folder, and replace it when they are done so that others can use it on their second round of reading. (If you have a very large group or a large room, place snapshot folders in several parts of the room [front and back] to cut down on the number of people sharing and movement in the room.) Facilitators can reuse these folders and handouts with other groups.

Handouts

All handouts can be found in the Chapter 4 folder on the CD-ROM.

- Facilitator Resource A1.1: K–12 Snapshots Facilitator Summary Notes (optional). This handout is for the facilitator only unless the group is made up of people who might use this activity themselves. If so, provide them with a copy of Facilitator Resource A1.1 after they have completed the snapshots.
- Handout A1.2: Agenda at a Glance
- Handout A1.3: Introduction to Mathematics CTS Snapshots—Scaffold
- Handout A1.4: List of Mathematics CTS Guides (If they have their own CTS books, you will not need this handout.)
- Handout A1.5: Anatomy of a Study Guide
- Handout A1.6: Snapshots
- Handout A1.7: Answer Key
- Handout A1.8: Recording Sheet
- Optional Handouts: If you do not have enough copies of the Mathematics CTS book, make handout copies of pages 27–30 and page 35 of that book.

DIRECTIONS FOR FACILITATING THE MODULE

Welcome and Overview (10 minutes)

Welcome and Introductions (5 minutes)

Have Module A1 PowerPoint Slide 1 showing as people arrive. Welcome participants and explain that this session will introduce them to CTS. (Show PowerPoint Slide 2.) Ask participants to introduce themselves at their tables and share something they hope to learn today. Briefly review the agenda using Handout A1.2: Agenda at a Glance.

Goals and Overview of CTS (5 minutes)

Ask participants to review the session goals on Slide 3. Using Module A1 Slides 4–7, explain to participants that CTS was developed by a National Science Foundation (NSF)–funded project. The project developed a set of tools and processes, using professional resources, to bridge the gap between national standards and research on learning and classroom practice and state standards (Slide 4). Ask for a show of hands of people who may have had some experience with CTS or heard about it prior to this session. Review what CTS is and what it is not (Slides 5 and 6) and describe how it has been called the "missing link" (Slide 7). (Review Chapter 2 of this book for more information on the project background.)

Figure 4.1 Snapshot Folders

Engagement (50–65 minutes)

Getting to Know the CTS Parent Book and Study Guides (20 minutes)

Ask participants to work with a partner or in table groups depending on how many books are available. Have them locate copies of the CTS parent book on their tables. Using Slide 8, start an exercise called First Glance, and tell the pairs or small table groups to open the book randomly and take a "first glance." Have each pair or small table group open to at least three spots in the book and take a "first glance" and discuss what they find.

Ask for a few volunteers to report on their first glance on any page up to page 109. Ask the following questions: What did you find? Why did that interest you? Then ask if anyone looked at one of the CTS guides that start on page 111 in the CTS parent book. Ask everyone to turn to these pages and look at a guide. Ask participants to report on what they found on the guides. Elaborate on what they say, explaining that there are 92 study guides and that they are the core resource for using CTS.

Explain that Handout A1.4: List of Mathematics Curriculum Topic Study Guides (alternatively page viii of the parent book if everyone has their own copy) lists the 92 different CTS guides and that the study guides are described in Chapter 2 of the parent book starting on page 21. Using Slides 9 and 10, point out the structure of a guide (including the website link at the bottom) and the six sections to the study guide that are used to answer different questions or issues related to mathematics understanding, teaching, and learning. Refer them to Handout A1.5: Anatomy of a Study Guide as you point out each section of the guide. For example, the readings in Section I address what adult literacy in the topic includes. Section II suggests instructional implications or suggestions of ways to effectively teach the topic. Section III identifies the concepts and specific ideas students learn at different grade bands. Section IV summarizes the cognitive research on student learning. Section V shows how the topic connects with and/or builds on or leads to other knowledge (as well as includes updated research on student learning in *Atlas*, Vol. 2). Section VI suggests reviewing state and local standards and curriculum documents for clarification. Tell participants they will come back to the study guides and work with them in a few minutes.

Use Slide 11, the Swiss Army knife, to point out the many functions of the versatile CTS process. Describe how there are times when you might use only one tool on your knife for a specific purpose. Other times you might use a combination of tools. What makes CTS so useful, just like a Swiss Army knife, is that the variety of tools ensures that you can find the right tool for the right purpose.

Getting to Know the Resource Books
(15–30 minutes, depending on which option is selected)

There are two options for introducing the CTS resource books. These options are described at the end of this chapter beginning on page 95, and the PowerPoint slides for each of the two options are included on the CD-ROM in the Chapter 4 PowerPoint folder. The process you select will depend on the amount of time you have in your agenda, number of resource books available, and participants' familiarity with the resource books. If time is limited, you can use a third option by merely holding up each book and describing it briefly to participants.

> **Facilitator Note**
>
> Point out that when CTS was published in 2006, the NCTM Focal Points and Common Core State Standards had not yet been developed. If you choose to include either of these resources, consider adding a graphic to the slide.

Show Slide 12. Explain that these are the resource books used in CTS. Mention that several of these resources or parts of these resources are available online and that the CTS website provides the URLs and a direct link to the online resources. You may wish to post the URLs on chart paper for your participants to record for their use later. Explain how having access to these books, which have significantly informed mathematics education, is like having a mathematics education expert available 24/7.

Show Slide 13 to point out that there is a parallel process and resource books for Science CTS and that several of the same books are used for both.

Your Selected Option

Follow the directions for the option you selected for introducing the CTS Resources on pages 95–98. Be sure the PowerPoint slide for the introduction you selected is inserted in advance to replace Slide 14, which is included as a placeholder. Introduce the resources using your selected option.

Introduction to CTS Scaffold (15 minutes)

Show Slide 15. Explain that the group will use a scaffold (a step-by-step guide) to guide their initial use of CTS to answer teaching and learning questions related to different curricular topics. Show Slide 16 and refer to Handout A1.3: Introduction to Mathematics CTS Snapshots–Scaffold. Quickly go through Slides 1 through 32 (these provide examples of what they will see on the scaffold and give them practice choosing the right section to focus on).

> **Facilitator Note**
>
> This should be a rapid paced practice session of how to find the right study guide. If everyone gets the process after the first few examples, you can skip over the other ones, although the last one is very useful in pointing out what is meant by reading only the "related sections."

Point out the CTS Reminders chart you posted earlier with reminders that include the following:

When Doing a CTS

1. Use *exact language* in Sections III and V. (Remind your group they should not rewrite or paraphrase goals; the standards developers chose the words used in the standards very carefully.)

2. Read only the text that is related to your specific inquiry. (See Slides 31–32 for an example of what is meant by related text.)

3. Write everything down that is related and important; cite the name of the book you used and page numbers so you can refer others back to the text later.

Elicitation (10–15 minutes)

Eliciting Prior Knowledge (10–15 minutes)

Show Slide 33 and refer participants to Handout A1.5: Snapshots. Explain that they will now dip their toe into the water to sample CTS. They won't be doing full topic studies, but rather short, partial studies called snapshots in order to practice using the guides and the resource books.

Show Slide 34. Explain that before they do their first CTS snapshot, it is important to take a few minutes to activate their prior knowledge so that after they do a CTS snapshot, they can compare what they knew before with what they gained from the CTS. Ask participants to review Handout A1.6: Snapshots and have them choose a snapshot that interests them. Give them a few minutes to write a brief response to the first question on Handout A1.8, based on their prior knowledge and/or experience. When everyone has finished, have them get up and stand by the letter on the wall that represents the snapshot they chose. In small groups or pairs, have participants share how they responded to the snapshot based on their own knowledge of teaching and learning. If some participants are the only ones who chose the snapshot and are unmatched, either have a facilitator converse with them or match them with others who are the only ones standing at their signs and ask them to exchange ideas. Once everyone has shared their pre-CTS ideas, have them return to their tables.

Exploration and Development (50 minutes)

Exploring and Practicing CTS (30 minutes plus a 10-minute break)

Show Slide 35. Tell the group that they will now have time to do the CTS on the snapshot they have chosen and just responded to with their initial ideas. Ask if there are any questions about using the steps on Handout A1.3: Introduction to Mathematics CTS Snapshots—Scaffold or about interpreting the study guides. Address any questions that come up. Remind them to record the CTS guide, section(s), and resource book(s) they used to do their CTS on Handout A1.8, Question 2, and summarize their findings on Question 3, after completing the reading. Ask them to specifically include any new knowledge or insights they gained after doing the CTS.

Invite participants to work individually or in pairs (with someone who chose the same snapshot) and practice using the scaffold going through Steps 1–7. Remind them not to skip steps the first time through. Encourage them to take notes as they read, recording information that is relevant to the question posed in the snapshot. Once they finish their snapshot, encourage them to try another one if they have time, recording their pre-CTS ideas, doing the CTS, and then recording new knowledge or insights gained from CTS. Remind them to start by jotting down their initial ideas before doing the CTS reading. Show Slide 36. (Keep this slide projected as they work on the snapshots.) Point out Handout A1.7: Answer Key, which they can use to make sure they are on the right category, topic, and section before they start their readings. Remind them to scan the reading and only read the text directly related to the questions on their snapshots.

As you walk around and check on groups, answer questions about the resources or the process as they complete their snapshots. If people seem confused or stuck, point them back to the scaffold on Handout A1.3: Introduction to Mathematics CTS Snapshots—Scaffold and to Handout A1.5: Anatomy of a Study Guide. Check that they are finding the right sections and readings referenced in the Study Guides. If CTS questions come up that you can't address at that time, ask the participants to write the content question on a sticky note and post it on the wall chart labeled CTS Content Questions.

Key Learning and CTS Process Debrief (10 minutes)

After participants have had time to complete at least one or two of the snapshots, ask the group to stand up again with Handout A1.8 in hand and meet at the snapshot wall sign with the same group or partner with whom they discussed their pre-CTS ideas. Give them time to discuss what new knowledge or insights they gained from doing CTS. After groups have had time to discuss their CTS findings, ask for a few report outs on how CTS addressed the snapshot questions and how CTS can be a valuable tool, even for experienced teachers, in answering questions about teaching and learning. Probe for the key CTS findings to come out. (Refer to Facilitator Resource A1.1: K–12 Snapshot Facilitator Summary Notes for the CTS findings that should be the main points of discussion at this point.) Ask participants to comment on how the process worked for them and what they found valuable in terms of addressing their snapshot question(s).

> **Facilitator Note**
>
> If any questions have been posted on the CTS Content Questions chart, this is a good time to read those to the group. Address any you can (given time constraints) and/or refer participants to other resources or people to talk with after the session.

Applications of CTS (15 minutes)

Context and Applications (15 minutes)

Ask participants to step back from the activity they have just done to think about different reasons why a mathematics educator might use CTS. Using the steps on Slide 37, have participants review the CTS application examples starting on page 35 of the Mathematics CTS parent book and ask for other examples. If everyone has access to a CTS parent book, have them turn to Chapter 4 on page 53 to scan examples of suggestions and support materials for using CTS in various content, curricular, instructional, assessment, or professional development applications. Point out the collection of Vignettes in Chapter 6 that illuminate how CTS is used in various contexts.

> **Facilitator Note**
>
> If there is only one CTS book per table, ask one person at each table to show these sections to the people at the table, or you can briefly describe to the group what is found in these chapters.

Reflection (10 minutes)

Show Slide 38. Ask participants to do a quick write (3–5 minutes of quiet time to write a reflection) that summarizes their thoughts on how CTS could be useful to them.

Use the group reflection exercise, Paired Verbal Fluency, to provide time for participants to share their reflection with one other person in the room. See directions for Paired Verbal Fluency in Chapter 3 on page 54 of this *Leader's Guide*.

Wrap-Up and Evaluation (10 minutes)

Wrap-Up (5 minutes)

Ask participants what questions they have about using CTS and answer any questions. Refer them to page 2 of the parent book for more information on the outcomes of using CTS and remind participants to visit the CTS website. Remind them that this was just a "taste of CTS" and that for their next experience, they should try a full topic study. (See modules for full topic studies in Chapter 5 of this *Leader's Guide* to plan a full topic study session.)

Evaluation (5 minutes)

Thank everyone for their participation and ask them to provide you with written feedback on the session.

Module A2

Introduction to CTS Resource Scenarios: Modeling, Facilitation Guide

BACKGROUND INFORMATION

Description of the Module

Module A2 uses mini-cases or what we call "resource scenarios" that raise specific questions teachers might have about a mathematics topic. The scenarios are used to explore how doing a CTS enriches understanding of a mathematics topic. For this session the scenarios focus on the Problem Solving and Processes topic of "Modeling." In small groups, participants reflect on what they already know about mathematical models and modeling in response to the scenario they are assigned. They read their assigned section from a resource book and record new knowledge gained from the readings. They compare the knowledge they started with to the knowledge they gained to recognize the "added value" of using CTS to enhance and expand upon the individual and collective knowledge of the group. Following completion of that task, they are introduced to a CTS study guide and then connect what they did with the resource scenario to the structure of a CTS study guide.

Audience

This session is designed for preservice and classroom teachers and other educators who work with or across Grades K–12 mathematics education and are interested in learning what CTS is and how it can be used in their work. The content focus of the session is "Modeling," an important process in solving and representing problems, making the experience applicable for people who work across different areas of mathematics.

Purpose

This CTS module provides a way to teach CTS to first-timers and novice users by focusing on a single topic and making a case for how the resources can lead to powerful learning. Use this session when you have a group of people who are new to CTS and you want them to see what can be gained by exploring the topic of mathematical modeling. The module allows participants to experience the process and learn the basics, including being introduced to the resource books. The approach used in this module leads participants to recognize the value added in using the vetted readings from national source documents and the CTS guides to build or enhance existing knowledge of content, teaching, and learning.

This session is especially useful if you have some participants who have strong content knowledge, but question what else they need to learn about the standards and mathematics teaching and learning. During the CTS field tests, participants with strong content knowledge, such as scientists, mathematicians, engineers, and teachers entering teaching from alternative, science, technology, engineering, and mathematics (STEM)-related careers without a mathematics education background, reported the great value they found in using CTS to identify what students should know at the different grade spans, considerations for effective teaching, and the research on student learning to inform their teaching.

Goals

The goals of this module are to

- develop awareness of the CTS process and the collective resources used for connecting standards and research on learning to classroom practice;
- provide guided practice in conducting a full CTS; and
- consider a variety of ways to use CTS in curricular, instructional, assessment, and professional development contexts.

Key Components

Key components of this introductory session include the following:

Time to Get Acquainted With the CTS Book

To support teachers in learning how to use CTS, this introductory session includes time for exploring the CTS parent book and what is in a CTS guide.

Embedded Practice Using the Resource Books and Selected Readings

Unlike Module A1 where participants explore and learn about the resource books and guides before doing CTS, this module uses a constructivist approach to embed the learning in the study process. After the participants have worked with the scenarios, the facilitator will link what they did to CTS by introducing the components of a CTS guide and connecting the purposes of each section of a study guide to a CTS resource.

Reading and Group Processing Strategies

CTS always involves reading and interpreting text from the CTS resources. Strategies that help participants to process what they are reading with a partner or group are embedded in this introductory module and others can be found in Chapter 3 of this *Leader's Guide*, beginning on page 49.

Application

For participants to apply what they learn and develop a commitment to using CTS, they need time to look at and discuss the different ways CTS can be applied to curriculum, instruction, assessment, and professional development. This module provides time for participants to identify applications that can be used in their own work.

SESSION DESIGN

Time

Approximately 2.5 hours (includes a 10-minute break)

Agenda at a Glance

Welcome and Overview (10 minutes)

- Welcome/Introductions (5 minutes)
- Overview of CTS (5 minutes)

Engagement—Preparing for CTS (5 minutes)

- Warm-up talk (5 minutes)

Elicitation—What Do We Already Know? (20 minutes)

- Form study groups and record individual responses to scenarios (10 minutes)
- Groups discuss and record initial ideas (10 minutes)

Exploration and Development of Modeling Ideas (40 minutes)

- Reading and studying about modeling (15 minutes)
- Developing modeling ideas (15 minutes)
- Reporting on modeling ideas (10 minutes)

Break (10 minutes)

Synthesizing Group Findings (15 minutes)

- Recapping findings (5 minutes)
- Context question (10 minutes)

Constructing an Understanding of the CTS Study Guides (20 minutes)

- Connecting back to the study guides (5 minutes)
- Linking the resource books to the study guide sections (10 minutes)
- Summarizing the resources (5 minutes)

Application and Reflection (25 minutes)

- Thinking about what we learned and how we can use it (10 minutes)
- Applying CTS in different contexts (10 minutes)
- Individual reflection (5 minutes)
- Partner reflection (5 minutes)
- Wrap-up and evaluation (5 minutes)

MATERIALS AND PREPARATION

Materials Needed by Facilitator

CTS Parent Book

Mathematics Curriculum Topic Study: Bridging the Gap Between Standards and Practice (Keeley & Rose, 2006)

Resource Books

One copy of each of the following resource books:

- *Science for All Americans* (AAAS, 1989)
- *Beyond Numeracy* (Paulos, 1992) (Optional)
- *Benchmarks for Science Literacy* (AAAS, 1993, or the 2009 online version)
- *Principles and Standards for School Mathematics* (NCTM, 2000)

Facilitator Note

It is important for CTS facilitators to have their own copies of both volumes of the *Atlas of Science Literacy*; but, for this module, Volume 1 is preferred. The "Mathematical Models" map in Volume 1 is available online through the National Science Digital Library Strand Map Service at http://strandmaps.nsdl.org/?id=SMS-MAP-1240.

- *Research Companion to Principles and Standards for School Mathematics* (NCTM, 2003)
- *Atlas of Science Literacy*, Vol. 1 (AAAS, 2000)
- *Atlas of Science Literacy*, Vol. 2 (AAAS, 2007) (Optional)

CTS Introductory Module A2 PowerPoint

The Module A2 PowerPoint presentation is included in the Chapter 4 PowerPoint folder on the CD-ROM at the back of this book. Review it and tailor it to your needs and audience as needed. Insert your date and location on Slide 1, add additional graphics as desired, and add your own contact information on the last slide.

Supplies and Equipment

- Computer and LCD projector to show PowerPoint presentation
- Flip chart, easel pad, and markers
- Blank paper for note taking
- Sticky notes (small and large)
- Optional: highlighter pens

Wall Charts

Post in pairs (side by side) twelve sheets of chart paper around the room to create six stations. Number each station (1–6) to correspond to the number of the resource scenarios. Label the first chart in each pair of charts Before CTS. Label the second chart in each pair After CTS. Post charts around the room where groups can stand by and record on them.

Prepare and post another chart labeled CTS Content Questions where participants can post sticky notes any time there is a content question that can't be answered in their group.

Facilitator Resources

- Facilitator Resource A2.1: Summary Notes for the Resource Scenarios found in the Chapter 4 folder under the A2 Handouts on the CD-ROM at the back of this book.
- Facilitator Resource Signs A2.5 found in the Chapter 4 folder under the A2 Handouts on the CD-ROM: One set of the 8.5-inch-by-11-inch signs for each of the CTS sections used with the resource scenarios: Modeling (IA, IB, IIA, IIB, IIIA, IIIB, IVA, IVB, V) along with the name of the resource printed on it.

Materials Needed by Participants

CTS Parent Book

Mathematics Curriculum Topic Study: Bridging the Gap Between Standards and Practice (Keeley & Rose, 2006).

Facilitator Note

Facilitators may choose to use the *Common Core State Standards for Mathematics* and/or the NCTM *Focal Points* for the CTS Section III readings. If these are used, see the Crosswalk Handouts 2.1 and 2.2 in the Chapter 2 folder on the CD-ROM for the selected readings that go with the "Modeling" CTS study guide.

Facilitator Note

As part of your preparation, carefully review the summary notes so you know the scenarios and the background on each before the session and can lead an effective report out and discussion.

Facilitator Note

Note that Section IB is not used for this session but the signs for these are included on the CD-ROM for you to use if you make your own resource scenarios or modify the session to include these sections. If using the *Common Core Mathematics Standards* or the NCTM *Focal Points,* you may wish to make up additional signs for these.

Ideally each participant will receive a book; but if that is not possible, provide at least one copy for every table group of about five to six people.

Facilitator Note

If you do not have copies of the CTS parent book for each participant, you will need to prepare copies of
- Pages 27–30—Descriptions of Resources Used
- Page 35—Examples of CTS Applications
- Page 203—Modeling Study Guide

CTS Resource Books

Choose one of the following options:

- Resource provision: one *Science for All Americans*, two *Benchmarks for Science Literacy*, one *Principles and Standards for School Mathematics*, one *Research Companion to Principles and Standards for School Mathematics*, and one *Atlas*, Vol. 1 (or "Mathematical Models" *Atlas* map) for a group of six people.

OR

- Copies of the CTS Study Guide reading sections from each of the above can be provided if there are not enough or no resource books available. The *Atlas*, Vol. 2 map on "Models" is available to print out from the Project 2061 website. See www.project2061.org.

Handouts

- Facilitator Resource A2.1: Modeling Summary Notes (this is for the facilitator, but you can provide a copy to participants if the group is made up of people who will use this session design with others later on).
- Handout A2.2: Agenda at a Glance
- Handout A2.3: Resource Scenarios—Modeling
- Handout A2.4: Anatomy of a Study Guide
- Copy of PowerPoint presentation (Optional)

DIRECTIONS FOR FACILITATING THE MODULE

Welcome and Introductions, and Overview (5–10 minutes)

Welcome and Introductions (5 minutes)

Welcome participants and explain that this module will introduce them to mathematics CTS. If your participants do not know one another, do quick introductions by either having people introduce themselves at their tables or choose your own introduction activity. (Add additional time as needed.)

Overview of CTS (5 minutes)

Review goals on Slide 2 and refer participants to the Handout A2.2: Agenda. Explain that this is an introductory session intended to introduce the CTS process, its purpose, and how to use the process. Suggest that once everyone learns the process, they may have a chance to go deeper by using CTS themselves or by attending follow-up sessions with CTS. Using Slides 3–6, explain to participants that CTS was a National Science Foundation (NSF)–funded project that developed a set of tools and processes, using professional resources, to bridge the gap between national standards and research on learning and classroom practice and state standards (Slide 3). Ask for a show of hands of people who have had some experience with CTS or heard about it prior to this session. Review what CTS is and what it is not (Slides 4 and 5) and describe how it has been called the "missing link" for implementing standards and research (Slide 6). (See Chapter 2 of this book for key points to raise during this part of the presentation.)

Engagement—Preparing for CTS (25 minutes)

Warm-Up Talk (5 minutes)

- Show Slide 7. Ask participants to have a quick discussion with an "elbow partner" (i.e., a person sitting next to them) using the prompt on Slide 7: "What role does modeling play in K–12 mathematics teaching and learning?" Allow about three minutes for this "warm-up talk" and then announce that the group is going to spend some time learning about modeling in mathematics. Rather than relying solely on the expertise within this group, we are going to access the prior knowledge we have and then build upon it by using readings from the CTS resource books.

- Show Slide 8 and tell participants they will use an activity called "Resource Scenarios" to learn the CTS process and deepen their knowledge of an important mathematical process-modeling. Refer them to Handout A2.3: Resource Scenarios—Modeling. Explain that each resource scenario is an example of a teaching or learning question related to mathematical models and modeling that an educator might need to learn more about to support their teaching. The scenarios will illustrate the value of using the CTS professional resources to improve and expand upon our existing knowledge and prior experience. The activity will also help them practice the difference between speaking from their own experience, beliefs, and knowledge base and speaking from and referencing a nationally validated, common body of knowledge—what we call "CTS Talk." To begin the process, we will start by forming "study groups."

Elicitation—What Do We Already Know? (20 minutes)

Form Study Groups and Record Individual Responses to Scenarios (10 minutes)

Use one of the strategies below to form study groups and record initial ideas before looking at any resource books.

- Ask participants to count off by sixes and assign each group to one of the scenarios on Handout A2.3: Resource Scenarios—Modeling. Show Slide 9 and give participants a few minutes to read their scenario and jot down any ideas they have about their scenario before doing the CTS. Remind them not to look in any of the resource books yet. They should record their response based on their own prior knowledge or experience.

OR

- Have each person refer to Handout A2.3: Resource Scenarios—Modeling and look over the scenarios. Ask them to mark one to two scenarios in which they are most interested and jot down their existing ideas for addressing their scenarios in the Before CTS Resource Reading box.

Show Slide 9 and ask everyone to follow the directions to write their ideas. Next, ask participants to stand by the wall chart for their scenario. If you used the second grouping option above, ask people to stand by their first choice or move to their second choice if there are too many people at their first choice. If some scenarios have few or no participants, ask for volunteers to work on them so that all are covered. Remind them to take their Handout A2.3: Resource Scenarios—Modeling with them.

Groups Discuss and Record Initial Ideas (10 minutes)

The groups should be standing by their scenario charts and have Handout A2.3 with them. Ask each group to read their scenario again and discuss any ideas they wrote down to address the scenario. Remind them that everyone should have a chance to share ideas and that this is not the time to tell their "individual stories." Remind them to focus on the Before CTS scenario task. Suggest that if the mathematics topic of modeling is unfamiliar to them, they can note that they have no firm ideas at this time or list some things they think they know on the Before CTS chart. Ask the group to record one to three key ideas on the chart marked Before CTS reading and then return to their seats.

Exploration and Development of Modeling Ideas (40 minutes)

Reading and Studying About Modeling (15 minutes)

> **Facilitator Note**
>
> Refer the participants to the Mathematics CTS book, or the copies of pages 27–30 you provided. Tell them there is more information on the resource books they are using starting on page 27.

Show Slide 10. Help participants locate their resource book needed for their scenario or a copy of the reading from the selected resource book. Ask participants to read their section quietly, making notes from their reading of information that enhances, adds to, or changes what they wrote on their Before CTS chart. Tell everyone that in a few minutes they will be asked to share ideas from the reading and cite the resource and page number used, so they should take notes or highlight text with underlining or sticky notes.

Developing Models Ideas (15 minutes)

When everyone in the group is done reading, show Slide 11 and ask them to meet back at their wall charts and discuss their readings as they relate to their scenario. Ask groups to examine the ideas they put up earlier and discuss what additional knowledge they would now add from reading their CTS section. Ask them to record at least three new or enhanced ideas they gained from reading the CTS resource. Remind everyone that this is the time that they should switch the discussion from talking about their own ideas or beliefs to citing the information in the resource readings (what we call "CTS Talk"). Ask them to make sure that anything that goes up on the second chart can be traced back to the readings and not a personal opinion, belief, or experience. Have each group prepare to report out one new insight they gained from the CTS reading. This could include changing something that they had on their Before CTS chart that they no longer think should be there, adding new knowledge they gained, or enhancing or building upon ideas they had previously identified.

Reporting on Modeling Ideas (10 minutes)

When groups are finished (or if some are taking longer, you may need to ask them to stop where they are), ask each group to stand by their chart. Ask a couple of the members of each group to take no more than one minute to briefly share one or two new insights they gained from CTS (not something they already knew). Thank the groups and have them return to their seats.

Break (10 minutes)

Synthesizing Group Findings (15 minutes)

Recapping Findings (5 minutes)

Provide a short recap of what you heard and observed from the group's learning. For example, you might emphasize a point such as a group learned that the basic idea of mathematical modeling is to find a mathematical relationship that behaves in the same way the system of interest does. Refer to Facilitator Resource A2.1: Summary Notes for the Resource Scenarios for each scenario and bring up any key points that may not have been mentioned or recorded by the groups. If you have a cofacilitator, one of you should record these synthesis points on a flip chart as you bring them up or ask a participant to chart the main points. This is a good time to remind everyone that if they have a content question they want to raise, they can write it on a sticky note and put it on the wall chart labeled CTS Content Questions.

Context Question (10 minutes)

Next draw the group's attention to the question on the bottom of Handout A2.3. Show Slide 12. Ask participants to read and jot down their thoughts on the question and then turn to a partner and discuss their ideas.

Constructing an Understanding of the CTS Study Guides (20 minutes)

Connecting Back to the Study Guides (5 minutes)

Show Slide 13. Refer participants to the "Modeling" CTS Study Guide on page 203 of the CTS parent book or to the handout of this page if everyone does not have a CTS book. Tell them this is the CTS guide that was used to identify the resources and readings they just used for the scenarios. Give them a minute to examine the study guide and ask them what they notice.

Linking the Resource Books to the Study Guide Sections (10 minutes)

Refer them to Handout A2.4: Anatomy of a Study Guide. Use Facilitator Resource A2.5 (these are signs made in advance for each of the scenarios with the book and the CTS Section used printed on it). Walk to the first scenario chart. Hold up your copy of the resource book used for that scenario (*Science for All Americans*) and tape the sign with the Section IA above the "Before and After" Charts (e.g., tape the sign "Section IA—*Science for All Americans*" above the charts for Scenario 1). Direct participants to Handout A2.4: Anatomy of a Study Guide to read about the purpose of Section I as you post the first sign. Do this for each of the scenarios, taping the sign for each section on top of the scenario charts and referring participants to review the purpose on Handout A2.4. After the last scenario, remind them of the purpose of Section VI in that it is always important to take the time to connect findings from a CTS back to your own state or local context.

Summarizing the Resources (5 minutes)

Show Slide 14 to remind them of all the resources they used to complete a CTS. Point out the additional resources they did not use for this topic that may be used in other topic studies (e.g., *Beyond Numeracy*). Point out that pages 27–30 of the *Mathematics Curriculum Topic Study* book describe each of these resources.

Explain that the CTS developers think of CTS as our Swiss Army knife (show Slide 15). It has the specific tools we need at different times for different purposes. Show Slide 16 and say there are parallel resources for science teaching and learning you can explore if you also work in science or with science teachers.

> **Facilitator Note**
>
> Add graphics for the *Common Core State Standards for Mathematics* or NCTM *Focal Points* if you added these resources.

Let everyone know there are also supplementary resources always being added to the CTS website to expand on the information in the standards and research. Show Slide 17. Point out that Volume 2 of the *Atlas* was released after the CTS book was published, but there is now a crosswalk of that resource to all the Science and Mathematics topics on the CTS website as well as on the CD-ROM in the back of this book. Crosswalks to the Common Core Mathematics Standards and the NCTM Focal Points can also be found on the CD-ROM and CTS website. Show an example of a supplementary resource related to modeling as an example of what they can find on the website (Slide 18).

Application (20 minutes)

Thinking About What We Learned and How We Can Use It (10 minutes)

> **Facilitator Note**
>
> If any questions have been posted on the CTS Content Questions chart, this is a good time to read those to the group. Address any you can (given time constraints) and/or refer participants to other resources or people to talk with after the session.

Ask participants to step back from the exploration they have just done to think about the value of the CTS tool. Refer to questions on Slide 19 and ask them to consider how CTS enhanced their knowledge of modeling and what people can learn from using CTS. Allow time for a short discussion of ideas (5 minutes) with table groups. Point out that one value of CTS is that it can make us more aware of important K–12 content we don't understand as well as we would like or may not have considered important to know.

Applying CTS in Different Contexts (10 minutes)

Ask participants to think about different reasons why a mathematics educator might use CTS. Using Slide 20, ask participants to review the CTS application examples on page 35 of the Mathematics CTS book and invite them to share other possible examples. Then ask them to turn to Chapter 4 beginning on page 53 to scan examples of suggestions and support materials for using CTS in various content, curricular, instructional, assessment, or professional development applications (if they do not have access to the CTS books, you can describe this briefly). Point out the collection of vignettes in the CTS book in Chapter 6 that illuminate how CTS is used in various contexts.

Show Slide 21. Ask participants to do a quick write (3–5 minutes of quiet time to write a reflection) that summarizes their thoughts on how CTS could be useful to them using these guiding questions.

Partner Reflections (5 minutes)

Show Slide 22. Ask everyone to find a partner (either make eye contact with someone across the room or find someone they haven't talked with yet) and share the ideas from their quick writes. Allow five minutes and remind people to "share the air time."

Wrap-Up and Evaluation (10 minutes)

Show Slide 23. Ask participants what questions they now have about using CTS and answer as many as time permits. Remind them they can go to www.curriculumtopicstudy.org for more information and that new tools and information are posted regularly on the CTS website.

Thank everyone for their participation and ask them to complete an evaluation of the session.

Module A3

Full-Day Introduction to CTS Resource Scenarios and Snapshots, Facilitation Guide

BACKGROUND INFORMATION

Description of the Module

This session is a combination of Modules A1 and A2. It provides a longer, in-depth introduction to Mathematics CTS. Participants begin by exploring "Resource Scenarios" that engage participants in answering specific questions teachers might raise about a mathematics topic. They use the scenarios to experience how CTS enriches a teacher's understanding of a mathematics topic. For this session, the scenarios focus on an important problem-solving process—"modeling." In small groups, participants reflect on what they already know about modeling in mathematics. They read an assigned section from a CTS resource book and record knowledge gained from the readings. They compare the knowledge they had with the knowledge they gained to recognize the "added value" of using CTS to enhance and expand upon the individual and collective knowledge of the group. Following this, they use fifteen snapshots that are questions or issues a teacher might raise and a CTS-guided scaffold to explore them, gain additional practice in using different sections of each topic study, and then identify next steps for using CTS in their work.

Audience

This session is designed for preservice and classroom teachers and other education professionals who work with or across Grades K–12 mathematics education and are interested in learning what CTS is and how it can be used in their work. In Part 1 of the module, a problem-solving process is used as one of the focus areas so that the experience is applicable across the different areas of mathematics. In Part 2 of the module, participants select from among mathematics topics applicable to Grades K–12 so they can explore areas of greatest interest to them. To tailor this session for specific grade levels or subject-area audiences, see the additional resource scenarios and snapshot examples in the Chapter 4 folder of the CD-ROM at the back of this book or on the CTS website at www.curriculumtopicstudy .org. You can also develop your own snapshots and resource scenarios following the directions at the end of this chapter on page 100. You can substitute one of those for the one(s) used in this module.

Purpose

Module A3 provides an in-depth experience to teach CTS to first-timers and novice users by first focusing on a single topic and making a case for how doing a full CTS on one topic can lead to powerful learning.

Part 1 of the module leads participants to recognize the value added in using the professional readings and CTS guides to build or enhance their existing knowledge of content, teaching, and learning. Part 2 of the module provides extended practice in using the CTS study guides with different topics, grade spans, and issues of teaching and learning.

Goals

The goals of this module are to

- develop awareness of Curriculum Topic Study (CTS) and the collective resources it uses for connecting standards and research on learning to classroom practice;
- provide guided practice in conducting a full topic study and several partial topic studies; and
- consider a variety of ways to apply CTS in curricular, instructional, assessment, and professional development contexts.

Key Components

The key components of Module A3 include the following:

Time to Get Acquainted With the CTS Book and Resource Books

Starting a topic study can be quite difficult if teachers have not been introduced to the basics of using the CTS parent book and CTS guides. To support teachers in learning how to use CTS, this introductory session includes time for exploring the CTS parent book and the structure and function of a CTS guide.

Embedded Practice Using the Resource Books and Selected Readings

An opportunity for getting to know the CTS resource books is embedded in the first part of this module. Participants are introduced to the CTS resource books and how they connect to the different parts of a CTS guide after they engage in focused readings and discussions about a topic. This allows participants to move right into the second part of the module with an understanding of the resource books and of the CTS section for which each book is used.

Scaffold

The multiple steps of CTS and the need to use different books for different purposes can be confusing at first, so we provide a scaffold for use in the second part of the module. The scaffold has step-by-step directions to guide novices through the process. After a few uses of the scaffold, teachers find they refer to it less and less as they learn the steps. Once they become familiar in the use of the CTS process, it becomes internalized and they no longer need the scaffold.

Reading and Group Processing Strategies

CTS always involves reading and interpretation of text from the CTS resources. Strategies that help participants to process what they are reading with a partner or group are embedded in this module. Other reading and group processing strategies are described in Chapter 3 of this *Leader's Guide*.

Application

For participants to apply what they learn and develop a commitment to using CTS, they need time to look at and discuss the different ways CTS can be applied to curriculum, instruction, assessment, and professional development. This module provides time for participants to identify applications that can be used in their own work.

SESSION DESIGN

Time

Approximately 6 hours (includes an hour lunch break and two 10-minute breaks).

Agenda

PART 1—RESOURCE SCENARIOS

Welcome and Overview (10 minutes)

- Welcome/Introductions (5 minutes)
- Overview of CTS (5 minutes)

Engagement—Preparing for CTS (25 minutes)

- Getting to know the CTS book and guides (20 minutes)
- Warm-up talk (5 minutes)

Elicitation—What Do We Already Know? (20 minutes)

- Form study groups and record individual responses to scenarios (10 minutes)
- Discuss and record initial ideas (10 minutes)

Exploration and Development of Ideas About Modeling (40 minutes)

- Reading and studying modeling (15 minutes)
- Developing ideas about modeling (15 minutes)
- Reporting on ideas about modeling (10 minutes)

Break (10 minutes)

Synthesizing Group Findings (15 minutes)

- Recapping findings (5 minutes)
- Context question (10 minutes)

Constructing an Understanding of the CTS Study Guides (20 minutes)

- Connecting back to the study guides (5 minutes)
- Linking the resource books to the study guide sections (10 minutes)
- Summarizing the resources (5 minutes)

Application (10 minutes)

- What we learned and how we can use it (10 minutes)

Lunch Break (1 hour)

PART 2—SNAPSHOTS

Engagement (15 minutes)

- Preparing for CTS snapshots (15 minutes)

Elicitation (10 minutes)

- Snapshots: Eliciting prior knowledge (10 minutes)

Exploration and Development (40 minutes)

- Snapshots: Exploring and practicing CTS (30 minutes)
- Key Learnings and CTS Process Debrief (10 minutes)

Break (10 minutes)

Applications (15 minutes)

- Applications for using CTS (5 minutes)
- Content, curricular, instructional, and assessment contexts (5 minutes)
- Vignettes (5 minutes)

Reflection (10 minutes)

- Quick write (5 minutes)
- Partner reflection (5 minutes)

Wrap-Up and Evaluation (10 minutes)

MATERIALS AND PREPARATION

Materials Needed by Facilitator

CTS Parent Book

Mathematics Curriculum Topic Study: Bridging the Gap Between Standards and Practice (Keeley & Rose, 2006)

Resource Books

One copy of each of the following resource books:

- *Science for All Americans* (AAAS, 1989)
- *Beyond Numeracy* (Paulos, 1992) (Optional)
- *Benchmarks for Science Literacy* (AAAS, 1993, or 2009 online version)
- *Principles and Standards for School Mathematics* (NCTM, 2000)
- *Research Companion to Principles and Standards for School Mathematics* (NCTM, 2003)
- *Atlas of Science Literacy*, Vol. 1 (AAAS, 2000)
- *Atlas of Science Literacy*, Vol. 2 (AAAS, 2007) (Optional)
- *Common Core State Standards for Mathematics* (Optional)
- NCTM *Focal Points* (Optional)

Facilitator Note

It is important for facilitators to have access to both volumes of the *Atlas of Science Literacy*. Either volume can be used for this session, but the "Mathematical Models" map in Volume 1 is preferred for the resource scenarios and addresses the snapshot questions.

CTS Module A3 PowerPoint

The module A3 PowerPoint is included in the Chapter 4 PowerPoint folder on the CD-ROM. Review and tailor the PowerPoint to your needs and audience. Insert your date and location on Slide 1, add additional graphics as desired, and add your own contact information on the last slide.

Supplies and Equipment

- Computer and LCD projector to show PowerPoint presentation
- Flip chart easel, pad, and markers
- Blank paper for note taking
- Sticky notes (small and large)
- Optional: highlighter pens

Wall Charts

Prepare the following charts and post in the meeting room prior to beginning the session:

- *Before CTS* and *After CTS* Charts: 12 sheets of chart paper posted in pairs (side-by-side) around the room to create six "stations." Number each station (1–6) to correspond to the number of the resource scenario used in the first part of this module. Label the first chart in each pair *Before CTS*. Label the second chart in each pair *After CTS*. Post charts around the room where groups can stand by and record on them.
- CTS Questions Chart: Post a chart labeled CTS Content Questions where participants can place sticky notes any time they have a content or CTS question that can't be answered in their group.

Prepare the following chart and post in the meeting room prior to beginning Part 2 of the session:

- CTS Reminders Chart

When Doing a CTS

1. Record the *exact language* in Sections III and V.
2. Read only the text that is related to your specific inquiry.
3. Take notes and include the name of the book and page numbers.

○ Print out signs of letters A through O from Facilitator Resource A1.9 found in the Chapter 4 A.1 handouts. Post these signs on a long wall or around the perimeter of the room where participants can see them. Spread them out so that small groups of participants can gather in front of the signs.

Facilitator Resources

- For the Summary Notes for the Resource Scenarios, use Facilitator Resource Handout A2.1 in the A2 handouts in the Chapter 4 folder on the CD-ROM at the back of this book. For the Resource Signs, use Facilitator Resource Handout A2.5. Print a copy of each sign.
- For the Summary Notes for the Snapshots, use Facilitator Resource Handout A1.1 in the A1 handouts in the Chapter 4 folder on the CD-ROM at the back of this book. For the Snapshot Signs, use Facilitator Resource Handout A1.9. Print a copy of each sign. Make additional signs for the Common Core Mathematics Standards or NCTM Focal Points if you add these resources to the CTS set.

> **Facilitator Note**
>
> As part of your preparation, carefully review these Summary Notes so you know the scenarios and the background on each before the session and can lead an effective report out and discussion.

Facilitator Note

If you do not have copies of the Mathematics CTS book for each participant, you will need to prepare copies of pages 27–30: Descriptions of Resources Used; page 35: Examples of CTS Applications; and page 203: Modeling Study Guide.

Materials Needed by Participants

CTS Parent Book

Mathematics Curriculum Topic Study: Bridging the Gap Between Standards and Practice (Keeley & Rose, 2006)

Ideally each participant will receive a book; if that is not possible, provide at least one copy for every table.

CTS Resource Books

For every six people, provide the following resources for Part 1—Resource Scenarios of this module.

- One *Science for All Americans*
- Two *Benchmarks for Science Literacy* (or access to online version)
- One *Principles and Standards for School Mathematics*
- One *Research Companion to Principles and Standards for School Mathematics*
- One *Atlas*, Vol. 1 (or "Mathematical Models" *Atlas* map)

Alternatively, copies of the sections from each of the above can be provided if there are not enough or no resource books available. The *Atlas*, Vol. 1 map on "Mathematical Models" is available to print out from the NSDL Strand Maps at http://strandmaps.nsdl.org/?id=SMS-MAP-1240. For Part 2 of this module, have at least one copy of all of the books used with the CTS guides available for each table group.

If not enough resource books are available to provide a full set for every four to five people, you can create "Snapshot Folders" in which multiple copies of each of the individual snapshot readings and CTS guides are placed in folders labeled A–O in large letters on the front of the folder. These folders replace the books or supplement a limited supply of books. Four copies of each individual snapshot reading and the CTS guides placed in each labeled folder work well for a group of up to twenty-five participants. You can add or decrease the number of copies, depending on the size of your group. These folders (A through O) are then placed in an area of the room where participants can come up and take a reading and study guide out of the folder and replace it when done so that others can use it on their second round. See Figure 4.1 on page 67.

Handouts

All of the handouts for this section are included in the A1 and A2 handout folders.

- Handout Facilitator Resource A1.1: Introduction to Mathematics CTS K–12 Snapshots Facilitator Notes (Note: These are for the facilitator but should be given as handouts also when your group includes people who will do this session with others later on.)
- Handout Facilitator Resource A2.1: Resource Scenarios Modeling: Facilitator Notes (Note: These are for the facilitator but should be given as handouts also when your group includes people who will do this session with others later on.)
- Handout A3.1: Agenda at a Glance
- Handout A2.3: Resource Scenarios—Modeling
- Handout A2.4: Anatomy of a Study Guide
- Handout A1.3: Introduction to CTS Snapshots—Scaffold
- Handout A1.4: List of Mathematics Curriculum Topic Study Guides (You will not need this handout if participants have their own copies of the CTS parent book.)
- Handout A1.6: Snapshots
- Handout A1.7: Snapshots Answer Key

- Handout A1.8: Recording Sheet
- Copy of PowerPoint presentation (Optional)

DIRECTIONS FOR FACILITATING THE MODULE

PART 1—RESOURCE SCENARIOS

Welcome/Overview (10 minutes)

Welcome and Introductions (5 minutes)

Show Slide 1. Welcome participants and explain that this session will introduce them to Mathematics CTS. If your participants do not know one another, do quick introductions.

Overview of CTS (5 minutes)

Review the goals on Slide 2 and refer participants to Handout A3.1: Agenda. Explain that this is an introductory session and that participants may have a chance to go deeper into CTS topics themselves once they learn to use the process and resources. Using Slides 3–6, explain to participants that CTS was a National Science Foundation (NSF)–funded project that developed a set of tools that help bridge the gap between national standards and research on learning and classroom practice and state standards (Slide 3). Ask for a show of hands of people who have had some experience with CTS or heard about it prior to this session. Review what CTS is and what it is not (Slides 4 and 5) and describe how it has been called the "missing link" for implementing standards and research (Slide 6) because it helps educators examine the standards and research on specific areas of interest and apply what they learn to their own work. For background information on this part of the presentation, see Chapter 2 of this *Leader's Guide.*

Engagement—Preparing for CTS (25 minutes)

Getting to Know the CTS Parent Book and Study Guides (20 minutes)

Ask participants to work with a partner. Distribute their CTS books if they are receiving one at the session or have them locate a copy of the CTS parent book on their tables and do the exercise as a table group. Using Slide 7, start an exercise called First Glance, and tell the pairs or small table groups to open the book randomly and take a "first glance." Have each pair or small table group open to at least three spots in the book and take a "first glance" and discuss what they find.

Ask for a few volunteers to report on their first glance on any page up to page 109. What did you find? Why did that interest you? Then ask if anyone looked at one of the CTS guides that start on page 111 in the Mathematics CTS. Ask everyone to turn to these pages and look at a guide. Ask participants to report on what they found in the guides. Elaborate on what they say, explaining that there are 92 guides and that they are the core resource for using CTS. Show Slide 8. Explain that the study guides are described in Chapter 2 of the Mathematics CTS Book. Using Slides 9 and 10, briefly point out the

structure of a guide (including the website link at the bottom) and the six sections to the guide that are used to answer different questions or issues related to mathematics understanding, teaching, and learning. Explain that they will revisit the structure of the guides in more detail after they have some experience with a topic study. Use Slide 11, the Swiss Army knife, to point out the many functions of the CTS process. Describe how there are times when you might use only one tool on your knife for a specific purpose. Other times you might use a combination of tools. What makes

> **Facilitator Note**
>
> You can point out that many schools and education organizations own these books but they do not use them—the CTS process can remedy that because it makes the resources more relevant and easier to use.

CTS so useful, just like a Swiss Army knife, is that the variety of tools ensures that you can find the right tool for the right purpose. Explain that for each CTS section you use different professional resources to get the information you need. Show Slide 12. It has images of all the front covers of the CTS resource books to let participants know what books they will be using. Ask people to raise their hands if they own a copy or have used one of these books. Explain to your group that the work today will be to experience a full topic study on the topic "modeling" and then to explore several different CTS sections on different topics.

Warm-Up Talk (5 minutes)

Show Slide 13. Ask participants to have a quick discussion with an "elbow partner" (i.e., a person sitting next to them) about the topic "Modeling" using the prompt on Slide 13 (Prompt: "What role does modeling play in K–12 mathematics teaching and learning?"). Allow about three minutes for this "warm-up talk" and then announce that we are going to spend some time learning about modeling in mathematics. Rather than relying solely on the expertise of this group, we are going to access the prior knowledge that we have and build upon it by using readings from the CTS resources. Show Slide 14 and say the activity we are going to do is called Resource Scenarios. Refer them to Handout A2.3: Resource Scenarios. Each scenario is an example of a teaching or learning question related to modeling that an educator might need to know more about. The scenarios will raise awareness of the value of using professional resources to improve and expand upon an individual's or group's existing knowledge. It will also help us experience the difference between speaking from our own experience, beliefs, and knowledge base and speaking from and referencing a common body of knowledge—what we call "CTS Talk." To begin the process, we will start by forming study groups.

 ### Elicitation—What Do We Already Know? (20 minutes)

Form Study Groups and Record Individual Responses to Scenarios (10 minutes)

Form groups using one of the strategies below.

- Ask participants to count off by sixes and assign each group to one of the six Scenarios on Handout A2.3: Resource Scenarios—Modeling. Give participants a few minutes to read their scenario and jot down any ideas they have about it before doing the CTS. Remind them not to look in any of the resource books yet. They should record their response based on their existing knowledge or prior experiences.

OR

- Have each person refer to Handout A2.3 and look over the scenarios. Ask them to mark one to two scenarios they are most interested in exploring and write down their ideas about those scenarios (before doing CTS readings).

Show Slide 15 that summarizes the directions for recording initial ideas and meeting in study groups to share initial ideas. Once participants have recorded their initial ideas, ask them to stand by the wall chart for their scenario. If you chose the second grouping option above, ask people to stand by their first choice or move to their second choice if there are too many people at their first scenario choice or move to their second choice if there are too many people at their first one. If some scenarios have few or no participants, ask for volunteers to work on them so that all are covered.

Groups Discuss and Record Initial Ideas (10 minutes)

The groups should be standing by their scenario chart with Handout A2.3. Ask them to focus on the Before CTS task by having each group read their scenario again and share and post the ideas they wrote down to address the scenario on the Before CTS chart. Ask them to be sure that everyone has a chance to share at least one idea; this is not the time to go into lengthy discussions. Tell the groups that if their mathematics topic is unfamiliar to them and they have no or few ideas, it is OK for them to write "we have no firm ideas at this time" or "some things we think we know are...." Ask the group to record one to three key ideas on the chart marked Before CTS reading and then return to their seats.

Exploration and Development of Models Ideas (40 minutes)

Reading and Studying About Models (15 minutes)

Show Slide 16. Help participants locate their resource or a copy of the reading from the selected resource. Ask participants to read their section quietly, making notes from their reading that enhances, adds to, or changes what they wrote on their Before CTS chart. Tell everyone that in a few minutes they will be asked to share ideas from the reading and cite the resource used, so they should take notes and/or highlight text with underlining or use sticky notes.

Developing Models Ideas (10–15 minutes)

When everyone is done reading, show Slide 17 and say they will be returning to their wall charts for a discussion in a minute. Before the groups return to their charts, tell them when they go back to the charts they will switch their discussion from talking about their own opinions or beliefs to citing the information in the resource readings (book and page number). Remind them to make sure they can trace anything that goes up on the chart back to the CTS readings and nothing posted on the After CTS chart is from a personal opinion, belief, or experience (what we call "CTS Talk"). Then give the directions for the task:

1. When participants return to their charts, they are to examine the ideas they put up earlier and discuss what they learned from the CTS readings.

2. They are to record at least three new or enhanced ideas gained on the *After CTS* chart.

3. When they are done, they are to choose one new insight to report out to the larger group such as something that was on the *Before CTS* chart that they no longer think should be there, new knowledge gained, or how they enhanced or built upon ideas previously identified.

Check to see if anyone has questions about "CTS Talk" or the directions and then ask them to meet back at their wall charts and discuss their readings as they relate to their scenario.

Reporting on Models Ideas (10 minutes)

When groups are finished (if some are taking longer you may need to ask them to stop where they are), ask each group to stay standing by their chart. Ask each group to take no more than one minute to share one new insight they gained from

Facilitator Note

This is a good time to remind everyone that if they have a CTS or content question they want to raise, they can write it on a sticky note and put it on the wall chart labeled CTS Content Questions during the break.

their readings. Clarify any content that is confusing, using your own knowledge and by referring to Facilitator Resource A2.1: Summary Notes for the Resource Scenarios. After hearing from the six groups, thank everyone and announce that there will be a short break.

Break (10 minutes)

 ### Synthesizing Group Findings (15 minutes)

Recapping Findings (5 minutes)

Provide a short recap of what you observed from the ideas reported by the scenario study groups. For example, you might emphasize a point such as a group learned that the basic idea of mathematical modeling is to find a mathematical relationship that behaves in the same way the system of interest does. Refer to Facilitator Resource A2.1: Summary Notes for the Resource Scenarios for each scenario and bring up any key points that may not have been mentioned or recorded by the groups. Ask how reading the resources added to their understanding of mathematical modeling and ask for a few responses from the large group.

Context Question (10 minutes)

Next, draw the group's attention to the context questions on the bottom of Handout A2.3: Resource Scenarios—Modeling and on Slide 18. Using an activity called *Think-Pair-Share*, ask participants to think about the questions themselves and jot down their thoughts. After a few minutes of quiet reflection, invite participants to pair up with a partner and spend a few minutes each sharing their ideas.

Constructing an Understanding of the CTS Study Guides (20 minutes)

Connecting Back to the Study Guides (5 minutes)

Show Slide 19. Refer participants to the Modeling CTS Study Guide on page 203 of their CTS book (or to the handouts of these pages you provided if everyone does not have a CTS book). Tell them this is the CTS "study guide" that was used to identify the resources and readings they just used for the scenarios activity. Give them a minute to examine the guide.

Linking the Resource Books to the Study Guide Sections (10 minutes)

Refer participants to Handout A2.4: Anatomy of a Study Guide. Starting with Section 1A, ask participants to review the purpose of that CTS Section. Use Facilitator Resource A2.5 (which are signs for each of the scenarios with the book and the CTS Section used printed on it). Walk to the scenario 1 wall chart. Hold up the resource book used for that scenario and tape the sign "Section IA—Science for All Americans" above the scenario 1 wall chart. Continue this for every scenario until all the signs are posted and the descriptions of each section on Handout A2.4 have been reviewed.

> **Facilitator Note**
>
> You might ask a few participants to hang the signs after you hold them up and connect them to the right scenario.

After the last scenario, remind them that the purpose of CTS Section VI is to connect findings from the national resources explored in CTS Sections I–V back to state and local contexts.

Summarizing the Resources (5 minutes)

Show Slide 20 to remind your group of the resources they used to complete the CTS. Point out the additional resources they did not use for this topic that may be used in other topic studies (e.g., *Beyond Numeracy*). Refer them to pages 27–30 of the CTS parent book for a description each of these resources if they want to read more about them after the session.

Show the Swiss Army knife slide again (Slide 21). Point out that just like the Swiss Army knife, CTS has the specific tools we need at different times. Show Slide 22 and say there are parallel resources for science teaching and learning you can explore if you also work in science.

Show Slide 23. Let everyone know there are supplementary resources always being added to the CTS website to expand on the information in the standards and research. Point out that Volume 2 of the *Atlas* was released after the CTS parent book was published, but there is a crosswalk of that resource to all the topics on the website as well as in the Chapter 2 folder on the CD-ROM. Also, show an example of a supplementary resource you can find on the website (Slide 24).

Application (10 minutes)

Thinking About What We Learned and How We Can Use It (10 minutes)

Ask participants to step back from the exploration they have just done to think about the value of CTS. Refer to questions on Slide 25. What did you learn and what can other people learn from using CTS? Allow time for a short discussion of ideas (5 minutes) at tables. Point out that one value of CTS is that it can make us more aware of content we don't understand as well as we would like.

Lunch Break (1 hour)

PART 2—SNAPSHOTS

Engagement (15 minutes)

Preparing for Snapshots (15 minutes)

- Welcome everyone back and show Slide 26. Explain that they will now do Part 2 of the session where they will use a scaffold (a step-by-step guide) to learn to use CTS to answer teaching and learning questions related to different curricular topics. Point out what is meant by a scaffold on Slide 26. Show Slide 27 and show the seven steps on the CTS scaffold. Ask participants to pull out the following handouts: Handout A2.4: Anatomy of a Study Guide (they already used this one in Part 1 of the session); Handout A1.3: Introduction to CTS Snapshots—Scaffold; and Handout A1.4: 92 Mathematics Curriculum Topic Study Guides. They will use these handouts to learn to use the scaffold.

- Tell everyone we are going to practice using the scaffold with several examples. Show Slide 28 and read the question. Ask participants to look at pages viii–ix in their CTS parent book or at Handout A1.4 and scan the seven categories of the CTS in which the CTS guides are organized. In what category should they look to find a topic to address the question? (Take responses—correct response is Numbers and Operations.) Then ask, "What topic guide would you consult?" (Take responses—correct response

> **Facilitator Note**
>
> This should be a rapid-paced practice session of how to find the right study guide. If everyone gets the process after the first few examples, you should skip over the other ones, although the last two are very useful in pointing out what is meant by reading only the "related sections."

is Percent.) Ask where they would find that topic guide in the CTS book. (Take responses—correct response is page 129.) Show Slide 29 and continue to engage the group in answering the questions. What CTS section would we look at to answer the question on Slide 29? (Take responses—correct response is Section II, which is focused on the outcome of raising instructional implications.) Quickly go through Slides 30–43 to provide examples of what they will see on the scaffold and practice choosing the right section to focus on.

- Show Slide 44 and point out that CTS takes practice and that is what the group will be doing next. Point out the chart you posted earlier with reminders, including the following:

When Doing a CTS

1. Use *exact language* in Sections III and V. (Don't paraphrase goals; the language used in the standards documents was chosen very deliberately.)

2. Read only the text that is related to your specific inquiry.

3. Write everything down that is related and important; cite the name of the book you used and page numbers.

Elicitation (5 minutes)

Eliciting Prior Knowledge (5 minutes)

Show Slide 45 and refer participants to Handout A1.6: Snapshots. Tell them they will now do some short, partial studies called snapshots in order to practice using the guides and the books. Explain that before they do their first CTS snapshot, it's important to take a few minutes to activate their prior knowledge so that after they do a CTS snapshot, they can compare what they knew before with what they gained from the CTS. Point participants to the Snapshots on Handout A1.6 and have them choose one that interests them. Give them a few minutes to write a brief response to the question, based on their prior knowledge. When they are done, have them set their response aside.

When everyone has finished, ask them to stand and move to the letter on the wall that represents the snapshot they chose. In small groups or pairs, have participants share how they responded to the snapshot based on their own knowledge of teaching and learning. If some participants are the only ones who chose the snapshot and are unmatched, either have a facilitator converse with them or match them with others who are the only ones standing at their signs and ask them to exchange ideas. Once everyone has shared their pre-CTS ideas, have them return to their tables.

Exploration and Development (55 minutes)

Facilitator Note

If you have assembled snapshot folders with the CTS guides and the readings in them, the participants will not have to find the CTS guide in the book or locate the correct resource book, but we still encourage them to use the scaffold to gain practice in how they would use this if they were using the material on their own.

Exploring and Practicing CTS (45 minutes)

- Show Slide 46. Tell the group that they will now have time to do the CTS on the snapshot they chose. Ask if there are any questions about using the steps on the scaffold or interpreting the study guides. If you do not have books available for everyone and are using the snapshot folders system for all the readings, point out where the folders are and how to use them. Remind participants they will be sharing these resources and to return them when they are done so others can use them.

- Invite participants to work individually or in pairs (with someone who chose the same snapshot) and use the scaffold, going through Steps 1–7 to find the guide and the resources they need. Remind them not to skip steps this first time through and to record the CTS guide, section(s), and resource book(s) they used to do their CTS on Handout A1.8 and summarize their findings after completing the reading. Ask them to specifically include any new knowledge or insights they gained after doing the CTS.
- Encourage participants to take notes as they read, recording information that is relevant to the question posed in the snapshot. Once they finish their snapshot, encourage them to try another one if they have time, recording their pre-CTS ideas, doing the CTS, and then recording new knowledge or insights gained from the CTS. Point out that there is an answer key they can check to make sure they are on the right category, topic, and section before they start their readings. (See Handout A1.7: Snapshots Answer Key.) Remind them to scan the reading and only read the text directly related to the question on their snapshot.
- Walk around and check on groups as they work, and answer any questions they might have about the process or resource as they complete their snapshots. If people seem confused or stuck, point them back to the scaffold and check that they are finding the right sections and readings referenced in the study guides. If CTS questions come up that you can't address at that time, ask the participants to write their questions on a sticky note and post them on the wall chart labeled CTS *Content Questions*.

Key Learning and CTS Process Debrief (10 minutes)

After participants have had time to complete at least one or two of the snapshots, ask the group to stand up again with Handouts A1.6 and A1.8 in hand, and meet at the snapshot wall signs with the same group or partner they discussed their pre-CTS ideas with. Show Slide 47. Give them time to discuss what new knowledge or insights they gained from doing the CTS. After groups have had time to discuss their CTS findings, ask for a few report outs on how CTS addressed the snapshot questions about teaching and learning. Ask volunteers to share what they learned from their snapshot. Probe to elaborate on what the standards and research suggested about the snapshot. Depending on the size of your group and the amount of time, you may only get to three or four snapshots. Clarify information and add in important information using Facilitator Resource A1.1: Introduction to CTS K–12 Snapshot Facilitator Notes.

> **Facilitator Note**
>
> If any questions have been posted on the CTS Questions chart, this is a good time to read those to the group. Address any you can (given time constraints) and/or refer participants to other resources or people to talk with after the session.

Applications of CTS (15 minutes)

Context and Applications (15 minutes)

Ask participants to step back from the snapshot activity they have just finished to think about different reasons why a mathematics educator might use CTS. In table groups, if you only have one CTS book per table, or in trios if you have enough books, use the steps on Slide 48 to have participants review the CTS application examples on page 35 of the Mathematics CTS book and ask for other examples. Then if they have their own books or a copy on the table, have everyone turn to Chapter 4 beginning on page 53 to scan examples of suggestions and support materials for using CTS in various content, curricular, instructional, assessment, or professional development applications. If they do not have access to the books, you can describe the applications briefly. Point out the collection of vignettes in Chapter 6 of the parent book that illuminate how CTS is used in various contexts.

Reflection (10 minutes)

Facilitator Note

See suggestions of reflection strategies in Chapter 3 starting on page 53.

- Show slide 49. Ask participants to do a quick write (3 minutes of quiet time to write a reflection) that summarizes their thoughts on how CTS could be useful to them.
- Show Slide 50. Have participants stand and find a partner and have a conversation about how CTS could be useful to them.

Wrap-Up and Evaluation (10 minutes)

Wrap-Up (5 minutes)

Ask participants to return to their seats. Answer any questions they have about using CTS and refer them to page 2 of the CTS parent book for more information on the outcomes of using CTS. Remind participants they can visit the CTS website at www.curriculumtopicstudy.org for more information and that new tools and information are posted quarterly. Suggest that as a next step they may want to do a full topic study. (See modules for leading full topic studies in Chapter 5 of this *Leader's Guide*.)

Evaluation (5 minutes)

Thank everyone for their participation and ask them to complete an evaluation.

OPTIONS FOR INTRODUCING THE CTS RESOURCE BOOKS

The introductory Module A1 in this chapter includes an introduction to the CTS resource books. Some of these books may be familiar to participants; others may be new to them. It is important to include enough time for participants to become acquainted with each of the resources before they engage in the CTS process. This can be done during Module A1, or you may want to provide an introduction as a separate session, for example, with a preservice class or as an introduction with the full topic studies in Chapter 5 if there are participants who do not know the books.

Two options are provided to introduce the books. The option you select will depend on the number of resource books you have available, the familiarity your participants have with the books, and the amount of time you have for your introductory workshop. Each option includes a slide to insert into the Module A1 PowerPoint slides or with one of the full topic studies in Chapter 5 if most of your participants are new to CTS. Check the slides and the script to see where to insert the slides.

Introduction to CTS Resources: Option 1

Overview

This option provides participants with a highly engaging, interactive way to explore the CTS resource books firsthand before using them to do CTS.

When to Use This Option

Use this option when you have multiple sets of the resources for participants and the time for them to explore the books firsthand.

Resources Needed

Ideally all six resources will be available for every six participants, or twelve if working in pairs. *Beyond Numeracy* can be optional. If *Research Companion* is not available, be sure *Benchmarks for Science Literacy* is available as it contains summaries of the research used in Section IV.

Time

Time needed is 25 to 30 minutes.

Preparation

Provide a set of available materials at each table group. The number of books determines the number of participants at each table, ideally a one-to-one match between the book and a participant. For example, if all six books are available, form table groups of six. If there are fewer resources available, participants can form pairs for this activity. If participants do not have their own copies of the CTS parent book, make copies of the resource descriptions on pages 27–30 of the CTS parent book. Insert the PowerPoint slide for this option in place of the Introduction to CTS Resources slide placeholder in the Module A1 facilitator's script or insert it into a Chapter 5 module if you are using it there.

Process

1. Ask groups to divide the resources on their tables among people at the table and follow directions on the PowerPoint slide found on the CD-ROM under Option 1. At their tables they should have stacks of the various resource books they will use for CTS.

2. Each person or pair will take one book and look through it, read the description of it from pages 27–30 of the CTS parent book, and become an expert on this book to later introduce it to the other people at their table. Allow about five minutes to review the book, examining its features and content described on pages 27–30. Tell everyone they will have just two or three minutes to introduce the books to each other, pointing out the main features and how they are used in CTS.

3. When they are done sharing the resources in their small groups, answer any additional questions the large group might have—you can refer to the descriptions of the resources provided in Option 2 below to provide additional information on the resources. Announce that participants will now use the resources they just explored to engage in the CTS process. Resume with the next slide in the module you are using.

Introduction to CTS Resources: Option 2

Overview

This option provides a quick way to introduce the resources. It is primarily a mini-lecture and does not provide an opportunity for much interaction.

When to Use This Option

Use this option when you do not have copies of the books available for table groups to use or there is limited time in your agenda. It can also be used if you know that many of the participants already own, have used, or have seen the books, and thus serves as a review for the group.

Resources Needed

The facilitator should have a set of the resources to hold up. After introducing each of the resources, the facilitator should put them on display at a "library table" where participants can go up during the break or after the workshop to look through them.

Approximate Time

Time needed is 10 to 15 minutes, depending on the detail you want to provide.

Preparation

Have each of the books ready to hold up and describe. If participants do not have their own copy of the CTS parent book, make copies of the resource descriptions on pages 27–30 of that book. Have a library area set up where the books can be on display for participants to look through during the break or after the session. Insert the PowerPoint

Slide for this option in place of the Introduction to CTS Resources slide placeholder in the facilitator's script.

Process

1. Refer participants to the descriptions of the resources on pages 27–30 of the CTS parent book as you lead them through a tour of the books. Hold up *Science for All Americans* (AAAS, 1989). Ask for a show of hands, how many people have used this book? How many have heard of it, but haven't used it? How many are learning about it for the first time? Explain that *Science for All Americans* was the first tool developed by the American Association for the Advancement of Science's Project 2061 to establish what all high school graduates should know in order to be prepared to be science literate citizens. *Science for All Americans* was developed with the input and consensus of hundreds of distinguished STEM professionals and educators. It provides an overall picture of what all adults (not just those who go on to higher education and STEM careers) should know after their K–12 experiences in order to be considered mathematically literate. It includes science, mathematics, technology, and social science and the interconnections among them. *Science for All Americans* is used with CTS Section IA, which identifies adult mathematics literacy.

2. Next show the adult trade book *Beyond Numeracy* (Paulos, 1992). Ask for a show of hands, how many people have used this book? How many have heard of it, but haven't used it? How many are learning about it for the first time? Explain that this book is authored by a well-known mathematician who writes about mathematics for public understanding. It describes mathematics concepts in ways the general public can understand when they encounter mathematics in their everyday lives. Besides addressing fundamental mathematics literacy ideas that are also part of *Science for All Americans,* it goes beyond the concepts we would expect every high school graduate to know and be able to use.

3. Next hold up *Benchmarks for Science Literacy* (AAAS, 1993). Ask for a show of hands for the following questions: "How many people have used this book?" "How many have heard of it, but haven't used it?" "How many are learning about it for the first time?" Explain that *Benchmarks* (like its companion, *Science for All Americans*) isn't just about science. It addresses science, technology, mathematics, and social sciences and lays out explicit learning goals for students to achieve in Grades K–2 in order to achieve the adult mathematical literacy described in *Science for All Americans.* Point out that the bulleted text lists specific benchmark learning goals at K–2, 3–5, 6–8, and 9–12 grade bands. These bullets are used with Section IIIA in the CTS guides. In addition, several of the benchmarks have been slightly revised, a few moved to other grade levels, and several new benchmarks have been added. These changes in the 1993 benchmarks can be seen on the online version of *Benchmarks for Science Literacy* available on the Project 2061 website at www.project2061.org. Besides the bulleted lists of learning goals, there are also grade span essays as well as an overview essay. These essays describe the implications for teaching the ideas and provide suggestions for curricular and instructional contexts. The essays are used with Section IIA, "Consider Instructional Implications," of a CTS guide. *Benchmarks for Science Literacy* also offers a summary of research about students' misconceptions, in the back of the book in Chapter 15.

These readings are used with Section IVA, "Examine Research on Learning," of a CTS guide.

4. Show the *Principles and Standards for School Mathematics* (NCTM, 2000). Ask for a show of hands, how many people have used this book? How many have heard of it, but haven't used it? How many are learning about it for the first time? Say while many of us are much more familiar with our own state and local standards, this document is important because it constitutes a consensus from the mathematics professional association of what is essential to know and be able to do in mathematics. Most state standards are based on the NCTM *Principles and Standards (PSSM)*, or its companion document *Focal Points*. In addition, states are now using the *Common Core State Standards for Mathematics (CCSM)*, which overlaps considerably with NCTM's standards. The *CCSM* does not give specific information on instruction like the *PSSM* provides; therefore, *PSSM* is an excellent companion to use with the *CCSM*. Like the *Benchmarks*, *PSSM* also includes bulleted lists of learning goals used for Section IIIB as well as essays used in Section IIB.

5. Next show the NCTM *Research Companion* (NCTM, 2003). Ask for a show of hands, how many people have used this book? How many have heard of it, but haven't used it? How many are learning about it for the first time? This book also provides summaries of the research on obstacles and difficulties students have with learning mathematics concepts and procedures in mathematics as well as research on effective teaching. Mention that the website for CTS has a searchable database where you can find additional recent research articles. This book is used for CTS Section IVB to examine research on student learning.

6. Finally, hold up Volumes 1 and 2 of *Atlas of Science Literacy* (AAAS, 2001, 2007; if both are available). Ask for a show of hands, how many people have used this book? How many have heard of it, but haven't used it? How many are learning about it for the first time? Explain that the *Atlas* organizes the explicit learning goals found in *Benchmarks* (as well as new or revised ones that are in the *Atlas*, but not in the 1993 version of *Benchmarks*) and statements from *Science for All Americans* into visual maps that show growth in understanding over a K–12 span, including prerequisite ideas that form the basis for subsequent ideas that build in sophistication over time. "Storylines" at the bottom of the maps show how the ideas related to that storyline unfold over time as you move up through each grade level. The maps show connections within and across topics. The *Atlas* is used with CTS Section V to examine coherency and articulation. The narrative that precedes each map can also be used with Sections II, III, and IV and includes updated summaries of the research on learning. Explain how Volume 2 of the *Atlas* was not available at the time the first edition of the CTS parent book was written. However, there is a crosswalk to the second edition that can be downloaded off the CTS website and is available in the Chapter 2 handouts in the CD-ROM at the back of this *Leader's Guide*.

7. Finally, hold up a copy of the state standards for the group you are working with, or if it is a multistate group, hold up a copy of any state standards document as an example. Explain how all the resources just mentioned are used to clarify state standards or the learning goals in local curriculum documents. These state or district-specific standards are used in Section VI of the CTS study guides.

8. Invite any additional questions and point out that the books will be on display in the room if they would like to browse through them. Announce that participants will now use the resources to engage in the CTS process. Resume with the next slide in the module you are using.

DEVELOPING YOUR OWN SNAPSHOTS AND RESOURCE SCENARIOS

As discussed in the introduction to this chapter, you may wish to develop your own snapshots and resource scenarios tailored directly to the needs and interests of your participants. The following instructions can be used to create your own session-specific snapshots or resource scenarios. Templates for designing your own are included in the Chapter 4 folder, Design Your Own Template, on the CD-ROM at the back of this book.

Designing Your Own Snapshots

1. Select the content and grade level that address the needs of your audience.

2. Identify the CTS study guide(s) that matches the concepts or skills.

3. Do your own brief CTS, using only the grade-level readings for the audience with which you will be working. Take notes on CTS findings for each section that could be useful to your audience.

4. Print out and review the templates for designing your own snapshots found in the Chapter 4 folder, Design Your Own Templates, on the CD-ROM. Decide whether you want to use a snapshot format for questions similar to the one provided in Module A1, Handout A1.5 (Snapshot Template 1—insert your own examples where indicated) or make up your own question starters (Snapshot Template 2).

5. Decide how many snapshots you would like to provide for your audience to investigate. A minimum of eight and no more than fifteen is suggested. Delete boxes on the Snapshot Templates (1 or 2) that you aren't using. Make sure you have a balance of questions across CTS Sections I–V.

6. If you are using Snapshot Template 2, scramble the snapshots so questions that use different sections of a CTS guide (and different topics if using more than one) are placed on the CTS snapshot template in different squares so they don't sequentially follow a CTS study guide. The idea is to provide practice in identifying which CTS study guide to use, which CTS section (I–V) to read, and what resource reading will answer the snapshot question. (Note: If you develop a set of snapshots on one topic, your participants will only use one CTS guide, so they can skip the step that involves identifying which CTS study guide to use.)

7. Use the questions on pages 39–41 of the Mathematics CTS book to guide your development of snapshot questions for Template 2, paying close attention to the purposes of the CTS Sections I–V.

8. Create an answer sheet like Handout A1.7 with the Category, Topic Study Guide, and CTS Section used so participants can check whether they selected the appropriate section(s) as they work through the scaffold.

Designing Your Own Resource Scenarios

1. Select a CTS topic guide that matches the needs of your audience.

2. Do the CTS readings for the topic yourself, taking notes from the readings that you might use in the scenarios.

3. Print out and review the templates for designing your own scenarios found in the Chapter 4 folder on the CD-ROM. Decide whether you want to use a resource scenario format for questions similar to the one provided in Module A2 (see Resource Scenario Template 1) or make up your own question starters (see Resource Scenario Template 2).
   - Make sure you have questions that target the first five sections of the CTS (I–V), different grade levels as appropriate, and use the different resource books (or include only the books you have available). Insert your own examples where indicated.
   - Use the guiding questions on pages 39–41 of the CTS parent book to help guide your development of the questions used in your resource scenario.
   - Try out your questions by going back to the CTS reading to be sure the CTS findings will address your questions adequately. If not, modify your questions.

NEXT STEPS AFTER CTS INTRODUCTIONS

After participants have been introduced to CTS, they are ready to use the tools and resources to conduct a full topic study. Examples of designs for leading a full topic study are described in the next chapter.

5

Leading Full Topic Studies

INTRODUCTION TO FULL TOPIC STUDIES

In the previous chapter, we described ways to introduce the curriculum topic study (CTS) process and the resources used with CTS. This chapter provides five comprehensive modules for leading full topic study sessions that afford the opportunity to delve deeply into important mathematics topics and directions for developing your own topic studies on mathematics content important to your work. The modules are designed to be used with participants who already have some familiarity with CTS; however, they can be adapted to use with audiences who have not experienced one of the Chapter 4 introductory sessions. Each module is intended to show the variety of ways a full CTS can be designed and facilitated (see summary of modules in Table 5.1). We have provided a sample script you can follow or adapt accordingly for your audience or presentation style. In addition, the CD-ROM at the back of this book includes a folder with the PowerPoint slides to use with each of the modules as well as the accompanying handouts and facilitator resources.

Table 5.1 Summary of CTS Topic Modules

Module	CTS Category	Grade Levels	Time (Approximate)	Application Used
B1: Number Sense	Numbers and Operations	K–5	3 hours	Tools for modeling base 10
B2: Fractions	Numbers and Operations	K–8	3 hours	Representations of fractions

(Continued)

Table 5.1 (Continued)

Module	CTS Category	Grade Levels	Time (Approximate)	Application Used
B3: Linear Measurement	Measurement	K–8	3 hours	Assessment probe with examples of student thinking
B4: Variables	Algebra	3–12	3.25 hours	Assessment probe with examples of student thinking
B5: Conjecture, Proof, and Justification	Problem-Solving and Processes	K–12	3.25 hours	Proof task with examples of student responses

Note: Grade levels can be modified according to the need and context of the audience. Times are approximate. Audiences with no or little experience with CTS will need additional time.

Table 5.2 CTS Learning Cycle Icons

Icon	CTS Learning Cycle Stage
	Engagement
	Elicitation
	Exploration
	Development
	Synthesis
	Application
	Reflection and Self-Assessment

Each of the module scripts, B1 through B5, uses the CTS Learning Cycle of Inquiry, Study, and Reflection described on pages 40–42 of Chapter 3 in this *Leader's Guide* as well as pages 38–48 in the parent book. Icons are used in the script and the agenda to indicate the stage of the CTS Learning Cycle (see Table 5.2).

It is important to note that a grade span has been designated for each module. This grade span indicates where the topic is most likely to appear in the K–12 curriculum. As such, the study process includes the grade levels for the designated grade spans. However, all the modules can be used with a K–12 audience to help start a conversation among K–12 teachers about vertical articulation. In addition, state standards may differ from national standards and district curriculum in relation to where a topic appears. For example, in the national standards, ideas related to linear relationships are targeted in Grade 8. In many districts, students do not study linear relationships until high school. Ultimately it is up to the facilitator to determine the appropriate grade level based on the K–12 progression of their state standards, district curriculum, and the audience attending the session.

In addition to the five modules, this chapter provides suggestions for developing your own full topic study as well as ways to combine two topics for an integrated topic study. These are not included as modules since they are not topic specific. The following are brief summaries of the five modules in this chapter that are described in Table 5.1.

Full CTS Modules (Half Day Sessions)

Module B1—Number Sense

In this session, participants will use the CTS guide "Number Sense" to develop a common definition of number sense and examine the implications for teaching and learning in elementary grades mathematics. Although different components of number sense are important at all grade spans, the main focus of this session is on early number sense. This session is primarily for teachers in Grades K–5 who teach mathematics or for leaders who work with teachers of mathematics at these levels; but it can also be adapted to address a K–8 or K–12 audience. Participants use their CTS findings to examine common tools used to build understanding of the base 10 system.

Module B2—Fractions

In this session, participants will use the CTS guide "Fractions" to develop a common understanding of teaching fractions and examine implications for learning. Although this is primarily a session for teachers in Grades K–8 who teach mathematics or for leaders who work with teachers of mathematics at these levels, it can be adapted to include other grade spans. Participants use their CTS findings to examine various representations of fractions and connect their findings to their own instructional materials.

Module B3—Linear Measurement

In this session, participants will use the CTS guide "Length" to develop a common understanding of teaching length measurement and examine implications for learning. This session is primarily for teachers in Grades K–8 who teach mathematics or for leaders who work with teachers of mathematics at these levels. Participants use their CTS findings to examine student work in which students are given a change in the intervals or a nonzero starting point.

Module B4—Variables

In this session, participants will use the CTS guide "Variables" to develop a common understanding of variables and examine implications for teaching and learning. This session is primarily for teachers in Grades 3–12 who teach mathematics or for leaders who work with teachers of mathematics at these levels. The module helps participants thoughtfully explore what students should understand about variables at the different grade levels. Participants use their CTS findings to examine assessment probes that uncover students' thinking related to variables.

Module B5—Conjecture, Proof, and Justification

In this session, participants use a CTS guide from the *Problem Solving and Processes* CTS category to develop a common understanding of conjecture, proof, and justification. This session is primarily for teachers in Grades K–12 who teach mathematics or for leaders who work with teachers of mathematics at these levels. The module helps participants thoughtfully explore the content, teaching, and learning implications related to conjecture, proof, and justification. Participants use their CTS findings to examine a framework that describes the development of proof concepts.

Additional Suggestions for Designing and Leading Full Topic Studies

This section of the chapter provides guidance and suggestions for how to use CTS templates and guidelines to develop your own full topic studies as well as how two topics can be combined into one full, combined study.

The next sections in this chapter provide the facilitation guides for the five comprehensive CTS full topic study modules (B1–B5). The handouts, facilitator resources, and PowerPoint presentations for each module are located in the Chapter 5 folder on the CD-ROM at the back of this book. Table 5.3 provides an at-a-glance summary of the Full Topic Study Modules.

Table 5.3 CTS Full Topic Study Sessions at a Glance

Module	Time Needed	Grade Level	Content	When to Use
Module B1: Number Sense	3 hours	K–5	Defining number sense; identifying the underlying concepts and skills; and instructional use of models	Group wishes to build common definition; need for teachers to consider the use of models in developing number sense
Module B2: Fractions	3 hours	K–8	Fraction as one meaning of a/b: a parts of size 1/b	Group wishes to enhance their own and their students' understanding of fractions and their various representations

Module	Time Needed	Grade Level	Content	When to Use
Module B3: Linear Measurement	3 hours	K–8	Foundational understandings of measurement including unit attribute relations, iteration, tiling, identical units, standardization, proportionality, additivity, and origin	Teachers wish to clarify the K–8 content for linear measurement and examine the research on learning to understand difficulties students have with this topic
Module B4: Variables	3.25 hours	3–12	How the understanding of the various uses of variables develops over Grades K–12; uses of variables including placeholders, generalized patterns, and covariation	Teachers wish to deepen understanding of the concepts and skills related to variables and examine the research on learning to understand difficulties students have with this topic
Module B5: Conjecture, Proof, and Justification	3.25 hours	K–12	The progression of understandings and skills related to proof, conjecture, and justification; clarification of terminology used	Teachers wish to understand how concepts and use of these processes develop over the K–12 grades

Module B1

Number Sense, Facilitation Guide

BACKGROUND INFORMATION

Description of the Module

In this CTS module, participants use the CTS Guide "Number Sense" to examine the understandings and skills younger children need for building number sense. Participants construct a definition of number sense, carefully analyze the specific ideas in the learning goals for the K–2 and 3–5 grade spans, and examine the research on learning to understand difficulties students have with developing number sense. Participants apply their CTS findings to examine several examples of ways models can be used to represent numbers and develop number sense.

Audience

This session is primarily for Grades K–5 teachers or specialists who work with elementary teachers.

Purpose and Goals

The overall purpose of this module is to improve participants' understanding of effective teaching and learning related to number sense. The goals of this module are to

- deepen understanding of the coherency and articulation of K–5 ideas related to developing number sense in the elementary grades,
- examine the research on learning and instructional implications related to developing the understandings and skills of early number sense, and
- consider how results from the CTS can be used to inform current practice.

SESSION DESIGN

Time

Allow about 3 hours (include a 15-minute break). This is an approximate time and will be adjusted based on the experience and needs of your audience.

Agenda at a Glance

Welcome and Engagement (10 minutes)

- Welcome and goals of the session (5 minutes)
- Engagement table talk (5 minutes)

Elicitation (15 minutes)

- Accessing prior knowledge by defining number sense (15 minutes)

Exploration (70 minutes, includes a 15-minute break)

- Preparing for the CTS (5 minutes)
- NCTM Number and Operation overview reading (10 minutes)
- CTS Section III card sort (20 minutes)
- Quiet read Sections I, II, IV, and V (35 minutes, includes a 15-minute break)

Development and Synthesis (40 minutes)

- Clarifying discussion (15 minutes)
- Synthesis of important points and gallery walk (25 minutes)

Application (25 minutes)

- Tools and modeling activity (25 minutes)

Reflection (10 minutes)

- Revisiting number sense definition (10 minutes)

Evaluation (5 minutes)

MATERIALS AND PREPARATION

Materials Needed by Facilitator

CTS Parent Book

Mathematics Curriculum Topic Study: Bridging the Gap Between Standards and Practice (Keeley & Rose, 2006)

Resource Books

One copy of each of the following resource books:

- *Science for All Americans* (American Association for the Advancement of Science [AAAS], 1989)
- *Beyond Numeracy* (Paulos, 1992) (Optional)
- *Benchmarks for Science Literacy* (AAAS, 1993 or 2009 online version)
- *Principles and Standards for School Mathematics* (National Council of Teachers of Mathematics [NCTM], 2000)
- *Research Companion to Principles and Standards for School Mathematics* (NCTM, 2003)
- *Atlas of Science Literacy*, Vol. 2 (AAAS, 2007)
- NCTM *Focal Points* or *Common Core Mathematics Standards* (Optional)

CTS Module B1 PowerPoint Presentation

The Module B1 PowerPoint presentation is located in the Chapter 5 folder on the CD-ROM at the back of this book. Review it and tailor it to your needs and audience. Insert your date and location on Slide 1, add additional graphics as desired, and add your own contact information on the last slide.

Supplies and Equipment

- Computer and LCD projector to show PowerPoint presentation
- Flip chart easel, pads, and markers
- Paper for participants to take notes
- Sentence strips (one for every participant); either buy sentence strips or make them by cutting multiple sheets of chart paper into thirds

Wall Charts

Prepare and post the CTS Reminders chart and the CTS Content Questions chart in meeting room prior to session (for description of these two charts, see Module A1 in Chapter 4, p. 65).

Facilitator Preparation

- Conduct your own "Number Sense" CTS prior to leading the session.
- PowerPoint slides for B1 (on CD-ROM). Insert your own graphics and additional information as desired.
- Review Facilitator Resource B1.1: CTS Facilitator Summary for Number Sense included in the Chapter 5 folder on the CD-ROM.
- Identify connections to state standards if necessary (e.g., if all the participants are from the same state).
- Prepare Facilitator Resource B1.2—CTS Section IIIB Cards for *Principles and Standards for School Mathematics (PSSM)* on yellow paper (or color of your choosing). Cut out and put in a resealable plastic bag.
- Prepare Facilitator Resource B1.3—CTS Section IIIA Cards for *Benchmarks* on yellow paper (or color of your choosing). Cut out and put in a resealable plastic bag.
- Choose the option for distributing and sharing readings (see Chapter 3 of this *Leader's Guide,* pp. 47–49) that best matches your audience.
- Prepare an evaluation form to collect feedback from participants.

Materials Needed for Participants

(*Note:* All handouts can be found in the Chapter 5 folder on the CD-ROM.)

- Handout B1.1: Agenda
- Handout B1.2: Number Sense Reading Assignments
- Handout B1.3: Tools and Modeling: Hundreds Chart
- Handout B1.4: Tools and Modeling: Ten-Frame
- Handout B1.5: Tools and Modeling: Open Number Line
- Handout B1.6: Tools and Modeling: Arithmetic Rack
- Section III Cards (See preparation for Facilitator Resource B1.2 and B1.3.)
- Optional: Copies of the PowerPoint Slides for Session B1 (on CD-ROM). Insert your own graphics and additional information you wish to add.
- If participants do not have their own CTS parent book, make copies for each participant of the CTS Guide "Number Sense" on page 127 of the CTS parent book.
- If not enough resource books are available, make copies of the selected readings from the CTS guide "Number Sense" on page 127 of the CTS parent book.

DIRECTIONS FOR FACILITATING THE MODULE

Welcome, Introductions, Goals, and Engagement (10 minutes)

Show Slide 1. Welcome the participants and review the agenda. If your group does not know one another, provide an opportunity for quick introductions. Show Slide 2 and review the goals for the session. Ask participants to briefly share at their tables why number sense is an important topic for mathematics teachers to study and what they hope to gain from studying this topic.

Elicitation (15 minutes)

Accessing Prior Knowledge (15 minutes)

Show Slide 3. Ask the participants to think about their definition of number sense and to write their definition on the sentence strips provided. Post the sentence strips on the wall for all to see. Ask participants to examine the group's definitions. Ask for examples that point out some of the common definitions as well as some of the unique ones. Encourage participants to keep these definitions in mind while reading and discussing ideas from the CTS.

Exploration (70 minutes, includes a 15-minute break)

Preparing for the CTS (5 minutes)

Explain that in order to examine the understandings and skills of number sense, we will conduct a curriculum topic study (CTS). Show Slide 4. Have participants turn to the Number Sense CTS guide on page 127 of the CTS parent book (or printed handout) and Handout B1.2, which provides a focus for the readings. Point out that the CTS guide lists the resources and page numbers that will be used to read about and study the topic "Number Sense." Provide a brief overview of the reading process that will be used and the purpose of each CTS study guide section (I–VI). Explain that the first two readings will be done by each individual person and the remaining readings will be divided among the group. Point out that although the learning goals for this topic continue into the middle and high school grades in the national standards, we will be focusing only on elementary number sense and therefore will study and discuss only those readings in the K–5 grade span.

Overview Reading From NCTM's Principles and Standards for School Mathematics (10 minutes)

Show Slide 5. Ask all participants to read the first reading listed on Handout B1.2—CTS Section IIB K–12 Number and Operations Overview in the *PSSM*, pages 32–33 (stop at the top of page 33). Explain that they will use the components of the definition described in the first paragraph of this overview as a lens during the activity they are about to engage in.

> **Facilitator Note**
>
> You may want to list the various components of the overview definition on chart paper. Number sense—(1) the ability to decompose numbers naturally; (2) use particular numbers as referents; (3) use the relationships among operations to solve problems; (4) understand the base-10 number system; and (5) estimate, make sense of numbers, and recognize the relative and absolute magnitude of numbers (NCTM, 2000, p. 32).

Section III Card Sort (20 minutes)

Show Slide 6. Explain they are now going to begin exploring the topic by examining CTS Section III: Identify Concepts and Specific Ideas related to the components of the number sense definition. Divide participants into groups of three, and give each group the sets of materials you put together from Facilitator Resource

B1.2 (*PSSM* cards) and B1.3 (*Benchmarks* cards). (Optional: Create additional cards using standards from the *Common Core State Standards for Mathematics*, NCTM *Focal Points*, or their state standards.) These are the Section III specific ideas cards (include both *Benchmarks* and *PSSM* cards in each grade span set and point out that the blue cards are ideas from *Benchmarks*, the yellow cards are expectations from *PSSM* and if you choose to use the *Common Core State Standards for Mathematics* or other standards, choose a third color. Each group will review and sort the ideas looking for the various components of the definition of number sense that were described in the *PSSM* Overview as well as similarities and differences among the ideas. After about ten minutes, ask for each group to respond briefly to each of the questions on Slide 7. What are some differences and similarities between the specific ideas from *Benchmarks* and *PSSM* (and add *Common Core State Standards for Mathematics* to the slide if you choose to add those)? How does this compare to your original definitions of number sense?

> **Facilitator Note**
>
> Depending on the number of small groups, choose at least one group to examine the difference between the K–2 and 3–5 ideas to add to the discussion on coherency and articulation.

Quiet Read (35 minutes, includes a 15-minute break)

Show Slide 8. Participants will now conduct a quiet read, depending on which option for distributing the readings was selected. Participants will read the sections below the dotted line on Handout B1.2 (participants have already looked at the sections above the dotted line). Adjust the time according to the reading option selected (for example, if participants wish to read all the sections, you will need to build in more time than you would assigning sections to each member of a group). Encourage participants to take notes that are relevant to the purpose of the section they are reading and that apply only to the knowledge needed to understand teaching and learning implications related to number sense. Again, explain that Handout B1.2: CTS Number Sense Reading Assignments reminds them of the focus for their reading so they know what to specifically extract from the reading.

> **Facilitator Note**
>
> You may wish to take a 15-minute break before or after the readings or build it into the reading time by telling participants they will have 35 minutes to use to complete their assigned readings (or more if each participant is reading all the sections) and take a break.

Development and Synthesis (40 minutes)

 ### Clarifying Discussion (15 minutes)

Depending on the option selected for distributing and sharing the readings, participants will discuss each of the readings in small groups and clarify findings related to the topic. Remind participants to refer to Handout B1.2 that describes what they should focus on during their reading and summarize the focus of that reading for the discussion.

 ### Synthesis of Important Points (15–25 minutes)

Show Slide 9. After groups have discussed the readings, ask them to list 3–5 important key points that emerged from the readings for the Number Sense CTS. The key points should be directly connected to their readings, not their own personal ideas. Have each group write their key ideas on chart paper and cite the CTS section (e.g., IVA Research on Learning), and post them on the wall. Have each group appoint a spokesperson or two to share one or two insights they gained from their CTS that changed or enhanced their initial ideas about number sense. Gather the larger group around each chart (or break into smaller groups if you have more than twenty participants). Allow about two minutes of talk at each chart and then move the group to the next one until all have visited all charts.

Do a short recap of what you observed in terms of the groups' learning. Bring up any key points that may not have been raised by the groups. Ask participants to share any other questions or comments about what they did and what they learned.

Application (25 minutes)

Instructional Context: Tools and Modeling

Show Slide 10. Review the following statement with participants: "Models can help students represent numbers and develop number sense. But using materials, especially in a rote manner, does not ensure understanding" (NCTM, 2000). Have the participants work in small groups of four people to examine four uses of common tools for modeling ideas related to building understanding of the base-10 number system. Divide Handouts B1.3–B1.6 among the four group members. Give five minutes for participants to review the information on their handout and prepare a summary for the other group members. Each person provides a two- or three-minute presentation to their group. When the group presentations are finished, ask participants to share any additional uses of models and modeling they have used that are designed to develop the understanding of the base-10 number system and other various components of number sense, and that reflect the CTS findings.

Reflection and Evaluation (10 minutes)

Show Slide 11. Ask participants to do a quick written response to these questions: How well did the CTS process help you meet your goals you established at the beginning of this session? What changes would you make to your initial number sense definition? Answer any questions, thank participants, and ask them to complete an evaluation.

Additional Facilitator Notes

- There are several examples of supplementary materials listed on the CTS website (go to the Products pull-down menu and click on Supplementary Database) that can be used to extend this session, including assessment probes that can be used to examine student work and videos of clinical interviews with children that reveal their misconceptions.

- This topic study can be followed by a book study of *Young Mathematicians at Work: Constructing Number Sense, Addition, and Subtraction* (Fosnot & Dolk, 2001), which can further delve into CTS Sections II and IV based on recent research intended for the classroom. In addition, *Fostering Children's Mathematical Development* (Fosnot & Dolk, 2004) includes short video clips from classroom situations, providing opportunities to observe, analyze, and discuss critical moments in children's number sense development.

- A number of probes in the *Uncovering Student Thinking in Mathematics* (Rose, Arline, & Minton, 2007) and *Uncovering Student Thinking in Mathematics in the K–5 Classroom* (Rose Tobey & Minton, 2011) can be used to explore number sense concepts.

- NCTM's Illuminations website includes videos of student interviews depicting beginning understanding of place value and number representation (http://illuminations.nctm.org/Reflections_preK-2.html).

Module B2

Fractions, Facilitation Guide

BACKGROUND INFORMATION

Description of the Module

In this session, participants engage in a full topic study on "Fractions" to examine what mathematically literate adults should know about fractions, the key conceptual understandings and skills for students at different grade spans, instructional implications for teaching fractions, and research on students' ideas related to understanding fractions. Although this is a K–8 topic study, high school teachers who teach struggling students, or leaders who work with teachers of mathematics at all grade levels, can also benefit from this module. The module helps participants think about fractions in different ways and thoughtfully examine what students should understand about fractions and be able to do with them at the different grade levels. The information will help teachers make informed choices about what important knowledge and skills students should develop at which grade levels and help them be more aware of the difficulties students encounter when learning about and using fractions.

Purpose and Goals

The overall purpose of this module is to help participants gain a better understanding of the teaching and learning implications related to fractions. The goals of this module are to

- deepen understanding of the coherency and articulation of ideas and skills related to fractions,
- examine teaching and learning implications related to the conceptual and procedural understanding of fractions, and
- consider how results from the CTS can be used to inform practice.

SESSION DESIGN

Time Required

Allow about 3 hours (includes a 15-minute break). This is an approximate time and will be adjusted based on the experience and needs of your audience.

Agenda at a Glance

Welcome and Engagement (10 minutes)

- Welcome and goals of the session (10 minutes)

Elicitation (15 minutes)

- Frayer Model for a/b (15 minutes)

Exploration (45 minutes)

- Preparing for the CTS (5 minutes)
- Quiet read (40 minutes, includes a 15-minute break)

Development and Synthesis (60 minutes)

- Clarifying discussion (25 minutes)
- Synthesis of key findings and gallery walk (25 minutes)
- Revisiting the Frayer Model (10 minutes)

Application (30 minutes)

- Representing fractions (5 minutes)
- Linking back to CTS (10 minutes)
- Linking findings to state standards and district curriculum (15 minutes)

Reflection and Evaluation (15 minutes)

- Revisit individual goals and new insights (10 minutes)
- Evaluation (5 minutes)

MATERIALS AND PREPARATION

Materials Needed by Facilitator

CTS Parent Book

Mathematics Curriculum Topic Study: Bridging the Gap Between Standards and Practice (Keeley & Rose, 2006)

Resource Books

One copy of each of the following resource books:

- *Science for All Americans* (AAAS, 1989)
- *Beyond Numeracy* (Paulos, 1992) (Optional)
- *Benchmarks for Science Literacy* (AAAS, 1993 or 2009 online version)
- *Principles and Standards for School Mathematics* (NCTM, 2000)
- *Research Companion to Principles and Standards for School Mathematics* (NCTM, 2003)
- *Atlas of Science Literacy*, Vol. 1 and Vol. 2 (AAAS, 2001, 2007)
- *Common Core State Standards for Mathematics*, NCTM *Focal Points*, or copies of State Standards (Optional)

CTS Module B2 PowerPoint Presentation

The Module B2 PowerPoint presentation is located in the Chapter 5 folder on the CD-ROM. Review it and tailor it to your needs and audience. Insert your date and location on Slide 1, add additional graphics as desired, and add your own contact information on the last slide.

Supplies and Equipment

- Computer and LCD projector to show PowerPoint presentation
- Flip chart easel, pads, and markers
- Paper for participants to take notes

Wall Charts

- Prepare and post the CTS Reminders chart and the CTS Content Questions chart in meeting room prior to session (for description of these two charts, see Module A1 in Chapter 4, p. 65).
- Prepare a wall chart of the Frayer Model used in Handout B2.3.

Facilitator Preparation

- PowerPoint slides for B2 (on CD-ROM). Insert your own graphics and additional information as desired.
- Conduct your own "Fractions" CTS prior to leading the session.
- Review Facilitator Resource B2.1: CTS Facilitator's Summary for Fractions included in the Chapter 5 folder on the CD-ROM.
- Identify connections to state or local standards if necessary.
- Choose the option for distributing and sharing readings (see Chapter 3, pp. 47–49) that best matches your audience.
- Decide whether to use the Handout B2.5: Representing Fractions application or substitute your own example related to the content teachers are learning in your professional development setting.
- Prepare an evaluation form to collect feedback from participants.

Materials Needed for Participants

(*Note:* All handouts are available in the Chapter 5 folder on the CD-ROM.)

- Handout B2.1: Agenda at a Glance
- Handout B2.2: Fraction CTS Guide—make copies if participants do not have a copy of the parent book. (Note: The first printing of the parent book included the wrong guide on p. 121. The title was correct but the readings in the guide were from the CTS study guide on the preceding page. Check to make sure your participants have the corrected version in their book or use this handout.)
- Handout B2.3: Frayer Model Template
- Handout B2.4: Fraction Reading Assignments
- Handout B2.5: Representing Fractions
- If not enough resource books are available, make copies of the selected readings from the CTS "Fraction" guide on page 121 (or Handout B2.2).

DIRECTIONS FOR FACILITATING THE MODULE

Welcome, Introductions, and Engagement (10 minutes)

Show Slide 1. Welcome the participants and explain that the purpose of this session is to use CTS to deepen their knowledge about fractions and consider how to apply what they learn to improve the teaching and learning of this important mathematics topic. If your participants do not know one another, do quick introductions by either having people introduce themselves at their tables or choose your own introduction activity. Show Slide 2 and review the goals of the session. Ask participants to think about their own personal goals for improving their understanding of the conceptual and procedural teaching and learning implications related to fractions. Ask them to write down two or three goals and save them to refer to later in the session.

Elicitation (15 minutes)

Accessing Prior Knowledge and Experience With a Frayer Model (15 minutes)

Show Slide 3 and refer to Handout B1.3: a/b Frayer Model. Tell participants that in order to examine the skills and understandings related to fractions, we need to first develop a common understanding of the definition and uses of the symbolic representation a/b. Explain that we will use an instructional strategy called the Frayer Model to document our prior knowledge about the representation a/b (Frayer, Frederick, & Klausmeier, 1969). Explain that a Frayer Model is a type of graphic organizer that helps students develop conceptual relationships and examples associated with a word or symbol. In mathematics, it provides students an opportunity to explain and elaborate with examples their understanding of a mathematical concept or technical term (Allen, 2007).

Ask everyone to look at the Frayer Model Handout: B1.3. Point out that a Frayer Model has four sections: Operational definition, characteristics/uses, examples, and nonexamples. Give the group about five minutes to individually fill in the four sections that describe the symbol "a/b." After individuals are finished, have participants exchange their Frayer Model with a partner and compare ideas. After pairs have had an opportunity to discuss the similarities and differences between their Frayer Models, assign one of the four sections to each small table group. Ask them to come up with a consensus on their section of the Frayer Model and share their idea with the whole group. Record each group's answer in the appropriate section on the large Frayer Model Chart you prepared and posted in the front of the room. Keep the chart posted, show Slide 4, debrief, and explain that we will go back to our Frayer Model clarification of the symbol "a/b" after we gain more information from the CTS readings.

> ### Facilitator Note
>
> The mathematics symbol (a/b) is placed in a circle in the center of the worksheet. Participants provide their own operational definition of a mathematical definition of the symbol in the upper left sidebar and characteristics or uses of a/b in the upper right box. Participants then list examples of mathematical uses of a/b, contrasted with examples that are not considered mathematical uses of a/b.

Exploration (45 minutes)

Preparing for the CTS (5 minutes)

Show Slide 5. Have participants turn to the CTS Guide, "Fractions" on page 121 or Handout B2.2 if they do not have a copy of the CTS guide, and Handout B2.4, which provides focus for the readings from each CTS section. Explain that in order to examine the concepts and skills related to fractions and consider the difficulties students have with these, we will conduct a Curriculum Topic Study on this topic. Show Slide 5 and go over each of the reading assignments. Describe how the readings will be distributed and shared, based on the option you selected in Chapter 3 pages 47–49. Make sure everyone is clear about which section(s) they are reading and remind them that the page numbers are listed on their CTS study guide.

> ### Facilitator Note
>
> If the group is large and you chose to do a jigsaw, it is suggested that you break up the Section IIB readings by grade span.

> ### Facilitator Note
>
> Adjust the reading time according to the option selected (for example, if participants wish to read all the sections for their grade level plus Sections I, IV, and V, you will need to build in more time. You may provide a 10–15-minute break after the readings or build a break into the reading time.

Quiet Read (40 minutes, includes a 15-minute break)

Ask participants to read their sections quietly using Handout B2.4 as a reminder of their assignment and focus. Encourage them to take notes that are relevant to the purpose of the section they are reading that apply only to the concepts and skills related to fractions.

Development and Synthesis (60 minutes)

Clarifying Discussion (25 minutes)

After the readings are completed, ask participants to work in small study groups of about five to six people to discuss their readings and clarify understandings related to the topic. Remind participants to refer to Handout B2.4 that describes what they should focus on during their reading and summarize the focus of that reading.

Synthesis of Key Findings and Gallery Walk (25 minutes)

Show Slide 6. After small study groups have discussed their readings, ask each group to develop a list of at least five key findings that came from their CTS readings and discussion on fractions that will be important to remember for their work. The key findings should focus on major ideas that can be traced back to the readings in the CTS. Ask each table group to write their key findings on chart paper and post them on the wall. Then invite everyone to walk around the room in small groups to do a "gallery walk." Ask them to examine the key findings on each chart, looking for similarities and differences from chart to chart. After the gallery walk, ask the large group what they noticed. What were some of the similar key findings identified by the group?

Revisiting the Frayer Model (10 minutes)

After all the summaries have been reported for each of the assigned readings, show Slide 7 and ask the participants to individually revisit the ideas recorded on their Frayer Model Template and add or change anything based on their CTS findings. Ask table groups to consider the following questions (Slide 7):

- Based on the group's CTS findings and the example Fractions Summary Chart (pp. 67–68 in Mathematics CTS), what additional ideas could you add to each section of the group's Frayer Model (point out the chart)?
- At which grade span should each of the different uses of fractions be introduced?
- At what level of understanding?

After participants have had time to discuss their "before and after" ideas, ask a few people to share with the full group.

Application (30 minutes)

Representing Fractions (5 minutes)

Show Slide 8. Have the participants review Handout B2.5: Representing Fractions at their table groups. Explain that this is an example of how a group of three to five teachers applied the information gathered through a CTS of fractions. After studying the topic, the group created this table to show the various representations of part/whole relationships. The group felt creating this chart was an important reminder to provide opportunities for students to see and use the various representations, to review instructional materials to highlight representations already incorporated, and to find possible gaps.

Facilitator Note

If the groups do not highlight the different meanings and uses of a/b, be sure to bring out these ideas.

Optional: Facilitators can extend this workshop even further to fit their own context by having participants examine their own instructional materials, critique representations and various uses of fractions in their materials, experience a model lesson, design a lesson that reflects the study findings, or examine student work.

Linking Back to CTS (10 minutes)

Show Slide 9. Give participants time to discuss how the findings from CTS are reflected in the Representing Fractions application (Handout B2.5) and how they might develop other applications to use with students (or teachers).

Linking CTS Findings to State Standards or District Curriculum (15 minutes)

Show Slide 10. If participants have their state standards available or are using common instructional materials, link to CTS Section VI and discuss how the "Fraction" CTS helped them clarify the meaning and intent of their state standards. Ask them to identify learning goals related to fractions in their state standards and compare them with the CTS findings. How does the "Fractions" CTS help teachers better understand or interpret their state standards? Which findings from CTS are reflected in the state standards? Which findings are not reflected in the state standards? Ask for any other comments about how CTS can help them implement their state standards.

Reflection and Evaluation (15 minutes)

Reflection (10 minutes)

Show Slide 11. Ask participants to revisit their individual goals from the beginning of the session and answer the questions on the slide: How well did the CTS process help you meet your goals? What else do you need to further your understanding of the topic of fractions?

Evaluation (5 minutes)

Answer any questions, thank participants, and ask them to complete a session evaluation.

Additional Facilitator Notes

- Consider having teams create CTS summaries as a record of their session. Examples of the Fraction CTS summary notes can be found on the CD-ROM in the Chapter 3 folder.
- This module can be adapted to focus on a single grade span, 3–5 or 6–8, keeping in mind the importance of examining the precursor ideas (CTS Sections III and V) and instruction (CTS Section II) from the previous grade span.
- This topic study can be followed by a book study of *Young Mathematicians at Work: Constructing Fractions, Decimals and Percents* (Fosnot & Dolk, 2002), which participants can use to further investigate CTS Sections II and IV based on recent research intended for the classroom. In addition, *Young Mathematicians at Work: Professional Development Materials* (Fosnot et al., 2004–2006) includes short video clips from classroom situations, providing opportunities to observe, analyze, and discuss critical moments in children's number sense development
- A number of probes in the *Uncovering Student Thinking in Mathematics* (Rose & Arline, 2009; Rose, Arline, & Minton, 2007) can be used to explore fraction concepts.

Module B3

Linear Measurement
Facilitation Guide

BACKGROUND INFORMATION

Description of the Module

In this session participants engage in a full topic study of an important concept and skill in mathematics, linear measurement, using the "Length" CTS guide. The module helps participants see how a coherent sequence of measurement-related ideas develops from Grades K–8. Participants also examine students' common errors and difficulties related to linear measurement.

Audience

This session is designed primarily for a K–8 audience. Since the national standards do extend learning goals related to linear measurement beyond Grade 8, the session could be extended for a K–12 audience so that high school teachers can examine precursor ideas that prepare students to apply extended ideas of measurement including ideas of precision and accuracy and informal concepts of limit in measurement situations.

Purpose and Goals

The overall purpose of this module is to examine the progression of K–8 ideas about measuring length and the teaching and learning implications related to this important mathematics concept. The goals for this module are to

- deepen conceptual understanding of ideas and skills related to linear measurement in the K–8 curriculum,
- examine teaching and learning implications related to linear measurement, and
- apply CTS findings to teachers' own curricular and instructional context.

SESSION DESIGN

Time

About 3 hours. This is an approximate time and will be adjusted based on the experience and needs of your audience.

Agenda at a Glance

Welcome and Engagement (10 minutes)

- Welcome and goals of the session (5 minutes)
- Engagement table talk (5 minutes)

Elicitation (20 minutes)

- Brainstorming foundational ideas (20 minutes)

Exploration (55 minutes)

- Preparing for the CTS (10 minutes)
- Quiet read (45 minutes, includes a 15-minute break)

Development and Synthesis (60 minutes)

- Clarifying discussion (30 minutes)
- Revisiting initial ideas (15 minutes)
- Gallery walk (15 minutes)

Application (20 minutes)

- Looking at student work (20 minutes)

Reflection and Evaluation (15 minutes)

- Quick write (10 minutes)
- Evaluation (5 minutes)

MATERIALS AND PREPARATION

Materials Needed by Facilitator

CTS Book

Mathematics Curriculum Topic Study: Bridging the Gap Between Standards and Practice (Keeley & Rose, 2006)

Resource Books

One copy of each of the following resource books:

- *Benchmarks for Science Literacy* (AAAS, 1993 or 2009 online version)
- *Principles and Standards for School Mathematics* (NCTM, 2000)
- *Research Companion to Principles and Standards for School Mathematics* (NCTM, 2003)
- *Atlas of Science Literacy*, Vol. 2 (AAAS, 2007)
- *Common Core State Standards for Mathematics*, NCTM *Focal Points*, or a copy of state standards (Optional)

CTS Module B3 PowerPoint Presentation

The Module B3 PowerPoint presentation is located in the Chapter 5 folder on the CD-ROM. Review it and tailor it to your needs/audience as needed. Insert your date and location on Slide 1, add additional graphics as desired, and add your own contact information on the last slide.

Supplies and Equipment

- Computer and LCD projector to show PowerPoint
- Flip chart easel, pads, and markers
- Paper for participants to take notes

Wall Charts

- Prepare and post the *CTS Reminders* chart and the *CTS Content Questions* chart in meeting room prior to session (see example in A1 Module, Chapter 4, p. 65).

Facilitator Preparation

- Conduct your own "Length" CTS prior to leading the session.
- Identify connections to state standards if necessary.
- Collect student work using the two probes What's the Measure? (Handout B3.3) and How Long Is the Pencil? (Handout B3.4); or use the optional student work in Handouts B3.4 and B3.5.
- Choose the option for distributing and sharing readings (see Chapter 3, pp. 47–49) that best matches your audience.
- Prepare an evaluation form to collect feedback from participants.

Materials Needed for Participants

(*Note:* All handouts are in the CD-ROM in the Chapter 5 folder.)

- Handout B3.1: Agenda at a Glance
- Handout B3.2: Length Reading Assignments
- Handout B3.3: What's the Measure? Probe 1
- Handout B3.4: How Long Is the Pencil? Probe 2
- Handout B3.5: What's the Measure? Sample Student Responses (use if you do not collect your own student work).
- Handout B3.6: How Long Is the Pencil? Sample Student Responses (use if you do not collect your own student work).
- Optional: Copy of PowerPoint Slides for Session B3 (on CD-ROM). Insert your own graphics and additional information you wish to add.
- If participants do not have their own CTS books, make copies of the CTS guide "Length" on page 171 for each participant.
- If not enough resource books are available, make copies of the selected readings from the CTS guide "Length" on page 171 that are used in Handout B3.2. Make sure everyone has a copy of the *Research Companion* reading, pages 180–182, used on PowerPoint Slide 4.

DIRECTIONS FOR FACILITATING THE MODULE

Welcome/Introductions and Engagement (10 minutes)

Welcome and Introductions (5 minutes)

Show Slides 1 and 2. Welcome the participants and explain the purpose of this session. Go over the agenda. If your group does not know one another, provide an opportunity for quick introductions.

Engagement Table Talk (5 minutes)

Ask participants to briefly share why "Linear Measurement" is an important topic for mathematics teachers to study and what they hope to gain from studying this topic. Review the goals for the session.

Elicitation (20 minutes)

Brainstorming Foundational Ideas (20 minutes)

Show Slide 3. Ask participants to brainstorm a list of important learning goals (concepts or specific ideas) that are foundational to the K–8 linear measurement topic of "Length." Divide the participants into groups of four to five to generate a group list. Ask them to indicate where in the K–8 sequence students should learn these ideas (label the ideas K–2, 3–5, and/or 6–8). Underline any terminology students are expected to know. Remind them to watch the time and honor all voices without passing judgment on others' ideas. This is a brainstorm. Post their charts on the wall. Later, after completing the CTS, they will reexamine their brainstormed lists. Facilitators may want to remind participants of the norms for brainstorming.

Exploration (55 minutes)

Preparing for the CTS (10 minutes)

Show Slide 4. Announce they are now going to explore the topic by doing a CTS to examine content, curricular, and instructional considerations related to the "Length" CTS measurement topic. Refer participants to the CTS guide on page 171 of the CTS parent book (or use a handout copy) and explain they will use selected (not all) readings from the CTS guide for this study. To guide the readings, refer participants to Handout B3.2: Length Reading Assignments, which identifies the selected sections from the CTS guide they will focus on during the session. To begin the CTS, everyone will start by reading pages 180–182 from Section IVB (*Research Companion*). Explain that they will use the eight foundations described in this reading as a lens to focus the grade-level CTS section readings they will be assigned. Explain that after everyone has read pages 180–182 from *Research Companion*, they will read the remaining sections assigned to them from Handout B3.2 to help them understand the foundations addressed in the research.

> **Facilitator Note**
>
> You may want to chart the eight foundations of measurement, (1) Unit attribute relations, (2) Iteration, (3) Tiling, (4) Identical units, (5) Standardization, (6) Proportionality, (7) Additivity, and (8) Origin, for participants and facilitator to refer to during the session.

Show Slide 5. Describe how the readings from Handout B3.2 will be distributed, based on the option you selected from Chapter 3 on pages 47–49. Review each of the reading assignments and the purpose of each CTS study guide section (I–VI). Point out that although the learning goals for this topic continue into Grades 9–12 in the national standards, we will focus only on the K–8 grade band for this session.

Quiet Read (45 minutes, includes a 15-minute break)

Participants will now conduct a quiet read of their CTS readings assignments, depending on which option for distributing readings was selected. Adjust the time according to the option selected (for example, if participants wish to read all the sections, you will need to build in more time). Encourage participants to take notes that are relevant to the purpose of the section they are reading and that apply only to the knowledge needed to understand linear measurement. Make sure groups know that all of the readings must be covered by their group. (Note: The connection to state standards and instructional materials [CTS Section VI] will be discussed by the whole group after examining

> **Facilitator Note**
>
> You may wish to take a 15-minute break after the readings or build it in to the reading time by telling participants they will have 45 minutes to use to complete the readings and take a break.

the selected CTS sections.) Give participants time to read their assigned sections on Handout B3.2. Remind them to look for findings related to the eight categories representing important measurement foundations (point to a chart if you previously recorded and posted them): (1) Unit attribute relations, (2) Iteration, (3) Tiling, (4) Identical units, (5) Standardization, (6) Proportionality, (7) Additivity, and (8) Origin. Remind participants as they read to look for CTS findings that directly describe the concepts or ideas.

Development and Synthesis (60 minutes)

Clarifying Discussion (30 minutes)

Facilitator Note

The latter is not to mean that they are not important, but rather they are not the ideas that are most essential for understanding linear measurement.

After participants have finished their assigned readings, have them discuss each of the readings in their small groups. Time and format of the discussion will depend on which of the options for distributing and sharing the readings was selected. Spend about five or ten minutes to pull out the main ideas from the study as a whole group discussion. (Refer to Facilitator Resource B3, Measurement Summary Chart of CTS Findings, for the main points that should be addressed.)

Revisiting Initial Ideas (15 minutes)

After concluding a debrief discussion of the main ideas, ask the small groups to return to their brainstormed lists posted on the wall and reconsider their initial ideas about the topic of Linear Measurement. Show Slide 6. Ask the group to reconsider their list of learning goals based on their CTS readings and discussions. Ask the groups to decide which things on the list, based on the CTS results, they should keep at a grade level, which ones to move to a different grade level, and which ones to discard.

Facilitator Note

Provide different colored markers from the ones participants used to make their brainstormed list so they can easily see changes they made in the chart and/or provide colored dots for groups to use to mark their Before CTS charts. For example, they can use colored markers to make a large green dot next to the idea that they want to keep, a red dot for something they will discard, and orange for ideas they will keep but move to a different grade span or change the wording. Or use the following key: K for keep as is, X for discard, and M for modify.

Ask groups to decide which terminology to leave in or change as well as any changes in the wording of the ideas to better match the statements in the CTS Section III or V standards. Encourage them to add any new ideas they gained from doing CTS. Have each group be prepared to give a short presentation to summarize how CTS changed and/or enhanced their initial thinking about the topic of linear measurement.

Topic Synthesis (15 minutes)

Gallery Walk (15 minutes)

Have each group appoint a spokesperson or two to share one or two insights they gained from their CTS that changed or enhanced their initial thinking about the topic. Gather the larger group around each chart (or break into smaller groups if you have more than twenty participants). Allow about two minutes of talk at each chart and then move the group to the next one until all groups' charts have been visited.

Do a short recap of what you observed in terms of the groups' learning. Bring up any key points that may not have been raised by the groups. Ask participants to share any other questions or comments about what they did and what they learned.

Application (20 minutes)

Looking at Student Work (20 minutes)

Show Slide 7 and refer participants to Handouts B3.3 and B3.4: What's the Measure? and How Long Is the Pencil? Based on their study of linear measurement, ask them to identify the concepts related to each probe. Ask which learning goal(s) seem to be most aligned with the context of the probe. Based on the CTS study results, ask them what commonly held ideas they might anticipate from the student work. Refer them to Handouts B3.5 and B3.6 or have them use their own student work or student work you brought to this session. Give participants time to examine the student responses and note any similarities and differences between the student responses. Have participants discuss how the students' responses reflect the research findings and understanding of the learning goal. Ask them to suggest how they would use the results of the CTS to design instruction that would address the students' ideas if these were their own students.

Reflection (10 minutes)

Show Slide 8. Ask participants to do a quick written response to the question, How will you use the results of this CTS? Ask for a few volunteers to share their next steps. Show Slide 9. Ask participants to reflect back on the personal session goal they identified and reflect on how the CTS helped them meet their goal.

Wrap-Up and Evaluation (5 minutes)

Answer any questions, thank participants, and ask them to complete an evaluation.

Module B4

Variables, Facilitation Guide

BACKGROUND INFORMATION

Description of the Module

In this session participants engage in a full topic study to deepen their understanding of the topic of variables in mathematics. Participants examine what all mathematically literate adults should know about variables, key concepts for students at the different grade spans, instructional implications, and the research on students' ideas related to this topic. Participants apply their CTS findings to examining student responses to an assessment probe that elicits common misunderstandings students have about variables.

Audience

This session is primarily for teachers in Grades 3–12 who teach mathematics or for leaders who work with teachers of mathematics at these levels. Although the activities in the module are more suited to an upper elementary through high school audience, K–2 teachers can also benefit from the CTS. The module helps participants thoughtfully explore what students should understand about variables at the different grade levels. The information will help teachers make informed choices about the important knowledge and skills related to variables that students should develop from one grade level to the next and the difficulties they often encounter when learning this topic.

Purpose and Goals

The overall purpose of this module is to improve teachers' content and pedagogical content knowledge related to the topic of variables. The goals of this module are to

- deepen understanding of the coherency and articulation of ideas related to the topic of variables over the 3–12 grade spans,
- examine how students' conceptual understanding and procedural use of variables develop over time, and
- consider how results from the CTS can be used to inform current practice.

SESSION DESIGN

Time

3.25 hours. This is an approximate time and will be adjusted based on the experiences and needs of your audience.

Agenda at a Glance

Welcome and Engagement (25 minutes)

- Welcome, introductions, and goals (5 minutes)
- Establishing a purpose (20 minutes)

Elicitation of Prior Knowledge (20 minutes)

- Uses of variables (5 minutes)
- Concepts and specific ideas brainstorm (15 minutes)

Exploration (65 minutes, includes a 15-minute break)

- Section III learning goal sort (20 minutes)
- Preparing for the CTS (5 minutes)
- CTS individual readings (25 minutes)

Development and Synthesis (55 minutes)

- Clarifying discussion (25 minutes)
- Revisiting initial ideas (15 minutes)
- Gallery walk (15 minutes)

Application of CTS Findings (20 minutes)

- Applying findings (10 minutes)
- Looking at additional contexts (10 minutes)

Reflection and Evaluation (15 minutes)

- Quick write and discussion (10 minutes)
- Evaluation (5 minutes)

MATERIALS AND PREPARATION

Materials Needed by Facilitator

CTS Book

Mathematics Curriculum Topic Study: Bridging the Gap Between Standards and Practice (Keeley & Rose, 2006)

Resource Books

One copy of each of the following resource books:

- *Science for All Americans* (AAAS, 1989)
- *Beyond Numeracy* (Paulos, 1992) (Optional)
- *Benchmarks for Science Literacy* (AAAS, 1993 or 2009 online version)
- *Principles and Standards for School Mathematics* (NCTM, 2000)
- *Research Companion to Principles and Standards for School Mathematics* (NCTM, 2003)

- *Atlas of Science Literacy*, Vol. 1 (AAAS, 2001)
- *Common Core Standards for Mathematics*, NCTM *Focal Points*, or copies of State Standards (Optional)
- *Uncovering Student Thinking in Mathematics Grades 6–12* (Rose & Arline, 2009) (Optional)

CTS Module B4 PowerPoint Presentation

The Module B4 PowerPoint presentation is located in the Chapter 5 folder on the CD-ROM. Review it and tailor it to your needs/audience as needed. Insert your date and location on Slide 1, add additional graphics as desired, and add your own contact information on the last slide.

Supplies and Equipment

- Computer and LCD projector to show PowerPoint presentation
- Flip chart easel, pads, and markers
- Paper for participants to take notes
- Optional: Green, red, and yellow dots or colored markers for the post-CTS chart activity

Wall Charts

- Prepare and post the CTS Reminders chart and the CTS Content Questions chart in meeting room prior to session (for description of these two charts, see Module A1 in Chapter 4, p. 65).
- Post three charts around the room to create three stations (or make two of each to create six stations depending on number of participants). Label with the following:

  1. Place Holder/Unknowns

  2. Generalized Patterns

  3. Covariation

- Conduct your own Variables CTS prior to leading the session, including CTS Section VI to identify connections to state standards if necessary.
- Review Facilitator Resource B4.1: CTS Summary Chart for Variables included in the Chapter 5 folder on the CD-ROM.
- Copy Facilitator Resources B4.2 and B4.3 on blue and yellow paper (or other colors if desired) and cut out cards.
- Choose the option for distributing and sharing readings (see Chapter 3, pp. 47–49) that best matches your audience.
- Prepare an evaluation form to collect feedback from participants.

Materials Needed for Participants

(*Note:* The handouts are available in the Chapter 5 folder on the CD-ROM.)

- Handout B4.1: Agenda at a Glance
- Handout B4.2: Probe: Is It True?
- Handout B4.3: Sample 8th-Grade Responses: Is It True?
- Handout B4.4: Variables CTS Reading Assignments
- Handout B4.5: Probe: Is It a Variable?
- Copies of PowerPoint presentation (on CD-ROM). Insert your own graphics and additional information you wish to add. (Optional)

- If participants do not have their own CTS books, make copies of the CTS guide "Variables" on page 146 in the parent book for each participant.
- If not enough resource books are available, make copies of the selected readings from the CTS "Variables" guide on page 146 that are used in Handout B3.4.

DIRECTIONS FOR FACILITATING THE MODULE

Welcome, Introductions, and Engagement (5 minutes)

Show Slide 1. Welcome the participants, do quick introductions if participants do not know each other, and explain that the session will engage them in using CTS to deepen their knowledge of the variables and consider how to apply what they learn to improve the teaching and learning of this important and often misunderstood concept.

Establishing a Purpose (20 minutes)

Show Slide 2. Point out the goals of the session. Ask participants to write down two or three personal learning goals they would like to achieve during the session to improve their understanding of the concept of a variable and the implications for teaching and learning about variables. Ask them to save their list of personal goals to refer to at the end of the session.

Show Slide 3. Ask participants to complete the Handout B4.2: Is It True? probe (if you have a copy of the book, hold it up for participants to see). Allow a few minutes and ask for a vote on which expressions they think are true when $m = 3$. Ask for show of hands for A, B, C, D, E, F, G, and H. After participants have voted on which expressions they think are true, explain that the correct responses are E and F. If some voted on E but not on F, point out that 3 times 5 represents the expression $3m$, even though it is not completely simplified. Explain that the CTS they are about to do will help us understand why some adults and students select the distracters A, B, C, D, G, and H.

Refer everyone to Handout B4.3: Sample 8th Grade Responses: Is It True? Show Slide 4. Have participants turn to a partner at their tables and discuss the students' ideas using the questions on Slide 4. Have participants briefly share why they think students have misunderstandings related to evaluating expressions. Explain that CTS can help us further examine this learning problem as well as other learning difficulties related to variables.

> **Facilitator Note**
>
> Take a few comments but do not go into details about the identified difficulties at this time. For facilitators' purpose, distracter A may reveal the misunderstanding that m is used as place value. Distracters B and C reveal whether a variable next to a number implies addition. Students who choose this distracter may be considering the rules of concatenation with mixed numbers when reasoning about this. For example, in students' prior experiences two numbers next to each other, as in 3 ½, has implied addition—3 and ½. Distracters D and H reveal whether students mistake variables with abbreviations for something. Distracter G reveals misunderstandings related to the letter m being used to represent the slope of an equation. Some students choose several different distracters based on the reasoning that $3m$ can mean addition, multiplication, or division; or that any distracter that has the numbers 3 and 5 in the answer must be right (Rose & Arline, 2009, pp. 181–182).

Elicitation of Prior Knowledge (20 minutes)

Uses of Variables (5 minutes)

Show Slide 5. Review the uses of variables on the slide and point out the information is from the *Principles and Standards for School Mathematics*. Explain they will be exploring these various uses further through the topic study. However, before they start the CTS, they will activate their knowledge about teaching variables by brainstorming what they think are important student learning goals and instructional considerations associated with the three uses of variables.

Brainstorm Pre-CTS Teaching and Learning Goals (15 minutes)

Divide participants evenly into groups by the three "use of variables" listed on the charts. Have participants meet with their groups and generate a brainstormed list following the directions on Slide 6 (without using the CTS resources yet) of what they think the important teaching considerations and learning goals are in their category based on their own beliefs and/or prior knowledge about standards and research on learning. After they generate their list, ask them to indicate where in the K–12 sequence they think students should be expected to learn the ideas or experience the teaching suggestions the groups generated. Have them develop a Before CTS wall chart that lists the ideas about teaching and learning they generated for their "use of variables" category by grade span K–2, 3–5, 6–8, and 9–12. Remind them to watch the time and record as many ideas as possible in the time given, honoring all voices without passing judgment on others' ideas.

> **Facilitator Note**
>
> Even though this is a Grades 3–12 CTS, it is important for Grades 3–5 teachers to identify ideas from the preceding grade span, K–2.

Exploration (65 minutes, includes a 15-minute break)

CTS Section III Card Sort (20 minutes)

Show Slide 7. Announce that we are now going to begin exploring the topic by first examining CTS Section III: Identify Concepts and Specific Ideas related to the uses of variables. Divide participants into groups of three, and give each group the sets of materials you made from Facilitator Resource B4.2 and Facilitator Resource B4.3. These are the Section III Specific Ideas cards. Include both *PSSM* and *Benchmarks* cards in each grade span set and point out that the yellow cards are expectations from *PSSM* and the blue cards are ideas from *Benchmarks*. (Optional: also include standards from the *Common Core State Standards* or from state standards using a third color.) Each group will sort the ideas into the three categories of "uses of variables": placeholders, generalized patterns, and covariation. After about ten minutes, ask for each group to respond briefly to each of the questions on Slide 8:

> **Facilitator Note**
>
> Participants should bring up the idea that many of the statements can be placed in more than one category and note that the statements from the *Benchmarks* are descriptions of the concept or idea, whereas the *PSSM* statements are expectations of what students should know and be able to do.

- What is the focus for each of the grade spans?
- Are there overlaps between grade spans?
- What are some differences and similarities between the learning goals from *Benchmarks* and *PSSM*? (Note: Include *Common Core* or *Focal Points* if added to this module.)

> **Facilitator Note**
>
> The *Beyond Numeracy* reading is optional, depending on your availability of this resource. Also, depending on your goals, you may suggest that your participants do the readings for the other CTS sections listed on the CTS guide on their own after the session.

Preparing for the CTS (5 minutes)

Show Slide 9. Refer participants to the CTS guide on page 146 in the CTS parent book (or use a handout copy) and explain that we will use selected (not all) readings from the CTS guide for this work. To guide the readings, refer participants to Handout B4.4: Variable CTS Reading Assignments, which identifies the selected sections from the CTS study guide we will focus on during this session. Remind them that if at any time they have a content question, they can write it on a sticky note and post it on the wall chart labeled "CTS Content Questions."

CTS Individual Readings (25 minutes depending on option selected plus 15 minutes for a break)

Have participants stay in their "uses of variables" group. Select one of the six options for distributing and sharing readings described on pages 47–49 in Chapter 3 of this *Leader's Guide.* Make sure groups know that all of the readings I–V must be covered by at least one person in their group. (Note: The connection to state standards and instructional materials will be discussed by the whole group after examining the selected CTS Sections I–V.) Give participants time to read their assigned sections on Handout B4.4. Remind them to look for findings related to the use of variables they were assigned to earlier.

> **Facilitator Note**
>
> If there are three or more people in a group, suggest they divide up the readings by grade level rather than read it all in order to save time. Ask participants to read other sections if they finish early.

Development and Synthesis (55 minutes)

Clarifying Discussion (25 minutes)

After finishing their assigned sections, have participants discuss each of the readings in their small groups as they relate to their "uses of variables" category. Time and format of the discussion will depend on which of the options for distributing and sharing the readings was selected. Spend about five or ten minutes to pull out the main ideas from the study as a whole group discussion. (Refer to Facilitator Resource B4.1, Summary Chart of CTS Findings, for the main points that should be addressed.)

Revisiting Initial Ideas (15 minutes)

After concluding a debrief discussion of the key points from the readings, ask the small groups to return to their brainstormed "Uses of Variables" chart posted on the wall and reconsider their initial ideas about teaching and learning related to their assigned use of a variable. Ask the group to reconsider their list of learning goals and teaching ideas based on their CTS readings and discussions to decide which things on the list to keep at a grade level, based on the study results, which ones to move to a different grade level, and which ones to discard.

Ask groups to decide which terminology to leave in or change as well as any changes in the wording of the goals to better match the ideas in the standards. Also ask them to add any new ideas they gained from doing CTS. Have each group be prepared to give a short presentation to summarize how CTS changed and/ or enhanced their initial thinking about the "uses of variables" category they were originally assigned.

> **Facilitator Note**
>
> The latter is not to mean that they are not important or can't be taught after students have achieved the basic ideas, but rather they are not the ideas that are needed to understand this particular use of a variable.

Gallery Walk (15 minutes)

Have each category group appoint a spokesperson or two to share one or two insights they gained from their CTS that changed or enhanced their initial ideas. Gather the larger group around each chart (or break into smaller groups if you have more than twenty participants). Allow about two minutes of talk at each chart and then move the group to the next one until all have visited all three categories.

> **Facilitator Note**
>
> Provide different colored markers from the ones participants used to make their brainstormed list so they can easily see changes they made in the chart and/or provide colored dots for groups to use to mark their *Before CTS* charts. For example, they can use colored markers to make a large green dot next to the idea that they want to keep, a red dot for something they will discard, and orange for ideas they will keep but move to a different grade span or change the wording. Or use the following key: K for keep as is, X for discard, and M for modify.

Do a short recap of what you observed in terms of the groups' learning. Bring up any key points that may not have been raised by the groups. Ask participants to share any other questions or comments about what they did and what they learned.

Application (20 minutes)

Applying Findings to Your Own Work (10 minutes)

Show Slide 10. Ask participants to step back from the CTS study they have just completed to think about the value of CTS. Allow time for several people to share their insights. If needed, point out that one value of CTS is that it can make us more aware of mathematics content we don't understand as well as we would like and affords the chance to explore what we need to know to better serve our students. Address any of the CTS questions that may have been posted on the CTS Questions Chart. Refer to the questions on Slide 10. Allow time for a short discussion of ideas at tables.

Looking at Additional Contexts (10 minutes)

Show Slide 11. Refer to Handout B4.5: Is It a Variable? probe. Have the participants discuss how the targeted concepts relate to the three uses of variables explored in the variables topic study.

Reflection and Evaluation (15 minutes)

Reflection (10 minutes)

Show Slide 12. Revisit the personal professional development goals identified at the beginning of the session. Have participants do a quick write and share with a partner the responses to the questions on the slide. Ask for a few final comments from the group.

Wrap-Up and Evaluation (5 minutes)

Show Slide 13. Invite any questions, thank participants, and ask them to complete an evaluation.

Additional Facilitator Notes

- There are several examples of supplementary materials listed on the CTS website that can be used to extend this session, including assessment probes that can be used to examine student work and videos of clinical interviews with children that reveal their misconceptions.

- A number of probes in the *Uncovering Student Thinking in Mathematics* resources (Rose & Arline, 2009; Rose Tobey & Minton, 2011; Rose, Arline, & Minton, 2007) can be used to explore additional uses of variables. More information about these resources can be found at www.uncoveringstudentideas.org.

Module B5

Conjecture, Proof, and Justification, Facilitation Guide

BACKGROUND INFORMATION

Description of the Module

In this session, participants engage in a full topic study from the Problem Solving and Processes category using the CTS study guide "Conjecture, Proof, and Justification." The module helps participants thoughtfully examine teaching and learning considerations at each grade level related to this topic, including the terminology used. The information will help teachers make informed choices about the important knowledge and skills students should develop at what grade levels, how these understandings and skills build over time, and the difficulties students encounter when learning about conjecture, proof, and justification. Teachers engage in a proof task and then examine students' responses to the same task.

Audience

This session is designed for a K–12 audience of teachers and/or mathematics specialists who work with K–12 teachers.

Purpose and Goals

The overall purpose of this module is to examine the K–12 teaching and learning implications related to conjecture, proof, and justification. The goals for this module are to

- deepen understanding of the coherency and articulation of K–12 ideas related to conjecture, proof, and justification,
- examine teaching and learning implications related to the process of conjecture and proof, and
- consider how results from the CTS can be used to inform practice.

SESSION DESIGN

Time

3.25 hours (includes a 15-minute break). This is an approximate time and will be adjusted based on the experience and needs of your audience.

Agenda at a Glance

Welcome and Engagement (10 minutes)

- Welcome and goals of the session (5 minutes)
- Table talk (5 minutes)

Elicitation (35 minutes)

- Word sort (35 minutes)

Exploration (45 minutes)

- Preparing for the CTS (5 minutes)
- Quiet read (40 minutes, includes a 15-minute break)

Development and Synthesis (50 minutes)

- Clarifying discussion (30 minutes)
- Synthesis of key findings (20 minutes)

Application (40 minutes)

- Applying CTS to your own context (10 minutes)
- Halving and Doubling Task (30 minutes)

Reflection and Evaluation (15 minutes)

- Think-Pair-Share (10 minutes)
- Evaluation (5 minutes)

MATERIALS AND PREPARATION

Materials Needed by Facilitator

CTS Parent Book

Mathematics Curriculum Topic Study: Bridging the Gap Between Standards and Practice (Keeley & Rose, 2006)

Resource Books

One copy of each of the following resource books:

- *Science for All Americans* (AAAS, 1989)
- *Beyond Numeracy* (Paulos, 1992) (Optional)
- *Benchmarks for Science Literacy* (AAAS, 1993 or 2009 online version)
- *Principles and Standards for School Mathematics* (NCTM, 2000)
- *Research Companion to Principles and Standards for School Mathematics* (NCTM, 2003)
- *Atlas of Science Literacy*, Vol. 1 and Vol. 2 (AAAS, 2001, 2007)
- *Common Core State Standards for Mathematics*, NCTM *Focal Points*, or copies of State Standards (Optional)

CTS Module B5 PowerPoint Presentation

The Module B5 PowerPoint presentation is located in the Chapter 5 folder on the CD-ROM. Review it and tailor it to your needs/audience as needed. Insert your date and location on Slide 1, add additional graphics as desired, and add your own contact information on the last slide.

Supplies and Equipment

- Computer and LCD projector to show PowerPoint presentation
- Flip chart easel, pads, and markers
- Paper for participants to take notes

Wall Charts

- Prepare and post the CTS Reminders chart and the CTS Content Questions Chart in meeting room prior to session (see example on p. 65).

Facilitator Preparation

- Conduct your own Conjecture, Proof, and Justification CTS prior to leading the session.
- Identify connections to state standards and core ideas if necessary.
- Choose the option for distributing and sharing readings (see Chapter 3, pp. 47–49) that best matches your audience.
- Prepare and post the CTS Reminders chart, CTS Content Questions chart, and CTS Words chart in meeting room prior to session.
- Prepare Word Sort materials from Facilitator Resource B5.1. Cut out the cards and clip a set of word cards together and a separate set of definition cards together. Place the two sets of cards in a resealable plastic bag to distribute at the beginning of the module.
- Prepare an evaluation form to collect feedback from participants.

Materials Needed for Participants

(*Note:* All handouts are in the Chapter 5 folder on the CD-ROM.)

- Handout B5.1: Conjecture, Proof, and Justification Agenda
- Handout B5.2: Word Sort Definitions
- Handout B5.3: Conjecture, Proof, and Justification CTS Jigsaw Reading Assignments
- Handout B5.4: Halving and Doubling
- Handout B5:5: Student Responses to Halving and Doubling Task
- Optional: Copy of PowerPoint presentation (on CD-ROM). Insert your own graphics and additional information you wish to add.
- If participants do not have their own CTS books, make copies of the CTS guide "Conjecture, Proof, and Justification" on page 201 for each participant.
- If not enough resource books are available, make copies of the selected readings from the CTS "Conjecture, Proof, and Justification" guide on page 201 that are used in Handout 3.
- Prepare an evaluation form to collect feedback from participants.

DIRECTIONS FOR FACILITATING THE MODULE

 ### Welcome, Introductions, and Engagement (10 minutes)

Welcome Participants and Share Goals (10 minutes)

Show Slides 1 and 2. If your group does not know one another, provide an opportunity for quick introductions. Review the goals for the session and have participants briefly share what they hope to gain from this session. Go over the agenda.

Elicitation (35 minutes)

Activating Prior Knowledge: Terminology Word Sort (35 minutes)

Show Slide 3. Explain that the "Conjecture, Proof, and Justification" CTS incorporates many mathematical terms that we will begin to clarify prior to the CTS readings. Some of the terms are not defined within the resources and may have different meanings to different people. To make sure we all have a common understanding of the terminology that is part of the CTS study, we will begin with a word sort activity. Have participants work in pairs with the cards prepared in advance for the word sort (Facilitator Resource 5.1) to sort the various terms and match each with a working definition. After matching, give the participants Handout B5.2: Word Sort Definitions. Allow participants to make adjustments to their matches and discuss terms as needed. Clarify any questions they may have.

Next, have participants sort the terms into grade span piles. Have them sort according to when they think the concept, idea, or skill is introduced, not the terminology. Show Slide 4 and give participants five minutes to discuss within their groups the following questions: (1) Were some of the terms more difficult to match than others? Why or why not? (2) How did you decide where to place the cards for the grade span sort? (3) How do you think CTS can help us explore these ideas further?

> **Facilitator Notes**
>
> Keep this conversation brief by reminding them they will be exploring these questions further during the topic study.

Exploration (45 minutes)

Preparing for the CTS (5 minutes)

Have participants refer to the "Conjecture, Proof, and Justification" CTS guide (p. 201) and Handout B5.3: Reading Assignments. Explain that in order to examine the K–12 content in the standards as well as the curricular and instructional considerations that build toward and contribute to an understanding of these mathematical processes, we will conduct a CTS. Show Slide 5 and point out that they will not be reading everything listed on the CTS guide on page 201. Explain they will use Handout B5.3: CTS Conjecture, Proof, and Justification Reading Assignments to focus on specific pages within the CTS guide readings for this session. Explain that they can go back and read the other sections on their own later. Describe how the readings will be distributed and shared based on the option you selected from Chapter 3, pages 47–49. Make sure everyone is clear about their reading assignment and remind them that the page numbers for the reading assignments are listed on their CTS study guide on page 201.

> **Facilitator Notes**
>
> The time indicated for this portion reflects the approximate time to read and make notes on one section. You may need to adjust accordingly.

Quiet Read (40 minutes, includes a 15-minute break)

Participants will read their sections quietly. Adjust the time according to the option selected. Encourage participants to take notes that are relevant to the purpose of the CTS section they are reading. You may wish to take a 15-minute break after the readings or build a break into the reading time.

Development and Synthesis (50 minutes)

Clarifying Discussion (30 minutes)

After participants complete the reading, ask them to discuss their readings in small groups and clarify content and pedagogical considerations related to the topic. Encourage participants to cite their text readings as they discuss the topic. Circulate and answer questions as needed.

Synthesis of Key Findings and Revisit Word Sort (20 minutes)

Show Slide 6. Refer everyone back to the terminology word sort activity. Ask table groups to consider the following statements (Slide 6): Based on your CTS findings, where would you now place these ideas? Have each group appoint a spokesperson or two to share one or two major insights gained from the CTS process about the knowledge and skills required of making conjectures and proving mathematical ideas.

Application (40 minutes)

Applying CTS to Your Own Context (10 minutes)

Ask participants to step back from what they have just done to think about the value of this CTS session in their own context. Refer to the questions on Slide 7: What new ideas or insights did you gain from this CTS that you will take back to your setting? What will you do with these new ideas or insights? Allow time for a short discussion of ideas at tables. Point out that one value of CTS is that it can make us more aware of K–12 content appropriate at different grade levels as well as mathematics content or processes we don't understand as well as we would like. For example, point out how CTS helps us understand why proof is not limited to high school geometry classes. There are many other important ideas that need time to develop first that form a foundation for formal proof in the secondary grades.

> **Facilitator Notes**
>
> Remind participants the level of proof can only be inferred from the brief student explanations provided.

Applying CTS to a Proof Task (30 minutes)

Show Slide 8. Refer participants to Handout B5.4: Halving and Doubling. Have a brief discussion on ways to prove that halving and doubling any two numbers will always produce new numbers with the same product as the original numbers (i.e., geometric and algebraically). In groups of three, have participants read the Grades 7–8 student responses to the task on Handout B5.5 and discuss how the level of their responses reflects expectations at their grade level for being able to engage in proof.

Reflection and Evaluation (10 minutes)

Reflection (5 minutes)

Show Slide 9 and refer participants back to the personal goals they established at the beginning of this session. Ask them to use Think-Pair-Share to reflect on whether or not the goals they listed were met or partially met by the Conjecture, Proof, and Justification topic study. If not, what further steps might they need to take to meet those goals?

Evaluation (5 minutes)

Show Slide 10. Invite any questions and then ask participants to complete an evaluation.

> **Additional Facilitator Notes**
>
> - Consider having teams create CTS summaries as a record of their session. Examples of summary notes can be found on the CD-ROM in the Chapter 3 folder.
> - This module can be adapted to focus on a single grade span, K–2, 3–5, 6–8, or 9–12, keeping in mind the importance of examining the precursor ideas (CTS Sections III and V) and instruction (CTS Section II) that happens in the previous grade span.
> - Encourage participants to search the CTS Supplementary Database on the CTS website for additional articles, websites, and materials that can further extend their understanding of proof, conjecture, and justification.
> - For working with leaders and facilitators, you might use Cathy Carroll and Judith Mumme's *Learning to Lead Mathematics Professional Development*, a case-based set of leadership modules. Module 1 includes a case using the halving and doubling concept (see Chapter 7 professional development strategy on CTS case discussions).

ADDITIONAL SUGGESTIONS FOR DESIGNING AND LEADING FULL TOPIC STUDIES

The previous five modules presented various examples of ways to design and facilitate a full topic study. Each example included standard features, such as incorporating stages in the CTS Learning Cycle, as well as unique nuances, such as engagement and elicitation strategies and ways to develop and debrief the group's understanding after small group study and discussion. These modules can be used as they are or adapted to fit your own context or topic. They can also be used to introduce participants to curriculum topic study. There may be times when a facilitator needs to use a topic situated in the work participants are doing such as a content institute, a particular topic with which students are struggling, for curriculum selection, or for other purposes. You are encouraged to modify any of the modules to fit your specific needs and facilitation style. The following guidelines are provided for facilitators who wish to design their own sessions using a topic other than the ones provided in modules B1 through B5.

DEVELOPING YOUR OWN HALF-DAY TOPIC STUDY

You will notice that each of the full topic study modules (B1–B5) share key components. You will use these same components to develop your own CTS full topic study for a selected topic and grade level. The following steps can be used to guide the development of your own CTS topic session.

1. Select a topic that is relevant to the group you are working with. Find the CTS guide that best matches the topic. Decide whether your topic will be fairly narrow and specific or wide and comprehensive. Develop goals for your session.

2. Decide whether the CTS will be K–12, two grade spans (elementary and middle or middle and high school), or a single grade span.

3. Conduct your own CTS on your chosen topic prior to designing your session. By doing the CTS yourself first, you will best learn which sections and readings to include and focus on in your session. Consider creating your own summary of the major findings from your CTS to refer to for planning and when conducting your session. (Examples of summaries can be found in the Chapter 3 folder on the CD-ROM or on page 67 in the CTS parent book.)

4. Examine the CTS study guide and decide if you are going to use all the readings or pare some of them down. Your decision will also be based on the availability of CTS resources during your session. Refer to Chapter 3 of this *Leader's Guide* for ways to distribute the CTS resources.

5. Decide whether to use the CTS guide as is or create a customized version for a specific grade level that includes only readings for that grade level. Use the Blank Create Your Own CTS Template in the Chapter 5 CD-ROM folder, Developing Your Own CTS, to create your guide. Follow the format used for the study guides in Chapter 7 of the parent CTS book. Add any supplementary resources from the CTS website you wish to include.

6. Decide whether to create a CTS Reading Assignments Handout such as the ones in modules B1 through B5. Consider how to break down the reading assignments in the best way for your group. Sample Blank Reading Assignment Templates are included in the Chapter 5 CD-ROM folder, Developing Your Own CTS, on the CD-ROM. Make sure to fill in your topics, sections, and page numbers that are marked with an XX on the templates.

7. Refer to the CTS Learning Cycle Guide on pages 38–48 in the CTS parent book (Keeley & Rose, 2006) to organize the different phases of the CTS process. Refer to modules B1 through B5 for different examples of ways to engage participants in each section of the CTS Learning Cycle.

8. Decide whether to select any supplementary materials from the CTS website database of CTS supplements to enhance the session, such as videos, assessment probes, and content readings. Embed these within the appropriate CTS Learning Cycle section, such as elicitation or application. If any of the vignettes in Chapter 5 of the CTS parent book match your topic, consider how to embed one of these in your session.

9. Review Chapter 3 of this *Leader's Guide* and choose the grouping, reading, and processing strategies you will use within each of the CTS Learning Cycle components.

10. Design your PowerPoint slides and any additional handouts. See those used for Modules B1 through B5 as examples to guide you.

11. If possible, try out your CTS design with a small group of colleagues. Gather feedback and make any needed modifications. Good luck designing and implementing your first CTS full topic study session design!

COMBINING SCIENCE AND MATHEMATICS TOPICS

Each of the sample modules B1 through B5 as well as the "Design Your Own Topic Study" illustrates how a full CTS topic study can be designed using one topic. Another option to consider is to combine two topic studies when doing a full CTS with science and mathematics teachers. This can be accomplished by splitting a group into two with one half doing one topic from the mathematics parent book and the other half doing a related topic from the science parent book (Keeley, 2005). During the Synthesis stage of the CTS Learning Cycle, facilitators encourage participants to make connections across both topics and discuss similarities and differences in teaching and learning the topic in science and mathematics. Some examples of combined science and mathematics topics are illustrated in Table 5.4.

CAUTIONS AND NEXT STEPS

This chapter presented various ways to design and facilitate a full topic study. These topic studies are best used after participants have had an introductory CTS session. (See Chapter 4 of this book for the introductory modules.) Facilitators are encouraged to include components from the modules in Chapter 4 if your group is unfamiliar with

| **Table 5.4** | Combined Mathematics and Science Topics |

Mathematics CTS Topic	Science CTS Topic
Line Graphs, Bar Graphs, and Histograms, or Graphic Representation	Graphs and Graphing
Summarizing Data	Data Collection and Analysis, or Summarizing and Representing Data
Scatterplots and Correlation	Correlation
Sampling	Scientific Sampling
Technology	Use of Computers and Communication Technologies
Reasoning	Scientific and Logical Reasoning
Communication in Mathematics	Communication in Science
Modeling	Mathematical Modeling
Problem Solving	Mathematics in Science and Technology
Proportionality	Scale
Constancy and Change	Constancy, Equilibrium, and Change
Measurement Systems or Measurement Tools	Observation, Measurement, and Tools

CTS. Look through the introductory slides and handouts in Modules A1 and A2 and incorporate some of these materials if you are doing a full topic study with CTS first-timers.

The next chapter provides examples of ways facilitators can extend a full topic study to include a variety of content, curriculum, instruction, and assessment applications.

6

Using CTS in a Content, Curricular, Instructional, or Assessment Context

INTRODUCTION TO CTS CONTEXT APPLICATIONS

Chapters 4 and 5 of this *Leader's Guide* described how to introduce mathematics educators to the curriculum topic study (CTS) tools and processes and described different approaches to designing and facilitating full topic studies. This chapter will address various ways leaders can help participants apply the knowledge gained from doing a CTS in the contextual applications of content, curriculum, instruction, and assessment. The application you select will depend on the purpose of your professional development session or program, the needs of your participants, and their familiarity with CTS. The applications in this chapter closely align with the descriptions on pages 53–91 of Chapter 4, "Utilizing Curriculum Topic Study for Different Contexts," in *Mathematics Curriculum Topic Study: Bridging the Gap Between Standards and Practice* (Keeley & Rose, 2006), the CTS parent book. To utilize the suggestions, tools, and designs in this chapter, it is recommended that you have the CTS parent book on hand, as several references will be made to it throughout this chapter. An outline of the context applications included in this chapter is provided in the box on page 140.

CONTEXT APPLICATIONS OUTLINE

A. CTS and mathematics content knowledge

    1. Adult content knowledge

    2. K–12 content knowledge

B. CTS and mathematics curriculum

    1. Curriculum coherence and articulation

    2. Curriculum selection

    3. Curriculum implementation

C. CTS and mathematics instruction

    1. Identifying appropriate strategies, representations, and contexts

    2. Reviewing and modifying lessons

    3. Instructional design

    4. Strengthening mathematical inquiry and problem solving

D. CTS and mathematics assessment

    1. Formative assessment probes

    2. Performance assessment

Within each of the four applications are specific tools and strategies leaders can use to either embed the context application into a full topic study or use the context application as the focus of a professional development session for participants who are already familiar with using CTS. For example, participants might engage in a full topic study on fractions using the session design provided in Chapter 5, Module B2, pages 112–117 of this *Leader's Guide*. The facilitator might choose to extend this module into a full-day session by having participants use the suggestions for "Reviewing and Modifying Instruction" described on page 76 in the CTS parent book and pages 175–176 of this *Leader's Guide*. Participants would then apply what they learned in the full Fractions topic study to improving an existing lesson on fractions.

Alternatively, the contextual application might be the focus of the professional development when working with participants who are familiar with the CTS tools and processes. For example, a facilitator might design a professional development session on how to develop formative assessment probes. Using the overview on pages 81–82 in the CTS parent book and the design provided on pages 181–185 in this chapter, participants are introduced to the CTS formative assessment probe design process. They then choose their own topics, conduct their own topic study, and apply their results to the development of an assessment probe that can be used in their own classrooms.

This chapter differs from Chapters 4 and 5 in that, with the exception of the Designing Formative Assessment Probes Module, it does not provide full session scripts accompanied by PowerPoint presentations and handouts. Instead it provides suggestions for ways to improve or enhance content knowledge, curriculum, instruction, and assessment by using CTS with a variety of strategies and tools provided in this chapter and in the Chapter 6 folder of the CD-ROM at the back of this book. The applications in this chapter can be used in the different stages of the CTS Learning Cycle when designing full topic studies. It is up to the discretion of facilitators to decide how best to use the suggestions and tools in this chapter based on the design of their professional development program, purpose of their work, experience of their participants, and adult and student learning needs.

Applications and the CTS Website

As you examine the material in this chapter and think about ways to use the resources that accompany Chapter 4 of the CTS parent book in your work, remember to check the CTS website at www.curriculumtopicstudy.org. As new tools and designs are developed to use with the CTS applications, by CTS leaders as well as CTS project staff, these will be shared on the CTS website.

CTS AND MATHEMATICS CONTENT KNOWLEDGE

Introduction to CTS Content Knowledge

As discussed in Chapter 3, one major goal of professional development is to continuously build understanding of mathematics content in order to support quality teaching and student learning. Teachers of mathematics strive to improve their content knowledge throughout their careers. CTS is particularly helpful to elementary teachers or other generalists who teach multiple subjects and have not had coursework in all the areas of mathematics they teach. Although many high school teachers specialize in a particular area of mathematics such as geometry, algebra, or calculus, they are sometimes faced with teaching a new course that includes topics outside of their specialty (for example, statistics or discrete mathematics). Some schools are using mathematics curricula that integrate across mathematics topics, such as Interactive Mathematics Program™ (IMP), that require teachers to learn new and nontraditional mathematics topics. Science teachers can also benefit from using mathematics CTS to improve their content knowledge since mathematics is a key component of inquiry and is an integral part of programs that take a cross-disciplinary science, technology, engineering, and mathematics (STEM) approach to teaching and learning.

When we refer to developing and enhancing teachers' content knowledge with CTS, we include the subject matter knowledge all teachers should have as a foundation to be considered mathematically literate. Adult mathematics literacy also includes the knowledge all students are expected to have at the end of their K–12 education. It also includes the mathematics knowledge that may exceed what some K–12 teachers teach. Teachers who are mathematically literate understand mathematics as a unique discipline used to solve quantitative, statistical, and spatial problems within a large range of everyday situations. A teacher who possesses a strong content background has a solid understanding of the curricular content he or she teaches as well as the curricular content that comes before and after a teacher's assigned grade level. It is important that teachers know what comes before their grade level so that they can effectively build on earlier key ideas. It is also important to know the next level of content in order to build the foundation students will need at the next grade level as well as to address the content learning needs of students who are ready to advance to higher levels of learning.

When a teacher has a strong knowledge and experiential background in mathematics content, he or she is able to be more versatile in quickly and effectively responding to students' ideas and learning needs. A teacher with strong content knowledge knows the next best question to ask to push student thinking and can guide learning down the most appropriate path. CTS can help strengthen teachers' content knowledge both directly and indirectly.

How Suggestions for Enhancing Content Knowledge Through CTS Are Organized

This section will provide suggestions, tools, and strategies for enhancing teachers' content knowledge using CTS. All of the resources and handouts for this section can be found on the CD-ROM at the back of this book by going to the Chapter 6 folder and opening the subfolder labeled Content Knowledge. An outline of the suggestions included in this chapter for using CTS to improve content knowledge is provided in the box on this page. Table 6.1 provides a description of the features of these suggestions and the examples provided in the text and on the CD-ROM that facilitators can use to plan inclusion of these suggestions in their CTS professional development.

OUTLINE OF SUGGESTIONS FOR ENHANCING MATHEMATICS CONTENT KNOWLEDGE

A. Adult mathematics content knowledge

  1. Ways of accessing content on demand

  2. Identifying and recording content for adult mathematical literacy

  3. Concept card mapping

  4. KWL

  5. Content vignettes

B. Knowledge of K–12 mathematics content

  1. Inventory of standards content statements

  2. Unpacking concepts and mathematical processes

  3. Ideas before terminology

  4. Examining the hierarchal structure of content knowledge in a topic

---

Table 6.1   Features of Tools and Strategies Used for Enhancing Content Knowledge

Strategy or Suggestion	Grade Levels	CTS Topic(s) Examples	CD-ROM Handouts	When to Use This Strategy or Suggestion
Ways of Accessing Content on Demand	K–12 and adult content	Not topic specific	6.1	To introduce CTS as a new strategy that can enhance adult and K–12 content knowledge on demand.
Identifying and Recording Content for Adult Literacy	Adult Content	Symbolic Relationships	6.2	Use once participants are familiar with using Sections IA and IB in the CTS guides.

Strategy or Suggestion	Grade Levels	CTS Topic(s) Examples	CD-ROM Handouts	When to Use This Strategy or Suggestion
Concept Card Mapping	Adult Content	Linear Measurement	6.3	Use with teachers who are already familiar with concept mapping.
KWL	Adult Content	Perimeter, Area, and Volume	6.4	Use once participants are familiar with using Sections IA and IB in the CTS guides.
Content Vignettes	Adult Content	Surface Area and Volume	Page 95 in parent book	Use to illustrate how a teacher might use CTS Sections IA and IB.
Inventory of Standards Content Statements	K–12, Grade 5 example	Symbolic Representation	6.5	Use with Sections II and III for teachers who are teaching unfamiliar content.
Unpacking Concepts and Scientific Processes	K–12; elementary, middle, and high school examples	Counting, Fractions, Graphic Representation, Algebraic Modeling	6.6	Use to deepen teachers' content understanding of the standards and the specific ideas and skills they target.
Ideas Before Terminology	K–12; K–2, 3–5, 6–8, 9–12 examples	Rates of Change, Scatterplots and Correlation, Place Value, Reasoning	none	Use to reveal conceptual understanding before introducing terminology. Especially useful at the K–5 level.
Hierarchal Structure of Content Knowledge	K–12; K–2, 3–5, 6–8, 9–12 examples	Counting, Fraction, Linear Relationships, Volume	6.7 6.8 6.9 6.10 6.11	Use when teachers have had considerable experience with CTS and have a fairly strong mathematics content background.

How CTS Reveals Gaps in Content Knowledge

There is a saying, "If you don't know what you don't know, you won't know to look for it." This condition of being "intellectually unconscious" is not unusual. Take the teacher who has been teaching the same mathematics unit for many years. She may feel competent and comfortable with what she is doing, yet not know that there is content she could learn that could improve her teaching. Sometimes teachers study a topic using CTS and gain indirect learning with respect to the content. They realize what they do not know about the topic and use CTS as an opportunity to identify important content goals for future professional development and learning. This may lead them to sign up for a workshop, summer institute, or university course to fill that identified gap.

CTS is not a replacement for formal mathematics coursework. However, the CTS process does build and enhance the subject matter knowledge deemed necessary to be considered a mathematically literate person. Chapter 4 in the CTS parent book contains a section on "CTS and Mathematics Content Knowledge" on pages 55–60. Facilitators of CTS are encouraged to read and become familiar with this section.

Content Knowledge and Mathematical Literacy

A mathematically literate person is one who has a basic understanding of the mathematics needed to be a productive and informed participant in today's society. A mathematically literate person is not necessarily one who has majored in mathematics in college or works in a mathematics-related career. Mathematical literacy applies to all adults, regardless of their postsecondary education or career choice. It applies to teachers of mathematics who have majored in mathematics as well as generalists, such as elementary teachers, who teach all subject areas, including mathematics. It is important when using CTS with teachers to reinforce what we mean by "mathematically literate" and emphasize that this also refers to the mathematics that all K–12 teachers are expected to know, regardless of what grade level they teach. According to the Organization for Economic Cooperation and Development (2003, pp. 24–25), a mathematically literate person is one who

- understands the role mathematics plays in natural, social and cultural settings;
- has knowledge of mathematical terminology, facts, and procedures as well as skill in performing certain operations and carrying out certain methods; and
- can formulate, solve, and interpret mathematical problems in a variety of situations.

Although CTS Sections I, III, V, and VI specifically target concepts, specific ideas, and skills, a careful study of all sections of a CTS study guide can contribute to teachers' subject matter knowledge—both the content they should know to be considered a mathematically literate adult and an understanding of the content that makes up K–12 learning goals. Figure 4.2 in the CTS parent book (Keeley & Rose, 2006) shows the connections between the sections of a CTS guide and teachers' subject matter knowledge. In Table 6.2, this chart is expanded to show how leaders can use CTS to enhance teachers' content knowledge.

> Facilitators can also choose to include the *Common Core State Standards for Mathematics* and/or the National Council for Teachers of Mathematics (NCTM) *Focal Points* in CTS Section III.

Table 6.2 Using CTS to Enhance Teachers' Content Knowledge

CTS Section and Resources	Ways to Enhance Teachers' Content Knowledge
Section I—*Science for All Americans*	• Identify and discuss the big, culminating ideas. • Identify examples that illustrate and explain the key ideas. • Identify relevant terminology and clarify definitions. • Find examples of ways the content integrates across science, mathematics, and technology.
Section I—*Beyond Numeracy*	• Provide explanations, real examples, and analogies for some difficult mathematics concepts. • Identify concepts, principles, properties, theorems, or generalizations.

CTS Section and Resources	Ways to Enhance Teachers' Content Knowledge
Section II—*Benchmarks for Science Literacy* and *Principals and Standards for School Mathematics* essays	• Examine and discuss the *Benchmarks* and *PSSM* K–12 overview essays to get a sense of what the "big ideas" are and why they are important. • Note places in the essays that need further content clarification such as suggestions for learning experiences where a term or representation is unfamiliar.
Section III—*Benchmarks for Science Literacy* and *Principles and Standards for School Mathematics* concepts and ideas	• Unpack and clarify key ideas in the learning goal statements. • Discuss the "boundaries" of a learning goal—what content it includes and what it does not include (exceeds the learning goal). • Identify and clarify key terminology used in the learning goal statements.
Section IV—Research Chapter 15 from *Benchmarks for Science Literacy* and *Research Companion*	• Clarify learning goals and adult content (I and III) before teachers examine the research on learning. • Clarify any statements in the research that are not understood. • Check for similar commonly held ideas among the teachers.
Section V—*Atlas of Science Literacy*	• Note the titles of the conceptual strands and clarify what they mean. • Note key terminology in the key ideas. • Analyze how one idea leads to another and how content understanding builds over time. • Analyze connections between ideas in different topics.
Section VI—State Standards or District Curriculum	• Unpack and clarify key ideas in the learning goal statements. • Discuss the "boundaries" of a learning goal—what content it includes and what it does not include (exceeds the learning goal). • Identify and clarify key terminology used in the learning goal statements. • Ensure the performance verb does not mask the intent and understanding of the content goal.

After examining the section "CTS and Mathematics Content Knowledge" on pages 55–60 in the CTS parent book, the following strategies and suggestions can be used by facilitators in their CTS sessions or professional development sessions to improve teachers' content knowledge. First, we will describe suggestions and strategies for enhancing adult content knowledge. Then we will follow that with suggestions and strategies for improving knowledge of the content ideas and skills taught at different grade levels.

Suggestions and Strategies for Using CTS to Enhance Adult Mathematics Content Knowledge

Typically many teachers seeking to improve their content knowledge will take a university course or participate in a summer content immersion institute. These learning experiences are geared toward adult learners and provide significant, interesting content deemed important by mathematicians and mathematics specialists for understanding the mathematical world. It is important for teachers to realize that the mathematics they are learning in their course or institute is sometimes intended to enhance their own content knowledge, and may not be directly applicable to their classrooms. Often teachers want to find a way to bring their own mathematics learning experience to their students. Rather than finding a way of modifying how they teach (as a result of their experience), they may actually try to re-create the same content experience for their students. They sometimes fail to see that the mathematics immersion experience was designed for them as adult learners, and that they can translate their new understanding in the classroom in subtle ways (such as an improved understanding of the application of mathematics in real-world contexts). This section addresses how to use CTS to enhance one's own adult understanding of mathematics in order to be more knowledgeable about the content and process of mathematics.

As teachers participate in content immersion experiences such as workshops, institutes, and courses that address mathematics knowledge, structure, and application beyond what is expected of students at their grade level, CTS can help them translate what they are learning as adults, to what all adults are expected to know about mathematics after their K–12 education. Using CTS Section I during a content immersion for adult learners can help teachers better understand the content being presented to them by seeing how it builds on and connects to fundamental ideas for mathematical literacy that are the capstone of a K–12 education and endure throughout one's lifetime.

A strategy teachers frequently use to gain or refresh their own adult content knowledge before teaching a new topic is to turn to textbooks, teacher guides, or the Internet to get the information they need. Textbooks often superficially cover content with an emphasis on terminology or procedures. Furthermore, they do not provide the rich descriptions, examples, and analogies included in mathematics trade books that are written to make mathematics interesting and accessible to the adult public.

CTS provides a different alternative to developing and enhancing adult content knowledge. Using the readings identified on a CTS guide to study a topic can considerably increase teachers' subject matter knowledge of the topics they teach as well as enhance the basic knowledge teachers need to be considered mathematically literate adults. The following are some suggestions and strategies for building adult content learning into your CTS professional development designs. All handouts in this section can be accessed by going to the Chapter 6 folder on the CD-ROM at the back of this book and opening the subfolder labeled "Content Knowledge."

Eliciting Teachers' Current Ways of Improving Content Knowledge on Demand

The following activity helps teachers recognize CTS as a valuable alternative to the typical ways they might brush up on their content knowledge prior to teaching a new or unfamiliar topic. When introducing CTS to teachers as a systematic way to improve teacher content knowledge, consider beginning your session by finding out what teachers currently do to enhance their content knowledge in situations where they do not have the time to take a course or experience a professional development session or institute prior to teaching a unit. Post a chart in the room such as the example provided on Handout 6.1: Enhancing Content Knowledge. Give participants the following scenario:

> Imagine you are teaching a new topic next month. You have limited familiarity with the topic and it has been a while since you had any formal coursework in that

topic. You don't have time to take a course and professional development is not offered until the summer. Before you prepare your instructional unit, you wish to strengthen or refresh your own understanding of the content. Put a check mark on the chart to indicate the strategy you typically use the most to improve your own adult content knowledge before teaching a unit.

Give teachers colored dots or have them go up and place a check mark next to the strategy they use most often in this situation. Typically you will see no or few checks next to the CTS strategy of reading and analyzing *Science for All Americans,* mathematics trade books, or national standards documents. Explain to teachers that the CTS session they are about to experience will provide them with a new strategy that they can use to improve their content knowledge before teaching a topic or working with other teachers to support their content knowledge. This strategy also reinforces why it is important for mathematics teachers to have access to the professional resources used in CTS to support their content learning. Prior to CTS, many teachers never thought of using resources, such as the ones used in CTS, to support their own learning in mathematics. For example, most mathematics educators do not know that *Science for All Americans* includes information about "mathematics as part of the scientific endeavor as well as mathematics as a process, or way of thinking" (American Association for the Advancement of Science [AAAS], 1989, p. 15).

Identifying and Recording Adult Mathematics Literacy Content Information From a CTS

Figure 4.2 in the CTS parent book shows the content information teachers record from CTS Sections I–V that can enhance their adult mathematical literacy. Handout 6.2 is an expanded version of this chart, focusing on CTS Section I. Use this handout when teachers are specifically focused on improving their own content knowledge using the CTS Section I readings. It can be embedded within the exploration and concept development phase of a full topic study. It can be used with both IA and IB readings, or facilitators can modify the handout if using only one of the Section I resources, or they may choose to add a content reading from the CTS Supplementary Resources on the CTS website or other resources. Facilitators should build in time to debrief the readings and discuss the content recorded on the handout. Time for reflection should also be included—encourage participants to reflect on new knowledge gained from the readings and how it will enhance their teaching.

For example, a group of middle school teachers may be assigned to teach the topic of "linear relationships" in their district curriculum. Linear relationships are addressed in the teachers' district's curriculum. Having a minimal background in algebra related topics, the teachers engage in a CTS using the "Linear Relationships" CTS guide to uncover the knowledge expected of a mathematically literate adult. Using CTS Section I in the "Linear Relationships" CTS guide, the facilitator guides small groups in recording content statements from their reading of *Science for All Americans.* As the small groups share their findings from the exercise with the whole group, the facilitator lists several of the major content statements, encouraging clarifying discussion of each concept and the terminology as it is listed. The facilitator guides a discussion around the importance of this background knowledge for the teachers and how it can help them be better prepared for teaching the topic. The following are examples of statements a group might generate from CTS Section IA around the topic of linear relationships. Note that these are basic ideas for mathematical literacy that come directly from the readings and do not get into the more complex mathematics related to algebraic relationships that a mathematician or engineer would need to know in order to have specialized knowledge in their field.

- Using mathematics to express ideas or solve problems has three phases: (1) representing some things abstractly; (2) manipulating the abstractions by rules of logic to find new relationships; and (3) seeing whether the new relationships say something useful about the original things.
- Numbers and relationships among them can be presented in symbolic statements to model, investigate, and display real-world relationships.
- Graphs are especially useful in examining relationships between quantities.
- There are many possible kinds of relationships between one variable and another, including directly proportional (one quantity always keeps the same proportion to the other) and inversely proportional (as one quantity increases, the other decreases proportionally).

The above example shows how CTS can be used to help teachers identify, discuss, and seek understanding of the important ideas and terminology every adult should know about a mathematics topic, such as linear relationships. For example, the teachers now recognize that mathematics can be used to describe the relationship between two changing quantities. Although there are many kinds of relationships, those that are linear include a proportional relationship. Although not all of the ideas in the readings may be taught at the middle school level, the background will help the teachers anticipate connections and respond to unanticipated questions that may arise during the teaching and learning process.

CONCEPT CARD MAPPING

Concept card maps are used to show how learners recognize relationships between concepts and ideas described in all or part of a CTS Section I reading. The strategy is used most effectively with teachers who are already familiar with concept mapping and want to improve their own adult knowledge of the topic. A concept card mapping activity used with CTS Section I takes approximately forty to sixty minutes, depending on whether you map all or part of the topic. To prepare for concept card mapping, the facilitator reviews the CTS Section I reading, selects key concepts from the reading that go with the topic or subtopic, and places them on cards. Each card contains a single concept. The number of cards varies according to the CTS topic or subtopic selected. Always be sure to provide some blank cards for teachers to write in additional concepts that may arise during their mapping. Handout 6.3 in the Chapter 6 folder on the CD-ROM is an example of using concept cards for conceptually mapping "Linear Measurement." The concepts were selected by the facilitator from the CTS Section IA *Science for All Americans* and CTS Section IVB *Research Companion* reading on the part of "Understanding Measure."

> Note: Although CTS Section I readings focus on the content adults are expected to know, facilitators should scan other CTS sections, especially Section IVB, for readings that contribute to understanding the content.

Facilitators can make up their own cards for the topics or subtopics they use in their professional development. The following directions describe how the facilitator uses the concept mapping cards with CTS:

Materials

- Packet of concept cards (no more than 15 cards)
- Blank sheet of paper or chart paper
- Glue stick

Directions

1. Distribute a packet of cards to groups of two to three teachers.

2. Give the teachers five minutes to sort through the cards, placing related cards in groups. Encourage participants to discuss and clarify the terminology on each card.

3. Lay the groups of cards out on a sheet of paper. Encourage teachers to arrange them according to any relationships between cards that make sense to them. They may add additional concepts to the blank cards to form relationships. They should discuss the relationships in their small groups and leave space between the cards to draw in connecting lines that describe the relationship.

4. When the group agrees on the arrangement of the cards and their relationships, have them glue them to their paper or chart.

5. Draw in connecting arrowhead lines between related concepts and insert an accompanying phrase that describes the relationship between the two concepts. For example:

Units ————————————→ **Iteration**
can be translated using

6. After completing their concept maps, have the participants read the section from which the mapping cards were taken in the CTS Section I reading.

7. Have groups revisit their maps and discuss the relationships based on their reading. Groups discuss any changes they might make after reading CTS Section I (or additional sections that enhance content understanding as assigned by the facilitator).

8. Debrief the maps with the whole group, asking for examples of key relationships they discovered through their reading. Provide additional content clarification as needed.

9. If time permits, groups can make a new map or write in new connections using a different color ink, based on new knowledge they gained from the CTS reading.

This strategy can also be done using sticky notes and chart paper, or the cards can be laid out on a table with strips of paper for writing relationships between the cards. After the CTS reading and discussion, participants can rearrange their sticky notes or table cards as needed or make new connecting statements. Figures 6.1 and 6.2 show a "before and after" example of concept card mapping of *Linear Measurement* using CTS Section IA and IVB from the "Length" CTS guide (p. 171 of the CTS parent book).

Another way to do concept mapping with a broad topic is to divide it into several subtopics and create concept cards for each of the subtopics. Small groups can be assigned a subtopic. After the mapping is completed, all groups share their maps and discuss the concepts as a whole topic. For example, the topic *Patterns, Relations, and Functions* can be broken down into four subtopics: Numeric Patterns, Linear Relationships, Nonlinear Relations, and Functions. Groups can be assigned one of the four subtopics.

KWL

KWL is a strategy used to list what participants think they already know (K) about the basic ideas all adults should know about a CTS topic, what additional content knowledge they want to gain (W), and what new content they learned after doing the CTS (L). Template 6.4 for using KWL with CTS is provided in the Chapter 6 folder on the CD-ROM. Facilitators should ask participants to fill out the first two columns before they begin the Section I (and other related sections) CTS readings. The last column is filled in

| **Figure 6.1** | Concept Map Before CTS |

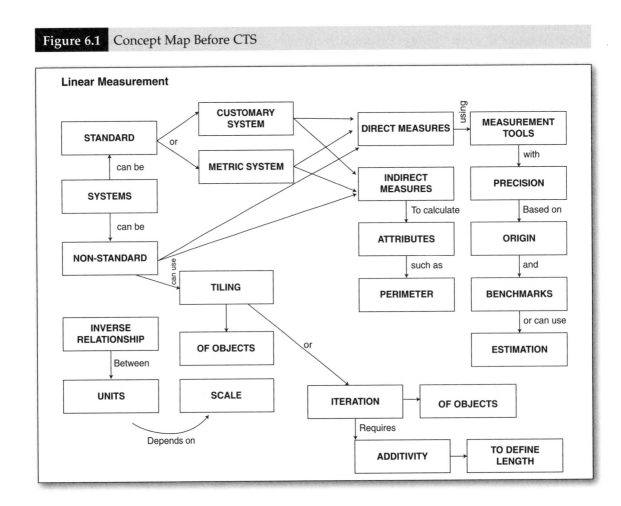

Figure 6.2 Concept Map After CTS

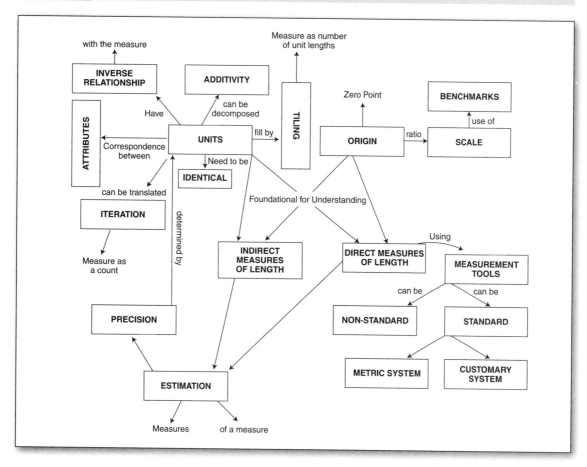

after completing and discussing the CTS readings. Facilitators might point out Figure 4.4 in the CTS parent book, which shows an example of how a teacher using the CTS guide on "Perimeter, Area, and Volume" might use KWL with CTS to enhance her content knowledge.

CONTENT VIGNETTES

The CTS parent book contains several images from practice that are useful for introducing teachers to the various ways CTS can be used in their practice. On page 95, "Vignette #5: A Middle-School Teacher Uses CTS to Understand Concepts of Surface Area and Volume" shows how a teacher used CTS to improve her own content knowledge. When introducing CTS as a way to improve upon or enhance one's content knowledge, consider using this vignette as a "mini-case" with the following questions:

- What is the teacher's content problem? Why did she decide to use CTS?
- What new content understanding did she gain from reading Section IA, *Science for All Americans*?
- How did she connect what she read in Sections II and III to Section IA?
- Summarize how CTS helped this teacher improve her content knowledge in preparation for teaching the topics of surface area and volume.

IMPROVING GRADE LEVEL (K–12) CONTENT KNOWLEDGE

Although teachers gain new understandings and an appreciation of mathematics content through university courses and other content immersion experiences, a drawback of these experiences is that they often fail to make a connection to what teachers teach, particularly at the elementary and middle level. Mathematicians deeply know their content and are able to excite and involve teachers in learning about and doing mathematics. What they often do not have is the specialized knowledge educators have about how to make the content accessible to K–12 students. In other words, they lack the pedagogical content knowledge of "school mathematics" needed to help teachers translate their knowledge and experience into knowledge and activities that are developmentally appropriate, standards-based, and effective in promoting learning with students at their grade level.

For example, a seventh-grade teacher might participate in a weeklong institute on engineering and learn a lot about the design process in the context of STEM, yet not know how to take what she learned and incorporate it into her seventh-grade curriculum in a way that students will see how mathematics is used in real-life applications and careers. Knowing how engineers use mathematics and learning about it in an adult context is very different from what one would teach seventh graders. However, incorporating the "Geometric Relationships" and "Geometric Modeling" topic studies into the teachers' learning experience can help her plan backwards to identify the prerequisite content that is related, but appropriate to teach at a seventh-grade level in the context of engineering.

In addition to the mathematics every adult is expected to know in order to be considered a mathematically literate person, as described in CTS Section I, Identify Adult Content Knowledge, sometimes there are content statements in the K–12 mathematics content standards and grade-level essays that may be unfamiliar to teachers who lack a strong mathematics background or who are strong in one mathematics domain but not another. Statements in the standards can be used to "unpack" content and identify the key ideas, skills, and terminology appropriate to use at different grade levels. It is important to take the time to clarify the content knowledge needed to understand and effectively teach the K–12 learning goals articulated in the standards. The following are suggestions and strategies used to improve teachers' knowledge of the content of the standards taught at their grade level. Handouts that accompany these suggestions and strategies can be found in the Chapter 6 CD-ROM folder in the subfolder labeled "Content Knowledge" on the CD-ROM.

INVENTORY OF STANDARDS CONTENT STATEMENTS

This is a strategy that can be used with CTS Sections II and III to improve teachers' content knowledge and clarify mathematical ideas and skills at the grade levels they teach. This strategy is used to identify important content and related content ideas taught at the specific grade level of the teachers' students. Table 6.3 shows an example of this strategy. The standards statements from the CTS Section III learning goals related to the topic are recorded in the left column as well as statements from the CTS Section II essays. These essays often contain content statements embedded within the description of instructional considerations. For example, the third statement on Table 6.3 comes from the *PSSM*

Grade 3–5 "Represent and analyze mathematical situations and structures using algebraic symbols" essay suggestion: "As students become more experienced in investigating, articulating, and justifying generalizations, they can begin to use variable notation and equations to represent their thinking" (NCTM, 2000, p. 161). Although the essay is describing an instructional implication, it also states three mathematical processes that demonstrate the use of variables and equations as a tool to represent thinking.

After participants have listed the content statements in the left column, they are asked to generate questions in the right column related to the content statements. These questions then are discussed in small groups and with the facilitator or content expert in the session. Discussion and clarification of the teacher raised questions enhances their knowledge of the content they will be teaching and prepares them for questions that might arise later during CTS as well as during classroom instruction and investigation. A template for using this strategy is provided on Handout 6.5 in the Chapter 6 folder on the CD-ROM at the back of this book.

Table 6.3 Example of an Inventory of Standards Content Statements and Questions— Symbolic Representation (Grade 5)

CTS Standards Content Statements	Questions
Students should represent the idea of a variable as an unknown quantity using a letter or a symbol (Section III—*PSSM*, p. 158).	Should the quantities be within a context? How can this be modeled so students understand the variable is representing the quantity and not the objects?
Students should express mathematical relationships using equations (Section III—*PSSM*, p. 158).	What operations should be used to form the equation? Are these only numeric equations or should one or more variables be used to express the relationship? What other ways can students represent relationships?
As students become more experienced in investigating, articulating, and justifying generalizations, they can begin to use variable notation and equations to represent their thinking (Section II—*PSSM*, p. 161).	What types of investigations and what type of generalizations are most useful in demonstrating the use of variables as a communication tool?
Mathematical statements using symbols may be true only when the symbols are replaced by certain numbers (Section III—AAAS, 1993, p. 218).	Should the statements be within a context? How can this be modeled so students understand what values make the statement true and what values make the statement false?
Tables and graphs can show how values of one quantity are related to values of another (Section III—AAAS, 1993, p. 218). In any case, graphs and tables, rather than equations, should be used to explore relationships between two variables (Section II—AAAS, 1993, p. 217).	What type of graphs? If not connected to an equation, what other ways can the relationships be described?

UNPACKING CONCEPTS AND MATHEMATICAL PROCESSES

Concepts or processes listed by themselves do not describe the key ideas or skills one must know to understand the concept and use the mathematical process. For example, proportionality is a concept that helps us understand a particular relationship between two quantities, but what is the relationship and what types of problems does understanding this relationship help us solve? Justification and proof are essential features of mathematical inquiry, but what does it mean to provide a justification or proof in mathematics? What exactly do students need to know about sampling? What do students need to know first before using a word like *correlation*? CTS can be used to answer these K–12 content questions through unpacking a concept or skill in the standards by

- Identifying the CTS topic guide that includes the core concepts and mathematical processes;
- Carefully examining the bulleted learning goals in CTS Sections III and V and identifying the concept or mathematical process to which they are related; and
- Breaking down the learning goals into key idea or skill statements related to the concepts and mathematical processes.

Table 6.4 shows examples of concepts, processes, key ideas, and skills at different grade levels that have been "unpacked" using CTS Sections III or V. This strategy can be used for single concepts or processes within a CTS topic or used with all of the concepts or processes that make up an entire CTS topic. Use this strategy after participants have completed and discussed the readings from CTS Sections III and/or V. Handout 6.6: Estimation, on the CD-ROM, shows an example of unpacking content in the learning goals by identifying the key ideas and skills in each concept or process. This handout provides facilitators with an example of unpacking an entire K–12 topic related to estimation.

Table 6.4 Examples of Unpacking Grade-Level Concepts, Key Ideas, and Skills

Concept or Process	Grade Level	CTS Guide and Key Ideas and Skills for Science Literacy (From CTS Section III or V)
Counting	K–2	• Numbers can be used to count things, place them in order, measure them, or name them. • A quantity is stated as a number and a label, such as 4 inches or 7 blocks. • Count with understanding and recognize "how many" in sets of objects. • Develop understanding of the relative position and magnitude of whole numbers and of ordinal and cardinal numbers and their connections. • Connect number words and numerals to the quantities they represent, using various physical models and representations.

Concept or Process	Grade Level	CTS Guide and Key Ideas and Skills for Science Literacy (From CTS Section III or V)
Fractions	3–5	• Sometimes in sharing or measuring there is a need to use numbers *between* whole numbers. • Use fractions and decimals, translating when necessary between commonly encountered fractions (halves, fourths, fifths, tenths, and hundredths) and their decimal equivalents. • Develop understanding of fractions as parts of unit wholes, as parts of a collection, as locations on number lines, and as divisions of whole numbers. • Use models, benchmarks, and equivalent forms to judge the size of fractions. • Recognize and generate equivalent forms of commonly used fractions, decimals, and percentages.
Graphic Representation	6–8	• The graphic display of numbers may help to show patterns such as trends, varying rates of change, gaps, or clusters that are useful when making predictions about the phenomena being graphed. • The scale chosen for a graph or drawing makes a big difference in how useful it is. • Model and solve contextualized problems using various representations, such as graphs, tables, and equations. • Use graphs to analyze the nature of changes in quantities in linear relationships. • Discuss and understand the correspondence between data sets and their graphical representations, especially histograms, stem-and-leaf plots, box plots, and scatterplots.
Algebraic Modeling	9–12	• Any mathematical model, graphic or algebraic, is limited in how well it can represent how the world works. The usefulness of a mathematical model for predicting may be limited by uncertainties in measurements, by neglect of some important influences, or by requiring too much computation. • Identify essential quantitative relationships in a situation and determine the class or classes of functions that might model the relationships. • Use symbolic expressions, including iterative and recursive forms, to represent relationships arising from various contexts. • Draw reasonable conclusions about a situation being modeled.

Ideas Before Terminology

Examining content statements in CTS Section III, particularly at the elementary level, can often reveal how conceptual understanding is developed before terminology is introduced. Developing ideas first provides an opportunity for students to construct a conceptual understanding and then be able to associate this understanding with the appropriate terminology. Often when words are introduced first, the emphasis is on memorizing definitions at the expense of conceptual understanding. The writers of the *Benchmarks for Science Literacy* (AAAS, 1993) were very intentional about word choice, often describing an idea conceptually before using the technical terminology. Encourage participants to look for examples in CTS Section IIIA where an idea in a learning goal is described before the mathematical term is given.

Table 6.5 shows examples of learning goals that describe conceptual understanding before introducing the mathematical terminology. When using Sections III, V, and VI, encourage teachers to look carefully at the learning goals for evidence of emphasis on developing the idea before including the terminology. As teachers discuss the conceptual ideas articulated in the content of the learning goal statement, ask them to identify the terminology that could be introduced after students have developed a conceptual understanding of the idea. Section IIIB goals often use specific terminology and can be used to compare the conceptual ideas in Section IIIA. Facilitators can also encourage participants to look at the Section III learning goals beyond their grade level to identify when it is appropriate to introduce technical terminology.

Table 6.5 Ideas Before Terminology

Terminology (Introduced After Developing the Concept)	Grade Level	Conceptual Idea (From Section IIIA Learning Goals)
Functions	6–8	Mathematical statements can be used to describe how one quantity changes when another changes.
Exponents	9–12	Express and compare very small and very large numbers using powers-of-10 notation.
Probability	3–5	Events can be described in terms of being more or less likely, impossible, or certain.
Fractions	K–2	Sometimes in sharing or measuring there is a need to use numbers *between* whole numbers.

Using CTS to Examine the Hierarchal Structure of Content Knowledge in a Topic

Leaders of CTS can use this option to help teachers think about the different levels of content knowledge in a topic ranging from discrete facts to big ideas to broad content and process standards. When teachers are engaged in examining and building a hierarchy of content knowledge, they often come to the important realization that the content emphasized in their curriculum or textbooks is often at the lower level of a content hierarchy (e.g., facts, terminology, and formulas) and fails to conceptually develop important big ideas and generalizations. The intellectual act of constructing a hierarchy helps teachers examine whether the instructional focus of their curricular topic is on lower level factual knowledge, what the key ideas and underlying concepts are in a learning goal, how they can build from the concepts and key ideas to construct understandings of "bigger ideas," and how to integrate ideas using unifying principles that cut across the disciplinary content areas of mathematics. The hierarchy is one of the more challenging applications of CTS. This application is most successful when teachers have had experience using CTS and understand the difference between facts, key ideas, concepts, "big ideas," and broad content and process standards.

For groups the facilitator feels are ready to try constructing a hierarchy of knowledge, this strategy proves to be one of the most intellectually challenging and invigorating applications of K–12 content knowledge. The end result is that it increases teachers' ability to modify curriculum and design instruction that promotes higher level use of knowledge and the development of big ideas, generalizations, and connections across areas of mathematics. However, facilitators need to be aware that this strategy is not an easy one to use if teachers do not have a strong understanding of the content they teach.

Pages 57–60 of the CTS parent book describe the structure of knowledge in a topic. It is important for leaders to read and become familiar with this section before using this application in a CTS session. Handout 6.7 is a revised graphic of the one shown on page 59 of the CTS parent book for facilitators to use when working with groups using this application. Embedding the "Hierarchal Structure of Content Knowledge" in a CTS session helps participants recognize the range of knowledge that a curricular topic can address, from the low level facts and "factlets" that often end up being memorized and later forgotten, to the really big ideas that cross-cut the content and process strands such as the ideas of proportionality and modeling. These bigger ideas are often overlooked when unpacking standards and teaching specific ideas.

Before using this application with a CTS topic, make sure the operational definitions of the terms used on Handout 6.7 have been discussed and clarified with the group. For example, there are many different definitions of what a concept is. For our purposes, we agree to define a concept as a one-word (or made up of few words) mental construct that represents a broad or specific idea. Note that the hierarchy example in the CTS parent book takes a topic and breaks it down using the elements described in the hierarchy. Breaking down a curricular topic can be quite demanding and cumbersome if participants do not have experience using a hierarchy of knowledge. A simpler way to start is with a concept that is part of a topic, rather than with a full topic. Once participants grasp the process using a single concept, they can then go on to construct a hierarchy of a full topic that includes several related concepts. The strategy described here will address the hierarchy at the concept level within a topic, rather than at the topic level as shown in the CTS parent book.

After participants complete a topic study and discuss the CTS findings for the topic, describe to participants that they will now use their CTS content ideas from Sections I, III, V, and VI to take a single concept in the topic and break it down into subconcepts (for some concepts that tend to be quite specific, you can skip the subconcept level), specific ideas, and facts, terminology, and formulas. This deconstruction process is a way of unpacking a concept. However, explain how the opposite direction is also important and is often the direction that is neglected when working with concepts. To go up, explain how they will construct a hierarchy of bigger ideas that builds on a concept. When they are done, they will see the structure of knowledge unfold from the top level of "really big ideas" to the lower level of factual, discrete information.

Refer participants to Handout 6.8 on the CD-ROM, which scaffolds the process of building a hierarchy starting with a concept (rather than a topic as described in the CTS parent book). Walk them through an example using one of examples on Handout 6.9, which shows four different grade-level examples of a concept hierarchy. Build in time to discuss each of the steps of the scaffold and examine how they link to the example(s) provided.

When participants have grasped the notion of a hierarchy, understand what the different levels are, and have had an opportunity to examine an example, they are ready to work in small groups to try out the scaffold with the CTS they completed. As a group, you might start by brainstorming a list of major concepts that were addressed in Section III of their CTS and then have groups select a concept to build a hierarchy around. Provide a copy of Handout 6.10 on the CD-ROM to guide their discussions in small groups as they work on their hierarchy. Handout 6.11 provides a template for creating a hierarchy chart. It is important to emphasize that while there is no one "right way" of doing this, it is the exercise in thinking about the structure of the knowledge that will inform how they teach the content that makes this a valuable learning experience. Provide time for participants to share their examples and reflect on the impact this application will have on their teaching. An extension of this activity is to write hierarchal essential questions to go with each of the levels identified.

CTS AND MATHEMATICS CURRICULUM

Another context application for which CTS is widely used is curriculum. Curriculum is broadly defined as the way content is designed and delivered. It includes the structure, organization, balance, and presentation of the content in the classroom (National Research Council [NRC], 1996). Leaders can use the CTS tools and process for a variety of curricular applications, including facilitating groups charged with designing a K–12 coherent scope and sequence, selection of curriculum materials that are standards and research based, and support for curriculum implementation.

This section provides suggestions, tools, and strategies for using CTS in a curricular context. All of the resources and handouts for this section can be found on the CD-ROM by going to the Chapter 6 folder and opening the subfolder labeled "CTS and Curriculum 6.12–6.21." The box on this page provides an outline of the suggestions included in this section for using CTS for curriculum-related work. Table 6.6 provides a description of the features of the tools, strategies, and examples provided in the text and CD-ROM used to help facilitators plan how to use CTS to support standards- and research-based curriculum.

OUTLINE OF SUGGESTIONS FOR CTS CURRICULAR APPLICATIONS

A. Curriculum Coherence and Articulation

   1. The Three Little Pigs metaphor

   2. Combining topics for broader study

   3. Choosing curricular priorities

   4. Creating clarification guides for curriculum topics

   5. Clarifying a state standard

   6. Developing Crosswalks to State Standards

B. Curriculum Selection

   1. CTS summary for curriculum materials review

   2. Summary review of curriculum materials

C. Curriculum Implementation

   1. Creating customized CTS guides for curriculum

   2. Developing CTS curricular learning paths

Table 6.6 Features of Tools and Strategies Used in a Curricular Context

Strategy or Suggestion	CTS Topic(s) Used as Examples	CD-ROM Handouts	Purpose of This Strategy or Suggestion
Three Little Pigs Metaphor	Not topic specific	6.12 6.13	To introduce CTS as a tool curriculum committees can use to develop a strong curriculum.
Combining Topics for Broader Study	All topics covered	none	To undertake a comprehensive study of all the content likely to be included in a K–12 science curriculum.
Choosing Curricular Priorities	Measure of Center (3–5)	6.14	To unburden the curriculum by deciding what to leave in and what can be left out.
Creating Clarification Guides for Curricular Topics	Fractions	6.15	To provide a summary of CTS findings teachers can use to clarify a topic included in their curriculum.
Clarifying a State Standard	Measurement Tools	6.16 6.17	To bring greater clarity to the meaning and intent of a state standard.
Developing Crosswalks to State Standards	Number and Operations, Geometry, Measurement	6.18a, 6.18b	To provide a tool states can use to link their standards to a CTS topic.
CTS Summary for Curriculum Materials Review	Addition and Subtraction of Whole Numbers	6.19	To provide a CTS template for determining what to look for in instructional materials.
Summary Review of Curriculum Materials	Addition and Subtraction of Whole Numbers	6.20	To provide a tool to examine instructional materials for the extent to which they reflect CTS findings.
Creating Customized Guides for Curriculum	Fractions; Customary Measurement	6.21	To create customized guides for a curriculum unit that is grade specific and combines parts of CTS topics.
Developing CTS Curricular Learning Paths	Geometric Shapes	none	Developing an at-a-glance road map to see the conceptual flow of a unit.

Curriculum Coherence and Articulation

"A coherent curriculum is one that holds together, that makes sense as a whole; and its parts, whatever they are, are unified and connected by that sense of the whole" (Beane, 1995, p. 3). This involves carefully thinking through the flow of ideas, how they interconnect, and how the process and content of mathematics are intertwined. Studying curricular topics and using the tools provided in this *Leader's Guide* can help curriculum committees make better decisions when grappling with the design and organization of a coherent K–12 mathematics curriculum.

CTS does not recommend a particular approach to designing and organizing a K–12 curriculum. There are a variety of ways to do this, and school districts often have their own formats for putting together the curriculum. The leader's work involves deciding how best to use CTS to inform the work of a curriculum committee. What CTS does provide is the information committees need to think through and make sound curriculum decisions. For groups interested in designs for organizing curriculum that utilize the *Benchmarks for Science Literacy* (AAAS, 1993) or another coherent set of learning goals, we recommend the book *Designs for Science Literacy* (AAAS, 2001), one of the science literacy tools developed by Project 2061 (recall that mathematics is included in science literacy). *Designs for Science Literacy* addresses the critical issues involved in assembling sound instructional materials into a coherent K–12 whole and proposes ways to choose and configure curriculum so it aligns with learning goals.

Suggestions for Using CTS to Develop and Articulate a Coherent K–12 Curriculum

Leaders who facilitate committees charged with developing or examining K–12 curriculum to align with standards should first become familiar with pages 60–75 in the CTS parent book. Figure 4.8 in the CTS parent book addresses five major considerations for curriculum when using CTS to study a topic. As committees make decisions about curriculum, use the questions in Figure 4.9 of the CTS parent book to guide or reflect on decisions. Other strategies and activities leaders can use when working with K–12 curriculum committees include the following:

Three Little Pigs Metaphor

Use the adaptation of the Three Little Pigs Story on Handout 6.12 on the CD-ROM to make a case for why curriculum committees would benefit from using the CTS tools to "build" a stronger curriculum. This activity is best used to engage curriculum committees in thinking about a different way to go about the process of developing, revising, or revisiting their K–12 scope and sequence curriculum. This process involves using CTS to ground the committee in the relevant content, appropriate ways to sequence learning goals, alignment of curriculum with standards, developmental appropriateness, and more (see Figure 4.8 on page 64 of the CTS parent book).

The Three Little Pigs metaphor clearly shows why tools, such as CTS, can strengthen the work teachers do in areas like curriculum. Ask for three volunteers to read the story aloud. Designate each volunteer to be one of the three pigs. As they read the story aloud, have the audience read silently along with them. When finished, distribute Handout 6.13 and have small groups or pairs respond to each of the questions (each person responds individually to the first question and places the sticky note on a chart that represents a histogram of Pigs 1, 2, and 3). After placing a sticky note on the wall graph, individuals meet in small groups to begin the discussion of the questions on the handout. Allow about thirty-five minutes for them to work through the task and then debrief ways they might think about using CTS to avoid the pitfalls of Pigs 1 and 2 and use some of the strategies of Pig 3 in the context of their own curriculum work.

Combining Topics for Broader Study

Dividing the 92 topic study guides up among a curriculum committee to study in order to inform their work is certainly not practical. Many committees look at the disciplinary content through the traditional organizers of Number and Operations, Algebra, Geometry, Measurement, Data Analysis, and Mathematical Processes; therefore, the listing below of 30 topic studies, taken together, should cover the entire K–12 mathematics curriculum. Curriculum committees can divide these up to study the K–12 content for a particular area of mathematics before assigning curriculum topics to grade levels. This study gives the curriculum committee a more connected view of the content within and across disciplinary boundaries. The following are suggestions for condensing the vast number of topics in the CTS parent book into a manageable number of topics that a curriculum committee can undertake over the span of their work. For example, when a committee is working on the geometry portion of their curriculum, they may choose to divide the seven topics listed under the Geometry category among their members and use the study results to inform their curricular decisions. This is more efficient than studying all 19 topics listed under the Geometry CTS category.

Number and Operation

- Comparing and Ordering Numbers
- Computation and Operations
- Fraction, Decimals, and Percent
- Number Sense
- Numbers and Number Systems
- Place Value

Algebra

- Algebraic Modeling
- Expressions and Equations
- Patterns, Relations, and Functions
- Symbolic Representation

Geometry

- Two-Dimensional Geometry
- Three-Dimensional Geometry
- Congruence and Similarity
- Coordinate Geometry
- Geometric Modeling
- Geometric Theorems
- Transformation and Symmetry

Measurement

- Measurement Systems
- Measurement Tools
- Perimeter, Area, and Volume
- Time, Temperature, Weight, and Capacity

Data Analysis

- Measures of Center and Spread
- Probability
- Summarizing Data
- Statistical Reasoning

Mathematical Processes

- Communication
- Modeling
- Problem Solving
- Reasoning
- Representations

Furthermore, leaders can develop customized CTS guides to study a broad area of curriculum at a particular grade level. For example, Table 6.7 shows how Grades K–2 and 3–5 topic readings from the Number and Operations topic studies were combined into one "Number and Operation" study guide. The curriculum committee used this guide to study a number and operation strand for their Grades K–5 scope and sequence. To prepare a combined guide, use the blank template for creating your own CTS found in the Chapter 5 folder, Templates for Developing Your Own CTS, on the CD-ROM. Make a list of all the readings from multiple topics for the grade level(s) that make up a particular strand that your committee wants to study. Combine repeated readings into one and list them on the template like the example shown in Table 6.7.

> Facilitators may choose to include readings from the *Common Core State Standards for Mathematics* or the NCTM *Focal Points* on the customized guide.

Table 6.7 Example of a Broad, Combined Topic for Elementary School Curriculum

Standards- and Research-Based Study of a K–5 Curricular Strand Number and Operation	
Section and Outcome	*Selected Sources and Readings for Study and Reflection—Read and Examine Related Parts of . . .*
I. Identify Adult Content Knowledge	*IA: Science for All Americans* • Chapter 9, *Numbers*, pp. 130–132 • Chapter 12, *Computation*, pp. 187–190; *Estimation*, pp. 190–191 *IB: Beyond Numeracy* • *Computation and Rote*, pp. 52–55
II. Consider Instructional Implications	*IIA: Benchmarks for Science Literacy* • 9A, *Numbers* general essay, p. 210; grade span essays, pp. 211–212 • 12B, *Computation and Estimation* general essay, pp. 288–289 *IIB: NCTM Principles and Standards for School Mathematics* • PreK–2 Number and Operations general essay, pp. 79–88; Connections, *What should connections look like*, p. 133; vignette, pp. 133–134 • 3–5 Number and Operations general essay, pp. 149–156

Section and Outcome	Selected Sources and Readings for Study and Reflection—Read and Examine Related Parts of . . .
III. Identify Concepts and Specific Ideas	**IIIA: Benchmarks for Science Literacy** • 9A, *Numbers*, pp. 211–212 • 12B, *Computation and Estimation*, p. 290 **IIIB: NCTM *Principles and Standards for School Mathematics*** • PreK–2 Number and Operations, p. 78/392 • 3–5 Number and Operations, p. 148/392
IV. Examine Research on Student Learning	**IVA: Benchmarks for Science Literacy** • 12 B, *Operations With Whole Numbers*, p. 358; *Operations With Fractions and Decimals*, pp. 358–359; *Calculators*, p. 359 **IVB: Research Companion** • Chapter 3, *A Framework for Mathematical Reasoning*, pp. 31–32 • Chapter 6, *Building Fluency*, p. 71; *Single Digit*, pp. 73–76 • Chapter 8, *Number Sense*, pp. 115–116 • Chapter 20, *Cardinality*, p. 290; *Ordinality*, p. 291 • Chapter 6, *Developing Mathematical Power in Whole Number Operations*, pp. 68–91 • Chapter 8, *Facts and Algorithms as Products of Students' Own Mathematical Activity*, pp. 114–121
V. Examine Coherency and Articulation	**V: Atlas of Science Literacy** • *Mathematical Processes*, p. 27 (Vol. 1) noting the conceptual strand "Computation and Operations" • *Numbers*, p. 65 (Vol. 2) • *Computation and Estimation*, p. 107 (Vol. 2)
VI. Clarify State Standards and District Curriculum	**VIA: State Standards**—Link Sections I–V to learning goals and information from your state standards or frameworks that are informed by the results of the topic study. **VIB: District Curriculum Guide**—Link Sections I–V to learning goals and information from your district curriculum guide that are informed by the results of the topic study.

Visit www.curriculumtopicstudy.org for updates or supplementary readings, websites, and videos.

Choosing Curricular Priorities

One of the difficulties curriculum committees often face when assembling a curriculum is deciding what is most important to leave in and what can be taken out. These decisions are often based on personal biases rather than a careful study of the concepts, key ideas, and skills that form a mathematical literacy core. The following quote from *Designs for Science Literacy* (AAAS, 2001) describes the dilemma educators face with an overstuffed, mile wide, inch deep curriculum:

Time in school for teaching and learning is not limitless. Yet many textbooks and course syllabi seem to assume otherwise. They include a great abundance of topics, many of which are treated in superficial detail and employ technical language that far exceeds most students' understanding. And even as new content is added to the curriculum, little is ever subtracted—students are being asked to learn with greater depth. Rarely is more time made available for accomplishing this. Coverage almost always wins out over student understanding, quantity takes precedence over quality. (AAAS, 2001, p. 211)

CTS provides a process that encourages justification of curricular decisions, based on standards and research, for reaching consensus on which concepts and ideas can be eliminated, which ones are essential to learning, and which ones could be included if mathematics learning goals are met and there is time for additional subject matter. The process also eliminates unnecessary redundancy and helps identify essential technical terminology in order to concentrate learning first on conceptual understanding and avoid the overemphasis on specialized vocabulary. Through a careful examination of CTS Sections III and V, in concert with examining local or state standards from Section VI, informed decisions can be made about which key ideas and skills are clearly emphasized in the standards and where the boundaries should be drawn in order to eliminate unnecessary instruction.

For example, the *Benchmarks* clearly show that by Grade 8 students should have a conceptual understanding of the possible relationships between two variables with an emphasis, as evidenced in the learning goals in both sets of national standards (CTS Sections IIIA and IIIB), to have middle school students learn about linear versus nonlinear relationships. Even though properties, classes, and symbolic representations of nonlinear relationships may be in the eighth-grade textbook, this can wait until high school, giving middle school teachers time to focus in more depth on the content that is most essential for students to understand at this grade level. An exception would be if a state decided, contrary to what is proposed in the national standards, to include ideas related to properties, classes, and symbolic representations of nonlinear relationships in their middle school learning goals. In this case, even though this idea is included at the middle school level, it is an indication to teachers that although they must teach this, they should probably place more emphasis, given the limited time teachers have for teaching, on the learning goals that are most central to the middle school curriculum.

The results from CTS Sections III, V, and VI form the center of the graphic shown in Figure 6.3 and used in Handout 6.14: Nested Priorities for Mathematics Curriculum. Curriculum committees can use this organizational chart to examine their current curriculum or curricular suggestions and make decisions about what to leave in or take out. The central content core is essential and focuses on a fewer number of key ideas. As one moves outward from the center of the diagram, the content becomes less essential, and if included, widens the curriculum. Keep in mind the wider a curriculum gets, the less opportunity students will have for in-depth learning. The four levels are described as follows:

Note: The *Common Core State Standards for Mathematics* were developed after CTS was published. These standards belong in the Essential Understandings Level 1 and can be used with CTS Section III as a third standards document or replace one of the others.

Level 1: Essential Understandings for Mathematical Literacy

These are the key ideas that come directly from the standards, including appropriate terminology. They are identified by using CTS Sections III, V, and VI. These are the important ideas that are central to the curriculum that all students are expected to learn at the grade level indicated.

Figure 6.3 Nested Priorities for Mathematics Curriculum

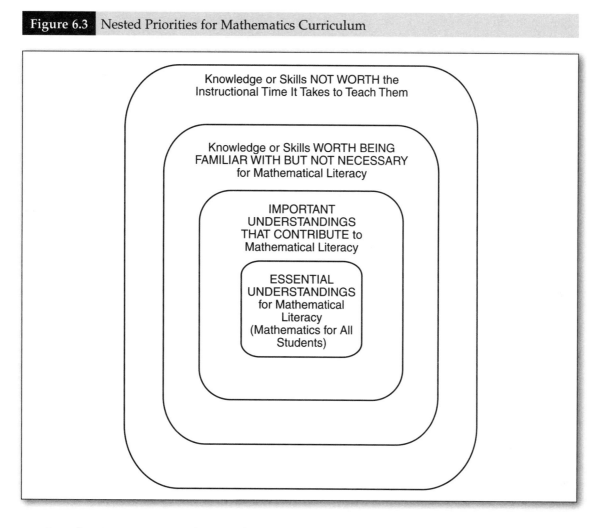

Level 2: Important Understandings That Contribute to Mathematics Literacy

These are ideas that can support learning the key ideas and are reasonable for students at the indicated grade level to learn without compromising the time needed to develop in-depth understanding.

Level 3: Knowledge or Skills Worth Being Familiar With but Not Necessary for Mathematical Literacy

These often include ideas that are included in curriculum materials and activities that may be interesting and possible for students to learn if they have first achieved the key ideas, and teaching these ideas does not replace the time needed to learn essential content. If they are eliminated from the curriculum, it does no harm. These may also be knowledge and skills that exceed mathematics literacy and are targeted for students who are ready to move beyond the standards for achieving mathematical literacy for all.

Level 4: Knowledge or Skills Not Worth the Instructional Time It Takes to Teach Them

These are ideas that exceed the readiness and ability of students at a specific grade level to comprehend, based on their prior knowledge and experience. They often include ideas that will be taught at a later grade span. It would take too much instructional time to be worth the effort to teach these ideas and may further confuse students. They should be eliminated from the curriculum for that grade span, but could be considered at a later grade.

Table 6.8 shows how a curriculum committee might use this graphic to make decisions about what to cover in the curriculum. The example shows the decisions made regarding the topic of Measures of Center taught in Grades 3–5 after teachers have done a CTS using "The Measures of Center and Spread" CTS guide.

When using the chart with curriculum committees, make a large chart out of Handout 6.14. Before studying a curricular topic, have participants list concepts, ideas, or skills that are typically taught in relation to the topic identified. Have them write each one on a sticky note and place it on the priorities chart according to where they think it belongs. After studying a topic using CTS, revisit the chart and have participants suggest any changes in the placement of their sticky notes. Invite them to add any additional concepts, ideas, or skills that should be included in the two central boxes as essential or important understandings.

Table 6.8   Curriculum Priorities for Teaching Measures of Center in Grades 3–5

Priority	*Examples*
ESSENTIAL UNDERSTANDINGS for Mathematical Literacy *Ideas from BSL—Benchmarks for Science Literacy* (AAAS, 1993) and the NCTM Standards—*PSSM* (NCTM, 2000)	• Spreading data out on a number line helps to see what the extremes are, where they pile up, and where the gaps are. *(BSL)* • A summary of data includes where the middle is and how much spread is around it. *(BSL)* • The shape and important features of a set of data can be described and compared with other related data sets, with an emphasis on how the data are distributed. *(PSSM)* • There are different ways to describe the measure of center. *(PSSM)* • Different representations of the same data can show important aspects of the data. *(PSSM)*
IMPORTANT UNDERSTANDINGS THAT CONTRIBUTE to Mathematical Literacy	• Median as the measure describing the middle point of the data set. • Mode as the measure of describing the data value that occurs most often. • Mean as the balance point for the data set. • Range as an indicator of spread of the data values. • Data sets can be represented with line plots and histograms. • Distributions of data sets are more easily compared when represented graphically.
Knowledge or Skills WORTH BEING FAMILIAR WITH BUT NOT NECESSARY for Mathematical Literacy	• Formal methods for determining median when describing data set with an even number of data points.
Knowledge or Skills NOT WORTH the Instructional Time It Takes to Teach Them at This Grade Level	• Specific algorithms for calculating the mean. • Creating and interpreting box plots. • Changes in data values have various effects on the different measures of center and spread.

Creating Clarification Guides for Curriculum Topics

After a curriculum committee has conducted a CTS, committee members can put together a summary of their findings to include in their district curriculum guides. These summaries help to clarify the content, learning goals, instructional considerations, possible misconceptions that may surface, and links to state standards. An example of a K–12 Curricular Clarification for the K–12 topic of fractions put together by a New Hampshire school district is shown on pages 67 and 68 in the CTS parent book. The clarification was included in the district curriculum binders all teachers received and provided a K–12 big picture summary at a glance of the specific ideas that underlie the state standards, research on learning that could be used to inform teaching, and implications for instruction at different grade levels. A copy of the template curriculum committees can use to electronically enter their CTS findings is included on Handout 6.15 in the CD-ROM. This template includes the *Common Core State Standards for Mathematics* or the NCTM *Focal Points*. Facilitators can delete any of the documents not used in the CTS.

Clarifying a State Standard

As curriculum committees work to align their curriculum with new or revised state standards or the adoption of the *Common Core Mathematics Standards* or improve the existing alignment, they often wrestle with the interpretation of a learning goal from their local or state standards. State standards are written at various levels of specificity from broad to very specific and are usually written with the inclusion of a performance verb. Sometimes the addition of a performance verb, particularly if the verb was arbitrarily chosen to ensure a range of levels of performance across standards rather than the cognitive complexity of the idea being assessed, can change or mask the specific mathematics idea that makes up a learning goal. Although almost all states have based their standards on the *Benchmarks for Science Literacy* or the *Principles and Standards for School Mathematics* (and will soon be including standards from the *Common Core*), they are seldom written word for word in their original language. Examining the national goal statement from which a state or local standard was derived can often reveal much more specific and detailed information about the intent and meaning of a learning goal. The steps facilitators can use to guide participants through the CTS process of clarifying a learning goal include the following:

1. Identify a learning goal from your local or state standards (CTS Section VI).

2. Identify the CTS topic study guide related to the learning goal.

3. Use CTS Section III to identify a similar learning goal from the national standards.

4. Break the national learning goal into its component parts, called "key ideas" (sometimes a learning goal consists of only one key idea). Use Section II as needed to extract more specific ideas from the essays.

5. Use CTS Section IV (or the narrative that precedes the *Atlas of Science Literacy* maps from Section V) to identify learning research related to the learning goal (not the entire topic).

6. Use CTS Section II to identify instructional implications for teaching the learning goal (not the entire topic).

7. Use CTS Section V to identify connections to other ideas as well as important prerequisite understandings that should be developed before introducing the learning goal.

Handout 6.16 in the CD-ROM shows an example of a goal clarification for a primary grades state standard: "Measures and uses units of measures appropriately and consistently, and makes conversions within systems when solving problems across the content strands" (New England Common Assessment Program [NECAP] Mathematics Grade-Level Expectations for Grade 2). What units are students expected to measure with? Using the "Measurement Tools" CTS guide, the committee was able to use CTS Section III to trace the state standard goal statement back to the national standard from which it was derived. After breaking down the NECAP standard into the key ideas students should be able to understand, further clarification from CTS Section IV was provided to grade-level teachers on what the research has found to be difficult for students as well as commonly held ideas. CTS Section II was used to describe considerations to take into account when planning instruction around these key ideas. In cases where the standard isn't a foundational goal, the *Atlas of Science Literacy* in CTS Section V points out important connections to the key ideas that will help support students' ability to explain the key ideas that make up the standard. Overall, the process of clarifying a single state standard, using a CTS topic guide, led to a greater understanding of the content, curricular, and instructional meaning and intent of the learning goal than what one could derive merely from looking at the goal statement. A template that can be used for this process of clarifying a state standard is provided on Handout 6.17 in the CD-ROM.

Developing Crosswalks to State Standards

Leaders who facilitate implementation of state standards can use the process described above to clarify a particular state learning goal. In addition, leaders who work extensively with a set of state standards might consider developing a crosswalk between their state standards and the CTS topic guides. The crosswalk provides an easy-to-use tool for teachers or other users of state standards to quickly cross-reference a CTS guide to a state standard that relates to the CTS topic. The CTS guide can then be used to clarify the standard. In addition, leaders who are considering the revision of their local or state standards can develop a crosswalk for committees to evaluate their existing standards and make modifications based on improved interpretation and current research on learning. Handouts 6.18 and 6.18.1 on the CD-ROM provide two different examples of crosswalks developed to cross-reference state standards with the CTS topic guides: the Wisconsin Model Academic Standards for Mathematics: Number Operations and Relationships Standard and the 2000 NECAP Mathematics Grade-Level Expectations: Geometry and Measurement Strand. In the Wisconsin example, a table was created that listed each specific Grade 4, 8, and 12 standard in the Wisconsin standards and matched it to the CTS topic study guides that could be used to clarify the standard. In the NECAP example, the CTS topic study guides were entered right into the standards document in italics to match the grade-level expectations. The CTS guides can be used to clarify the meaning and intent of an expectation.

Please note that states periodically update their standards and that these example crosswalks may differ from current standards. However, the examples provided in Handouts 6.18a and 6.18.b are intended to show what a CTS crosswalk might look like.

Using CTS for Curriculum Selection

In many districts, the process of selecting curriculum materials has been simply to pick something popular with a few teachers, or worse, have all teachers use their own materials with little coordination. Increasingly districts are engaging in more thoughtful analysis of the curriculum and its alignment with standards and research (Loucks-Horsley, Stiles, Mundry, Love, & Hewson, 2010). CTS can be a useful tool for selecting curriculum materials that are based on standards and reflect the research on learning. Curriculum selection leaders and committee members should first read pages 66–69 in the parent CTS book. This section describes how CTS can be used for curriculum selection. The following tools can be used by curriculum selection committees to deepen their understanding of the standards and research on learning that should inform curriculum materials and evaluate the extent to which curriculum materials reflect CTS findings.

CTS Summary for Curriculum Materials Review

If the goal of a curriculum selection committee is to select standards-based and research-informed materials, then doing a CTS prior to examining and selecting new curriculum can make selection committees more aware of what to look for in the material. Publishers often claim that their materials are "standards-based" and developed with the latest research in mind. However, upon close examination, the alignment is often at a topical level or may miss the key ideas at the grade level specified in the standards. For example, the material may include a basic number combination (commonly referred to as "facts") strand to develop fluency but at closer look the instructional approach does not match what is recommended in the CTS readings. The CTS readings on addition and subtraction facts focus on developing fluency and accuracy by "(a) developing the relationships within addition and subtraction combinations and (b) eliciting counting on for addition and counting up for subtraction and unknown addend situations" (NCTM, 2000, p. 84).

Handout 6.19 provides a template selection leaders and committee members can use to summarize findings from a CTS study that are then used as a lens through which to rate the material according to the extent to which there is evidence that matches the CTS results. To create a CTS summary guide for curricular review, the committee first chooses the CTS topic guide that best matches the topic of the curriculum materials or unit that will be examined. For example, on page 70 in the parent CTS book, an elementary committee is examining a primary grade unit on addition and subtraction of whole numbers. The committee does a CTS and records the following information in a concise format that can be used at a glance to examine the curriculum material:

- *Concepts for Teacher Background Information:* Use CTS Section I and the K–12 overview essay in CTS Section IIA to identify content background material that should be provided for teachers using the curriculum. Record the major concepts identified in these CTS sections. (Note: A concept is a word or short phrase that provides a mental construct for the key ideas.)
- *Students' Content Knowledge:* Use CTS Sections III, V, and VI to list specific ideas that should be included in the learning objectives of the curricular unit.
- *Instructional Implications:* Use CTS Sections II and IV to identify instructional strategies, appropriate learning contexts, or developmental considerations that should inform the lessons that make up the unit.

- *Student Difficulties and Misconceptions:* Use CTS Sections II and IV to identify any difficulties students may have learning the ideas in the topic or potential misconceptions students may develop or bring to their learning. This information will be used to look for explicit mention of these in the teacher's guide or evidence of activities designed to address these difficulties and misconceptions.
- *Prerequisite Knowledge:* Use CTS Sections III and V to examine ideas that are developed in the grade level before or precursor ideas within the grade level that should be taught before introducing other ideas. This information will be used to look for evidence in the teacher's guide that alerts teachers to the prior knowledge students will need or activities that consider and build upon prerequisite skills and knowledge.
- *Connections to Other Topics:* Use CTS Section V to look for connections that can be made to other curricular topics. Look for evidence of these connections in the activities or descriptions of extensions in the teacher's guide that connect to other lessons or units. (Note: Occasionally Section II will provide useful information about connections.)

Once this review has been completed and recorded by the committee, it will be used as an overview-at-a-glance of the things a curriculum committee should look for in the unit. The committee then uses this information to rate material on how well it addresses the standards and research on learning that are revealed through the CTS process. However, the review process only looks at how well it reflects the CTS findings. It does not evaluate the pedagogical design of the materials or likeliness of instructional effectiveness.

CTS Summary Review of Curriculum Materials

Now that you have the CTS information to guide the review of the material you selected, the next step is to examine the material by looking at the extent to which it addresses the information revealed through the CTS. Handout 6.20 on the CD-ROM provides a template for reviewing the curriculum materials using evidence from the summary completed in Handout 6.19. A description of this tool and an example of how it was used with a CTS topic study and a curriculum unit on Addition and Subtraction of Whole Numbers is shown in Figures 4.11 and 4.12 in the parent CTS book. There are five ratings, ranging from 1 to 5, with a "1 being no evidence of the CTS findings in the material and a 5 including strong evidence of the CTS information in the materials as well as additional appropriate features that build from the standards and research that may exceed the basic threshold recommendations of CTS but still contribute to student learning in a meaningful way."

Selection committee members go through each of the sections of Handout 6.20, discussing where they see evidence of the CTS findings in the curriculum materials. The group comes to a consensus on the rating and summarizes their reasons for the rating. The discussions among curriculum selection members significantly increase their knowledge of standards and research and increase their ability to look carefully at curriculum materials and not be misled by superficial features.

Doing a CTS on the topic of the materials prior to conducting an analysis of curriculum materials provides a lens through which to make evidence-based decisions regarding the likelihood that the materials address standards and research on learning. However, it does not ensure that students will learn the mathematics from the materials. Further analysis on instructional effectiveness, including an examination of the pedagogy, would be suggested if the committee is looking at the instructional quality of the material. For groups interested in taking the analysis further, we recommend that some leaders may want to use CTS with the Project 2061 Curriculum Materials Analysis Process that rigorously examines content alignment and instructional quality of mathematics textbooks and curriculum materials. This process is not described in this *Leader's Guide* or the CTS parent book, but can be accessed at http://www.project2061.org/publications/textbook/default.htm.

CURRICULUM IMPLEMENTATION

Supporting teachers to learn mathematics content and pedagogical content knowledge that is directly connected to their curriculum materials increases the likelihood of changes in classroom teaching (Loucks-Horsley et al., 2010). Many districts use teacher leaders and instructional coaches to support implementation of new curriculum materials. One of the ways leaders can help teachers understand the content in their curriculum and know why it is presented and sequenced in such a way to promote learning (which requires teachers not to skip over or pick and choose only the activities they like or feel comfortable with) is to conduct a CTS with the teachers prior to examining the curriculum materials and experiencing the activities. By doing a CTS first, the teachers develop a common understanding of the content, reasons why certain instructional practices and activities are used, common difficulties and potential misconceptions to anticipate, and connections between lessons and content. The common understandings gained through the CTS process deepen the teachers' understanding of the intent of the curriculum and the importance of maintaining the fidelity of implementation. CTS leaders are encouraged to read pages 69–75 in the CTS parent book. This section provides a background on using CTS to support curriculum implementation. The following are suggested CTS tools and strategies that support curriculum implementation.

Creating Customized CTS Guides for Curriculum Units

To use CTS in the context of supporting curriculum implementation, leaders first must identify the CTS guide(s) that most closely match the curricular unit or create a customized guide that combines elements from two or more guides to address the curricular unit. Figure 4.13 on page 73 in the parent CTS book shows an example of a customized guide for Grade 6 that combined readings from the "Fractions" CTS guide and the "Customary Measurement" CTS guide to create a guide that addressed the MathThematics Module, "Creating Things." Notice the readings focus only on Grades 6–8 and combine readings from both topics. Handout 6.21 on the CD-ROM provides a custom template for creating your own topic-specific guides for curriculum units that target a specific grade level rather than doing a full K–12 CTS. If there is a process skill being developed, your customized guide can include links to readings for that skill as well. *Common Core State Standards* or NCTM *Focal Points* can be added to CTS Section III.

Once you select or create your own CTS guide for the unit being implemented, the leader should first do the CTS, making note of findings that specifically relate to the curriculum unit being implemented. Following the suggestions in Chapter 5 in this *Leader's Guide* for conducting a full CTS with groups, lead participants through the CTS, discussing the results as a group. For the application stage of a full CTS study, refer participants to the curriculum materials. Guide teachers through each of the lessons, encouraging them to make links to the CTS findings from each CTS study section that supports the materials or refer to the CTS findings when teachers have questions about the materials. By doing a CTS first, the teachers have a lens through which to view their materials and focus their instruction.

Developing CTS Curricular Learning Paths

CTS curricular learning paths provide a one-page graphic for teachers to see at a glance the content in a curricular unit. The paths visually organize the intended learning from each activity by subconcepts that are unpacked from the major concepts that make up the unit. Curricular learning paths can be created by the CTS leader and used to support curriculum implementation or can be created collaboratively with teacher leaders supporting the implementation of new curriculum materials. Figures 4.14 and 4.15 in the CTS parent book show the development of a CTS Curricular Learning Path for the Math in Context unit Triangles and Beyond. The Hierarchal Structure of Content Knowledge described on pages 57–60 of the CTS parent book and on pages 156–157 of this *Leader's Guide* chapter is used to unpack concepts for the learning paths as well as identify big ideas and connecting themes. The learning paths help classroom teachers plan their instruction while following the flow of the unit. They also identify the CTS guides if teachers wish to explore further by doing their own CTS on the topic of the unit. Leaders interested in developing or facilitating the development of CTS learning paths for curriculum can use the following steps to construct their own learning path.

Part 1: Groundwork

1. Browse through the unit and become familiar with the content and lessons included in the material. You will keep referring back to the unit as you develop the background information and learning path using CTS.

2. Select a CTS guide that seems to be the primary topic of the unit. For example, the *Triangles and Beyond* Math in Context unit seemed to best match the CTS guide "Geometric Shapes."

3. Examine CTS Sections III and V to identify major concepts that make up the topic at the intended grade level and are included in the unit. For example, after examining CTS Sections III and V, polygons, transformation and symmetry seemed to be concepts related to both the "Geometric Shapes" CTS guide and the curricular unit. Record the concepts. These will be your starting point for unpacking the content.

4. Look for subconcepts included in the unit that may be a subset of the major concepts you identified in Step 3. List these subconcepts. These will be used to group the lessons. In Figure 4.14 in the CTS parent book, you will see several subconcepts listed that make up the concepts described above them on the chart. For example, the subconcepts of polygons for this unit include triangles and quadrilaterals.

5. List learning goals from your state standards (CTS Section VI) that relate to the concepts or subconcepts. In the example shown on page 75 of the CTS parent book, the listed Vermont standard is related to the concepts and subconcepts of the unit.

6. Examine CTS Sections II, III, IV, and V for specific ideas from the learning goals (CTS Section III) as well as specific ideas that can be synthesized from the essays (CTS Section II overview essay and grade level essay), research on learning (CTS Section

IV), and connections to and from the maps (CTS Section V). List any specific ideas gleaned from these CTS sections that relate to the lessons in the curriculum material. You might look at related CTS guides connected to the content. For example, in this unit, the CTS guide "Connections" helped in describing specific ideas about connecting ideas about geometric shapes outside the discipline of mathematics.

7. Examine the material as a whole and look for big ideas in CTS Section I and the K–12 Overview essay in CTS Section II that describe the major, overarching ideas developed by the material. For example, the big idea that "shapes can be classified by characteristics and properties" is a big idea that comes from several of the lessons in the unit.

8. Identify the broad content and/or process standards that provide connections between the big idea, concepts, and specific ideas. For example, Geometry, Measurement, Reasoning, and Proof are all broad standards that overarch this unit.

The preceding describes the CTS groundwork that is done in concert with examining the lessons in the material. The information is now used to create a one-page curricular learning path to help a teacher understand the conceptual flow and learning objectives of the lessons. The following describes how to construct a learning path using a format similar to the one on page 75 in the CTS parent book:

Part 2: Development of the Flow Chart

1. Start with the title of the unit and the grade level(s).

2. Describe the big ideas and major concepts identified from the groundwork.

3. Examine the activities. Create boxes that describe the name of the activity or lesson and a brief description of what happens in the lesson. Refer to the specific ideas from CTS when developing the description. Don't list the specific idea from CTS but rather try to use it to concisely describe the lesson so that it connects to a CTS idea. However, keep in mind that some lessons may not connect directly to CTS findings but are needed in order to maintain coherency.

4. Group these lessons/activities by related subconcepts. Sometimes there may be only one lesson to address a single subconcept, two or more lessons addressing one subconcept, or a cluster of lessons addressing related subconcepts.

5. Draw arrows, use connectors, or arrange in rows to indicate when a new lesson or cluster of lessons targets a new subconcept(s). The flow chart continues by grouping related lessons that develop a subconcept and contribute to the next set of lessons that focus on a new subconcept. For example, on page 75 in the CTS parent book, the paths are broken into the subpaths of triangles; triangles, polygons and circles; quadrilaterals; and transformations. Collectively, all the lessons will build an understanding of the major concepts listed at the top of the chart.

6. Review your chart to see if the conceptual path makes sense and that the activities align with the subconcepts.

7. At the bottom of the chart, list specific skills that are used to develop content understanding through the activities. This is particularly important for process-based units.

8. List the major CTS guide that was used to examine the curriculum material and inform the structure of knowledge.

9. List any related CTS guides to which the user of the curriculum might refer in order to learn more about the concepts and skills.

10. List the learning goals from your state standards that are aligned with the material.

11. *Optional*: List the specific ideas identified during the groundwork stage.

When completed, the CTS curricular learning path provides a conceptual road map for teachers to follow. In addition, listing the CTS guides related to the unit provides information for curriculum users to use CTS to further their understanding of the important ideas that are developed throughout the curriculum.

These are just a few of the many suggestions for ways to use CTS to support the multifaceted nature of curriculum. As you become more familiar with the use of CTS and strategies for leading a topic study, you may find additional ways to support curriculum.

CTS AND MATHEMATICS INSTRUCTION

Many professional development programs provide opportunities for teachers to develop their own lessons or modify existing lessons to improve their alignment and instructional quality. Pages 76–80 in the CTS parent book describe ways CTS can be used in an instructional context to target important content-related ideas and skills. Leaders should take the time to read through this section in the parent book. Table 6.9 shows the instructional components, content examples, and CD-ROM handouts described in this section.

Table 6.9 Instructional Components, Content Examples, and CD-ROM Handouts

Instructional Component	CTS Topic Examples	CD-ROM Handouts
Identifying appropriate instructional strategies, representations, or contexts	Fractions, Decimals, and Percents; Rates of Change	6.22
Reviewing and modifying lessons	Probability	6.23, 6.24, 6.25, 6.26, 6.27
Developing a standards- and research-based lesson	Division and Remainders	6.28, 6.29
Strengthening mathematical inquiry and problem solving	Spatial Visualization; Functions; Ratio and Proportion; Modeling; Problem Solving; Conjecture, Proof and Justification	none

These suggestions and strategies can be used by leaders to help teachers improve instruction that targets important learning goals in a curricular unit. They are described as follows:

Identifying Appropriate Instructional Strategies, Representations, or Contexts

A careful study of CTS Section II reveals implications for instruction that connect to important learning goals included in CTS Sections III and VI. As teachers study CTS Section II, encourage them to identify examples of effective strategies, representations, or contexts described in the essays. If mathematics is the science of patterns, representations are the means by which those patterns are recorded and analyzed (NCTM, 2000, p. 360). The *PSSM* standards for representation include three core expectations for all students. They include the ability to

1. Create and use representations to organize, record, and communicate mathematical ideas;

2. Select, apply, and translate among mathematical representations to solve problems; and

3. Use representations to model and interpret physical, social, and mathematical phenomena.

The "Representations" CTS, Section IIB readings highlight the types of representations expected at each of the K–2, 3–5, 6–8, and 9–12 grade spans. In addition, Section IIB content topic essays are rich in examples of representations. For example, in the "Fractions, Decimals and Percents" CTS, Grades 6–8, reading provides examples of concrete representations that may be helpful in teaching about fractions.

The context in which students learn mathematical ideas is also important. For example, Section IIB of the grades "Rates of Change" topic study includes an essay titled "Analyze change in various contexts" for each of the grade spans. These essays point out the importance of designing instruction that uses situations and data students are familiar with. Handout 6.22 provides a template teachers can use to link key ideas in a curricular topic using CTS Section III to instructional considerations from CTS Section II such as teaching strategies, representations, and effective contexts. Teachers can then refer to the handout during their instructional planning to make decisions informed by CTS.

Reviewing and Modifying Lessons

Page 76 in the CTS parent book provides suggestions for reviewing and modifying existing lessons. These lessons may come from teachers' instructional materials or may be teacher developed. The CTS process for reviewing and modifying existing lessons strengthens the lesson's alignment to learning goals and improves its instructional quality. This application can be used with any CTS full topic session in which improvement of lessons is used as the context in which teachers apply their CTS findings. It is also useful in helping preservice and novice teachers understand how to improve a lesson's alignment to standards and instructional quality, as well as to address commonly held ideas noted in the research on learning. Handout 6.23 in the CD-ROM provides a scaffold leaders can use with teachers to guide them through the CTS lesson review and modification process. Handout 6.24 provides a worksheet for participants to use as they record their CTS findings that relate to the lesson and track modifications they can make to strengthen the lesson, based on their CTS findings.

An example of the lesson modification process is included on the CD-ROM. Handout 6.25 is a copy of an original middle school lesson. A middle school teacher found this lesson on the Internet and adapted it to address the concepts of theoretical and experimental probability. She felt this lesson would provide understanding of theoretical probability;

however, although the lesson was good, the teacher felt it could be strengthened by including a conceptual development approach that took into account students' existing ideas about informal understandings of chance moving toward a numerical approach incorporating concepts of ratio. She brought the lesson to her grade-level team, and they decided to use CTS to strengthen and improve the lesson. After conducting a CTS on related topic studies, using the results to modify the lesson, and adding instructional strategies that reflect the wisdom of the practitioner, the teacher and her colleagues produced the version shown in Handout 6.26. Handout 6.27 shows how the teacher and her colleagues used the CTS results to record and track suggestions for modifying the lesson. The following options can be used to introduce the CTS lesson review and modification process:

- Option 1: Choose a lesson that matches the CTS topic of your session that has potential but needs improvement. After participants have completed and debriefed their CTS, have them read page 76 in their CTS book (or provide a handout of that page) and explain that there are materials that elaborate on this description of lesson review and modification that you will introduce to them. Provide a copy of the scaffold (Handout 6.23) and guide participants through each step of the scaffold using the existing lesson you previously identified and the CTS results. Provide participants with a copy of Handout 6.24 to record their CTS findings and track suggested modifications to the lesson. As a whole group, discuss and record how to best modify the lesson, justifying decisions based on CTS as well as knowledge of effective teaching.
- Option 2: Provide copies of Handouts 6.25 and 6.26. Ask participants to examine the two lessons and describe the differences they see in the CTS modified lesson (Handout 6.26). Distribute a copy of Handout 6.27 to show how CTS was used to inform the modifications. Discuss and debrief evidence in the lesson that shows how the teacher used CTS to make modifications. Provide a copy of the scaffold (Handout 6.23) and blank worksheet (Handout 6.24) for participants to use in a follow-up session (or as an assignment) to modify a lesson that is related to the topic of the session or a new topic of their choosing. (This will depend on your purpose for using CTS. If it was in a content institute for a particular topic, everyone should be using related CTS guides. If it was for introducing CTS, participants can choose a topic relevant to their own curriculum.)
- Option 3: Obtain materials and model and teach the lesson described in Handout 6.26 (participants do not need a copy of the lesson). After teaching the lesson and giving participants a chance to experience it as learners, compare the lesson they experienced to the original one (pass out Handout 6.25). Ask them to comment on the differences in the lesson. Refer to the scaffold (Handout 6.23) and Handout 6.27 to show how a teacher used the scaffold and CTS results to modify the lesson. Give participants an opportunity to reflect on the connections they see between CTS and the revised lesson. As a follow-up, have participants use the scaffold and the worksheet (Handout 6.24) to modify a lesson of their choice.

Developing a Standards- and Research-Based Lesson

Exemplary instructional materials take into account the specific concepts and ideas in the national standards (CTS Section III), prerequisite knowledge and skills and connections among ideas in mathematics (CTS Section V), effective instruction related to specific content (Section II), and the research on learning (CTS Section IV). These considerations inform the targeted learning goal(s), instructional context, and strategies used in a lesson. However, there are times when a teacher may not have access to exemplary instructional materials, or state standards or the local curriculum require supplementary lessons be taught to address gap(s) in existing materials. In this case, teachers often have to develop their own lesson(s).

The CTS standards- and research-based approach to lesson design (SRB lessons) uses a backward design approach that begins with a CTS study in order to more effectively address the alignment of specific mathematics content and content-appropriate pedagogy. Although there are other excellent generic lesson design processes, such as *Understanding by Design* (Wiggins & McTighe, 2005), the added value CTS brings to these processes is the clarification of the mathematics content, key ideas in the standards, and research on learning before designing instruction to address learning goals. The steps in the process are described in the CTS parent book on page 77 and Figure 4.16, on page 78. Handout 6.28 in the CD-ROM provides a scaffold, based on Figure 4.16, that can be used to design SRB lessons. This lesson design process can be used as an application after teachers have conducted a full CTS on a mathematics topic.

Handout 6.29 shows an example of an SRB lesson designed by a fifth-grade teacher to address her state standard's division of whole numbers goal. Leaders can use the scaffold and CTS results to guide teachers in developing similar lessons that align with local and national standards and incorporate effective instructional strategies for the specific content.

To introduce the value of using CTS to guide instruction without going through the process of designing an SRB lesson during your CTS session, you can instead have participants read *Vignette #7: An Intermediate Teacher Uses CTS to Prepare for a Unit on Probability* on pages 104–105 in the CTS parent book. The vignette describes how a teacher plans to modify her instruction, based on the information she gained from using CTS. This vignette helps teachers see the value of doing a CTS first before they design a lesson.

Strengthening Mathematical Inquiry and Problem Solving

Pages 77–80 in the CTS parent book address ways to strengthen a lesson's connection to inquiry and problem solving. When leading CTS sessions that include an opportunity to develop or modify lessons that incorporate the skills and understandings of mathematical inquiry and problem solving, leaders can connect a content CTS guide from the "Number and Operations," "Algebra," "Geometry," "Measurement," and "Data Analysis" categories to one of the guides in the "Integrated Topics" category such as "Constancy and Change," "Equivalence," and "Proportionality" and to one of the process guides in the "Problem Solving and Processes" category, such as Modeling, to develop lessons that link process skills, processes, habits of mind, and content.

Encourage teachers to use the questions on pages 79–80 as they think about ways to strengthen mathematical inquiry or other crosscutting skills and process standards connections to their lessons. Provide them with one of the following examples to illustrate how CTS can be used to strengthen inquiry.

Example 1: A fourth-grade teacher decides to have her students enhance their modeling skills while learning about two-dimensional views of three-dimensional objects. She selects the "Spatial Visualization" and "Modeling" CTS guides. She is particularly interested in instructional implications and methods of allowing students to get a hands-on approach to understanding the relationships between the nets and the three-dimensional figures. As she uses the questions for CTS Section II on page 79, she finds out that students should use spatial visualization about the relationships by using physical models as well as mental models and that technology could help develop a bridge from the concrete models to the mental models. She designs the activity based on the "E-example" mentioned on page 169 of the *Principles and Standards for School Mathematics* to first have students predict which nets would create a cube and then test their predictions by trying to create the cube from the net. To bridge to other three-dimensional shapes, she plans to use a three-dimensional object technology-based application to continue to build toward students having mental images.

Example 2: A seventh-grade teacher decides to include a problem-solving context to accompany a unit on ratio and rates. He wants his students to build an understanding of a unit rate or to use a unit rate to solve problems within a real-world context. His state's standards include "problem solving" as a mathematical practice but he isn't sure what the "practice" involves beyond that of the typical problem-solving approaches in his textbook that integrates many different math topics to teach various approaches. He turns to CTS and does a study of "Problem Solving." Using the questions on page 79 for CTS Sections II and III to guide his study, he learns how students can build mathematical knowledge through problem solving and considers how to scaffold various problems in order to move students' understandings from ratio to unit rate to applying unit rates.

Example 3: An Algebra II teacher wants to design a lesson that will involve students in looking at various representations to determine the class of the function. She wants them to use critical reasoning skills to justify the classifications. She uses the CTS guide "Conjecture, Proof, and Justification" to learn more about how to create an instructional setting for students to engage in a justification as well as any research related to student difficulties with this process skill. Using the guiding questions for CTS Sections II and IV on page 79, she learns that students' conceptual understandings affect what they can accept as valid justification and that justification relies on what the classroom community has as shared understandings. She decides to focus the first part of the activity on developing ideas around the properties and characteristics of the classes of functions in order to have students use these properties and characteristics within their justifications of the classification of the representations during the second part of the activity. She also includes a third part to the lesson where justifications are shared and compared to determine criteria for valid justifications within this mathematics context.

Overall, the strategies and tools for linking instruction to CTS findings can result in changes that focus instruction more deeply on learning goals and provide improved opportunities for students to learn concepts and skills through lessons selected and taught by a teacher who has experienced CTS. The instructional applications can be combined with a full topic workshop to create a full-day session in which teachers select, modify, or design lessons based on the CTS topic they studied.

CTS AND MATHEMATICS ASSESSMENT

Pages 80–85 in the CTS parent book describe how CTS can be used in an assessment context. The box on this page provides an outline of the suggestions included in this chapter for using CTS in assessment. All of the resources and handouts for this section can be found in the CD-ROM Chapter 6 folder labeled Assessment.

OUTLINE OF SUGGESTIONS FOR ENHANCING CTS AND MATHEMATICS ASSESSMENT

A. Formative Assessment

   1. Introduction to CTS assessment probes

   2. Professional development module—Developing CTS Assessment Probes

B. Performance Assessment

   1. Introduction to CTS performance assessment

   2. Designing CTS performance assessment tasks

Table 6.10	Assessment Tools and Strategies	
Assessment Application	*CTS Example Used*	*CD-ROM Handouts*
Developing Formative Assessment Probes	Probability, Expressions, and Equations	Handouts 6.30–6.37
Designing Performance Assessments	Symbolic Representation	Handouts 6.38–6.40

The CTS parent book describes the different purposes of assessment and provides suggestions for using CTS to design two types of assessments: assessment probes that are used for diagnostic and formative assessment, and performance tasks that are used for culminating classroom formative or summative assessments. Table 6.10 describes the tools and strategies for the assessment context applications included in this chapter. In addition, "Developing Formative Assessment Probes" is a full-session module that includes a facilitator script and PowerPoint slides.

Assessment Probes

An explicit link between a standards-based key idea and a commonly held difficulty or misconception noted in the learning research can be used to develop a type of formative assessment item called an assessment probe. These assessment probes reveal much more than simply an answer. They provide an opportunity for teachers to probe students' ideas and thinking in order to uncover conceptual barriers that may be hidden from the teacher. These conceptual barriers can be uncovered prior to or throughout instruction by using a CTS-developed assessment probe.

Mathematics CTS assessment probes allow teachers to target specific areas of difficulty as identified by the research on learning. Being aware of and eliciting common misunderstandings and drawing students' attention to them can be a valuable teaching technique (Griffin & Madgwick, 2005). Examples of commonly held misconceptions elicited by a CTS mathematics assessment probe include ideas such as *multiplication makes bigger* and *the larger the denominator, the larger the fraction* (Rose, Arline, & Minton, 2007). Applying CTS to the development of assessment probes provides teachers with the tools they need to engage in continuous assessment of student learning.

In our work with CTS, we have found significant interest in the development of assessment probes. Page Keeley and Cheryl Rose Tobey, authors of this *Leader's Guide*, have authored a series of books on formative assessment that include diagnostic/formative assessment probes developed by using the CTS assessment probe design process described in the CTS science and mathematics parent books. To learn more about this work, visit the Uncovering Student Ideas website at www.uncoveringstudentideas.org.

Cheryl Rose Tobey, coauthor of this *Leader's Guide,* is the primary author of the *Uncovering Student Thinking in Mathematics* series (Rose & Arline, 2009; Rose et al., 2007; Rose Tobey & Minton, 2011) published by Corwin. These mathematics probes are accompanied by extensive teacher notes and a chapter that describes how CTS was used in the development process. Handouts 6.30 and 6.31 show the assessment probe described on pages 81–83 in the CTS parent book, along with the accompanying teacher notes that reflect the CTS findings. This probe has been published in *Uncovering Student Thinking in Mathematics* (Rose et al., 2007). Table 6.11 lists the information provided in the *Uncovering*

| Table 6.11 | Linking *Uncovering Student Ideas* Teacher Notes to CTS |

Uncovering Student Thinking in Mathematics *Teacher Notes*	*CTS Section Used to Inform Development of the Teacher Notes*
Questioning for Student Understanding and Uncovering Understandings	Sections II and III
Examining Student Work	Sections II and IV
Seeking Links to Cognitive Research	Sections II and IV
Teaching Implications	Sections II and IV
Additional References	Includes several of the CTS resource books as well as supplementary resources from the CTS website
Curriculum Topic Study	Lists the CTS guides used to inform the development of the probe

Student Ideas teacher notes and shows the link between this valuable teacher information and CTS.

Teachers who have used these probes and experienced the impact they have made on their students' learning, their instruction, and the classroom climate have taken the next step to learn how to use CTS to develop their own probes. The following is a workshop module leaders can use to facilitate the CTS assessment design process. From our experience with facilitators of CTS and CTS users, this has been the most used application of the CTS contexts described in Chapter 4 of the CTS parent book.

Module C1

Developing CTS Assessment Probes

DESCRIPTION OF THE MODULE

This module introduces participants to the CTS process of developing assessment probes. This context application module takes participants through a cycle of learn, practice, and apply. During this module, participants

- *Learn* about a CTS process for developing assessment probes that elicit students' ideas and inform instruction;
- *Practice* using CTS to unpack specific ideas in the standards and research related to an assessment topic; and
- *Apply* by developing an assessment probe using the CTS assessment probe development process.

Goal of a CTS Assessment Probe Development Session

The overarching goal of this module is to help participants learn how to use CTS to develop their own assessment probes.

Audience

This session is designed for K–12 teachers and assessment developers. The examples used in this introductory module target Grades 3–12 ideas from the "Expressions and Equations" topic study guide, but participants are encouraged to focus on just one grade span when they use CTS to develop their own probe.

Use of a Scaffold

The CTS Assessment Probe development process involves several sequential steps. A scaffold is provided to guide novices through each of the steps until they become proficient in the process.

Guidelines for Leading a Session on CTS Assessment Probe Development

Obtain the Following

- At least one copy of the CTS parent book, *Mathematics Curriculum Topic Study: Bridging the Gap Between Standards and Practice* (Keeley & Rose, 2006).
- At least one copy of *Benchmarks for Science Literacy* (AAAS, 1993), *Principles and Standards for School Mathematics* (NCTM, 2000), and the *Research Companion* (NCTM, 2003) for each group of two to three participants if they are going to develop additional probes after the introduction to the process. (Other books that can also be used but are optional include *Atlas of Science Literacy*, Vol. 1 (AAAS, 2001) and *Atlas of Science Literacy*, Vol. 2 (AAAS, 2007). *Common Core Mathematics Standards* or NCTM *Focal Points* can also be used.

- Flip chart easel, pads, and markers
- Paper for participants to take notes
- Optional: A copy of any of the books from the *Uncovering Student Ideas in Mathematics* series (Rose & Arline, 2009; Rose et al., 2007; Rose Tobey & Minton, 2011).

Duplicate the Following

(See CD-ROM Chapter 6 Assessment subfolder for all handouts.)

- If participants do not have their own CTS parent books, make copies of "CTS and Assessment" on pages 80–83 of that book and the CTS Guide "Expressions and Equations" on page 136.
- If not enough resource books are available, make copies of the selected readings from CTS Sections IIIA and IV from CTS guide "Expressions and Equations" on page 136.
- Optional: Handouts 6.30 and 6.31 if participants are not familiar with the *Uncovering Student Thinking in Mathematics* probes.
- Print copies of Facilitator Handouts 6.32 and 6.33, one copy per group of two to three. Facilitator Handout 6.32 should be copied on yellow paper and Facilitator Handout 6.33 should be copied on blue paper. If you choose to add learning goals from the *Common Core* or NCTM *Focal Points*, add those to Handout 6.32 prior to printing out the handout.
- Handout 6.34: Assessment Probe Scaffold
- Handout 6.35: Scaffold Step 4: Expressions and Equations Chart
- Handout 6.36: Five Types of Probes
- Handout 6.37: Probe Development Worksheet

Prepare

- PowerPoint slides for *Designing Assessment Probes* (on CD-ROM) in the Chapter 6 assessment folder. Insert your own graphics and additional information. Optional: Print out copies of the PowerPoint slides for participants.
- Cards for matching activity—cut out yellow and blue cards from Facilitator's Handouts 6.32 and 6.33, and place cards in a resealable plastic bag.

Time

Introducing the process and practicing with the examples provided takes approximately 2 hours. After completing the introduction, if participants are going to develop their own probe using a topic of their choice, add an additional 1 to 1.5 hours. This session can be extended into a full day if participants are working in groups to develop a collection of probes.

DIRECTIONS FOR LEADING CTS ASSESSMENT PROBE DEVELOPMENT

The following directions describe how to lead an introductory CTS probe development session for first-timers using the "Expressions and Equations" CTS as an example.

- Show Slides 1 and 2, and go over goals for the session. Include introductions if participants do not know each other. (3 minutes)
- Show Slide 3, and give participants an opportunity to discuss the difference between the three types of assessment. Debrief with the large group and explain how this session will instruct them in how to develop their own assessment probes that are used to elicit and identify students' ideas (diagnostic use) and use information about students' thinking to inform instruction (formative use). (5 minutes)

- Show Slide 4. In pairs or groups of three, have participants take turns summarizing each paragraph of the reading to gain background knowledge on formative assessment and the probe development process. Provide time for questions. (15 minutes)

- Show Slide 5 to describe what a formative assessment probe is. If participants are not familiar with the *Uncovering Student Thinking in Mathematics* probes developed by the coauthor of this leader's guide, Cheryl Rose Tobey, pass out Handouts 6.30 and 6.31 and provide a few minutes for participants to look at the probe and teacher notes. Explain how CTS formative assessment probes are different from summative assessment testing items, which are used after instruction to measure the extent to which a student has met a learning goal. Show Slide 6 to explain that there are many terms used to describe the ideas students bring to their learning. During this session, we will call them "misconceptions," using this term in a general way to refer to all the different types of ideas students have that are not completely accurate. (5 minutes)

- Show Slide 7 and explain that we are going to look at how a CTS assessment probe is developed. Explain that the development process consists of three steps: (1) identifying a specific idea or ideas from the standards using CTS Section III (or V or VI); (2) identifying findings from the research on student learning that relate to the specific idea (CTS Section IV); and (3) forming from these two components the basis of the assessment probe, which leads to the development of the context of the probe (prompt), the selected responses (distracters and correct answer[s]), and a justification that asks students to explain their thinking and provide reasons for their answer. (5 minutes)

- Show Slide 8 to show an example of using the "Computation and Operations" CTS guide to identify specific ideas related to multiplication. This slide shows a specific idea from the *Principles and Standards of School Mathematics* (NCTM, 2000) that relates to the idea of the effect of operating with fractions, decimals, and integers. Identifying ideas from the standards is the first component of probe development. We have now targeted a specific idea in the standards about arithmetic operations, while our focus is on multiplication. The next component involves looking for a match between the idea(s) in the standards and the research on learning that helps us understand how students think about the effect of multiplication. Show Slide 9 to see an example of a match to the research that comes from examining CTS Section IV. Now these two components can be put together to develop a probe that can be used across multiple grade levels to find out if students misunderstand the effect of multiplying by a number between 0 and 1. (5 minutes)

- Show Slide 10 to illustrate the third component—choosing the prompt, selected responses, and asking for a justification. If you have a copy of *Uncovering Student Thinking in Mathematics* (Rose et al., 2007), you can mention that this probe came from this book and that all the probes in this book were developed using the CTS process. In this example, a format called a "multiple selections response" was used to see if students repeatedly used the idea of multiplication makes bigger disregarding the numbers used in each set. Point out how the last part of the probe asks students to explain their thinking and justify their answer. Reinforce how this probe was developed by connecting the research from CTS Section IV to the specific ideas about arithmetic operations in CTS Section III. Show Slide 11 and provide a few minutes to discuss the questions in small groups and debrief with the larger group. Point out how CTS provides the information and a process to make an assessment link between a key idea and the research on student learning. These types of assessments are important because they help us uncover strongly held preconceptions students bring to their learning that if not addressed through careful instructional planning, will go unchanged from one grade level to the next. (10 minutes)

- Show Slide 12 and refer participants to Handout 6.34: Assessment Probe Scaffold. Describe how a scaffold provides the support one needs to undertake a task. Show Slide 13 and refer participants to the first step on the scaffold. For the purpose of learning how to develop a probe, we will practice with the topic of expressions and equations. Our first step is to look at the "Expressions and Equations" CTS study guide on page 136 in *Mathematics Curriculum Topic Study* (Keeley & Rose, 2006). Show Slide 14 and point out that they will focus primarily on Sections III and IV when using CTS to develop assessment probes. Section III will help them find the specific ideas that are related to expressions and equations. Although foundational ideas within this topic begin in the K–2 grade span, we will only look at the 3–5, 6–8, and 9–12 concepts and ideas in the *Principles and Standards for School Mathematics* and *Benchmarks*. Point out Section III on the slide to show what part of the study guide they will focus on. Then point out Section IV and explain how this section will help them identify misconceptions and learning difficulties that are noted in the research on learning. Point out the readings from Sections IVA and IVB that will be used for assessment probe development. (7 minutes)

- Show Slide 15 and refer to Step 2 on the scaffold. Point out the bag of yellow and blue cards— one bag for each small group. Ask participants to take out the yellow cards. Tell them if they were doing their own CTS, these would be the ideas they would identify and record from CTS Section III. The CTS has already been done and the ideas have been placed on cards for this practice activity. Have them spread out the cards and arrange them by grade level. (5 minutes)

- Show Slide 16 and refer to Step 3 on the scaffold. Ask participants to take out the blue cards and spread them out. If they were doing the CTS, these would be the misconceptions and learning difficulties recorded from the CTS Section IV reading. (3 minutes)

- Show Slide 17 and refer to Step 4 on the scaffold. Group similar ideas on the yellow cards using the concept categories in the left column on the slide. Repeat with the blue cards using the concept categories on the right column. Explain how this is done in order to make a match between similar clusters of ideas, especially across grade spans. Pass out Handout 6.35 to show how the CTS results are organized for the probe development process, reflecting what participants have done with the cards. (Note: The cards are used for practicing CTS probe development. The handout illustrates how the CTS Sections III and IV are organized when actually doing CTS for the purpose of developing assessment probes.) (8 minutes)

- Show Slide 18. Explain how Step 4 involves finding a close match between a standards idea and a research finding. This match will lead to possible questions that inform the development of the probe. Explain how the standards idea and the research finding shown on the slide address writing expressions to describe a relationship. This match will lead to the development of an assessment probe that will determine whether students consider the relationship between two quantities or just translate the problem directly. (5 minutes)

- Show Slide 19 and refer to Step 5 on the scaffold. Pass out Handout 6.36 and have participants pair up to read and discuss the five different types of selected response probes. Explain that any of these formats can be used to inform the development of a probe that assesses whether students directly translate a relationship. Show the next slide as an example of a Justified Multiple Choice probe. (5 minutes)

- Refer to Step 6 on the scaffold. Looking at the example on Slide 20, point out the prompt, distracters, and correct response that make up the first tier of a two-tiered assessment probe. Point out the justification in the second tier of the probe that asks for an explanation. (3 minutes)

- Show Slide 21 and summarize the remaining Steps 7 and 8 on the scaffold. Ask if there are any questions about the assessment probe development process before participants work in small groups to develop their own. (5 minutes)

- Show Slide 22 and explain that the CTS summary on Handout 6.35 can be used to develop other expressions and equations probes by finding additional matches between key ideas in the standards and the research on learning. Have participants work in small groups to develop a new expressions and equations probe by following the probe development process on the scaffold. Provide Handout 6.37 and explain that this worksheet can be used to track and provide a record of their work. (30 minutes)

- Provide time for participants to share their work through either a gallery walk or brief presentations to the whole group. Provide time for feedback. Feedback should include how closely the probe matches the key idea selected, whether the distracters are likely to reveal misconceptions, and the familiarity of the context and wording used. Remind participants to examine each other's probes with an eye to whether the information revealed will be useful to the teacher. Explain how the next step would involve piloting with students, revising, and then using the probe to gather data on student thinking for the purpose of informing instruction. Ask each small group to briefly discuss with one another how the student data from the probe could be used to adjust their instruction. (10 minutes)
- Conclude the session with the reflection on Slide 23.

Extension

After completing the introduction to CTS Assessment Probe Development using the expressions and equations example, this session can be extended into a 3- to 3.5-hour session by having participants develop a probe using a topic of their choice. If you are working with a group on a long-term basis, you might consider having teachers come back again after they have refined their probe, used it with students, and collected student work to examine in a subsequent session.

Facilitator Note

Assessment probe development is an iterative process that usually takes several revisions before it is in final, polished form. Make sure participants know that they are not expected to produce a final, finished product during the workshop. Rather, it is their idea for a probe that can be used to address a student learning difficulty and the experience of developing the first probe that is important.

CTS and Performance Assessment Tasks

Performance assessment involves tasks that "use one's knowledge to effectively act or bring to fruition a complex product that reveals one's knowledge and expertise" (Wiggins & McTighe, 2005, p. 346). A well-designed CTS performance task simultaneously provides an opportunity for students to (1) draw upon their existing knowledge and skills, (2) deepen their conceptual understanding of mathematics, (3) further hone their process skills, and (4) demonstrate their content understandings and ability to use mathematical practices.

Performance assessments are more challenging and complex than traditional short answer types of assessments. They require more work by the teacher to create and more effort from the student to complete. Nevertheless, teachers and students frequently prefer these types of assessments because they are engaging, have multiple entry points, require students to do mathematics, access higher level thinking skills, and allow students to demonstrate their understanding in more than one way.

CTS performance assessment tasks are designed by a teacher or teams of teachers for use in the classroom. They are usually embedded within a curricular unit as part of the teaching and learning cycle. CTS performance assessment tasks differ from other types of performance assessments in that they are used by the teacher for both instruction and assessment purposes and closely mirror the curricular and instructional context in which students are learning the ideas. They can be both formative and summative, providing an opportunity for feedback and revision as well as measuring the extent to which students have achieved a learning goal. Other types of performance assessment tasks are used for large-scale or districtwide assessment in which results are used for documenting student achievement for accountability purposes. These external summative performance assessments undergo rigorous field-testing and validity and reliability checks. Although CTS classroom-based performance assessment tasks are a vital part of classroom assessment, it is important to understand they do not undergo the same level of rigorous analysis used with their high-stakes counterparts.

CTS performance assessment tasks align with and build on the important learning goals targeted by the curriculum. They are strategically placed in a curricular unit to enhance learning and encourage students to pull their mathematics knowledge and skills together, resulting in a product or performance to "show what they know." They can range from a short activity completed within a single classroom period to longer, culminating projects that involve group work and time outside of the classroom. CTS performance tasks can be developed from scratch (with the use of CTS) or they can be adapted from certain types of instructional activities. With modification, a mathematics activity can be adapted for a performance assessment if it targets clear knowledge and skill goals and has the potential to provide evidence of the extent to which students can use the knowledge and skills to complete the task.

CTS Performance Assessment Task Design and Teacher Learning

Teacher collaboration is a major feature of CTS professional learning. Collaborative efforts to develop a classroom-based performance assessment task after engaging in the study of a curricular topic is a powerful way to apply CTS learning. At the same time it results in a standards- and research-based product that can be used in the teachers' classrooms. When teachers work together, using their CTS findings to develop performance assessment tasks, use a peer review process to give each other constructive feedback, and plan together to refine their work, they are engaged in high levels of adult learning.

After the performance tasks have been developed, teacher learning can be extended by having the teachers use their performance tasks in their classrooms and collect authentic achievement data. Teachers may choose to come together again to examine and score the student work. By examining the strengths and weaknesses in the student work, and referring back to the CTS results for "evidence-based" conversations about teaching and learning, the tasks provide ongoing data to help teachers plan for continuous improvement in helping all students achieve high standards of learning.

A CTS Process for Developing Performance Tasks

Pages 83–85 in the CTS parent book briefly describe how CTS can be used to develop performance tasks. The example provided shows how a topic study of "Symbolic Representation" was used to inform development of a task that would demonstrate students' understanding of the relationship between two given quantities and ways to represent these relationships using words, symbols, tables, and graphs. It also shows how a learning goal from the "cross-cutting" process standard of "Conjecture, Proof, and Justification" was used to explain and justify the choice of representation and choice of CD club. The teacher notes, shown in Figure 4.20 in the parent book, informed by doing the CTS, provide the background material teachers need to administer the task as well as understand the intent of the task and the instructional considerations that support readiness for students to undertake the task.

Facilitators who lead performance task development using the Understanding by Design process (Wiggins & McTighe, 2005) or similar backwards-design models may find CTS to be a powerful tool to use in their performance assessment work. In any design work undertaken by teachers, it is important to provide them with relevant resources to support their work. CTS provides a collective set of resources that are essential for developing standards- and research-based performance tasks in mathematics. Having participants do a CTS first provides a much sharper focus for aligning content, instruction, assessment, and opportunity to learn—all factors that must be considered when designing complex performance tasks that target important learning goals in mathematics.

Performance assessment provides a way for teachers to observe, give feedback on, and document how students use mathematics, not just what they know about it within discrete applications. Rich problem-based performance tasks can be developed that combine a disciplinary content CTS topic with the cross-cutting integrated and process standards CTS topics in mathematics as shown in Table 6.12.

Table 6.12 Performance Task Content

CTS Performance Assessment Tasks Combine Learning Goals From CTS Topic Categories	
Disciplinary Content From	*With Cross-Cutting Content and Processes From*
Number and Operation Algebra Geometry Measurement Data Analysis	Constancy and Change Equivalence Estimation Proportionality Modeling Conjecture, Proof, and Justification Representation Problem Solving

By doing a full study of a CTS content topic and an integrated or process topic before engaging in the design process, teachers deepen their content knowledge and better understand what is reasonable and fair to expect from students. They also have a much fuller view of the likely misconceptions or learning difficulties that might surface during the task and the kinds of instructional experiences and prior knowledge that precede the task.

CTS Performance Task Development Tools

Many grade level teams, schools, and districts are engaged in the work of developing performance assessments ranging from tasks used by teams of teachers for instructional purposes to districtwide common performance assessment tasks for benchmarking or summative assessment. It is important for leaders to first become familiar with the tools, templates, and processes their own districts and teachers are using to create performance assessment tasks and to determine how CTS can best fit into and complement the work being done in their local context.

The following tools and templates are provided for leaders to use (or adapt to fit a district context) in facilitating the development of CTS performance assessment tasks. If participants have access to computers, it is suggested that leaders provide the template electronically. These tools and templates can be found in the Chapter 6 Assessment folder in the CD-ROM:

Handout 6.38: Steps in CTS Performance Task Development

This handout outlines the steps for developing performance tasks. These steps outline the development of CTS performance assessment tasks starting with the CTS groundwork that lays the foundation to inform the development of a content and instructionally aligned task.

Handout 6.39: Criteria for Developing CTS Performance Assessment Tasks

This handout presents established criteria teachers can use as a guide to develop quality, appropriate tasks that provide an opportunity for all learners to demonstrate their knowledge and skills.

Handout 6.40: Guidelines for Drafting Scoring Guides or Rubrics for CTS Performance Tasks

This handout includes criteria for writing a scoring guide/rubric as well as suggestions for writing descriptors.

Template 1: CTS Groundwork

This blank template is used with Part 1 in Handout 6.38. The template provides space for task developers to record their CTS findings used to inform development of the task.

Template 2: CTS Task Development

This blank template is used with Part 2 in Handout 6.38. The template provides space for task developers to record ideas and track their development work as they design their task.

Template 3: CTS Performance Task Teacher Notes

This blank template is used with Step 14 in Handout 6.38. The template is used as a guide to develop the teacher notes that provide the background material on the performance task.

Introducing the CTS Performance Assessment Task Application

To introduce teachers to the CTS Performance Assessment Task Development process using the example provided in the CTS parent book, the following serves as a guide for CTS leaders. (Note: Make copies of pages 83–86, 145, and 201 in the CTS parent book if participants do not have their own copy of CTS.) Leaders are encouraged to make modifications based on the assessment experience of their group and the local context for assessment development. The times given are approximate and depend on the modifications the leader makes to fit their unique context. Overall, the introduction to the CTS process takes approximately 2 hours.

- Ask participants what the purpose of performance tasks is and how they differ from other types of assessments. Discuss their ideas and explain what a CTS performance assessment task is and how these tasks can be used in their classrooms. (Note: If working with a school or district, become familiar with the local approach to performance assessment development, such as *Understanding by Design*, and determine how CTS best fits in to that approach.) (5 minutes)
- Describe the purpose of this session. Will the session be used to introduce participants to the process of CTS Performance Task Development, using the topic and example already provided, or will they be choosing their own topics and developing their own tasks after the introduction? If you are only introducing the process, build in at least one hour to walk participants through the example. If they are going to develop their own tasks, they will need at least a half-day to develop a draft task.
- Ask participants to describe what they would look for in quality, classroom-appropriate performance assessment tasks. Review Handout 6.39: Criteria for Developing CTS Performance Assessment Tasks. Give participants time to discuss and clarify each of the criteria. Provide an opportunity for participants to examine a variety of performance tasks available through their district (*optional*) or use the example on page 85 in the CTS parent book. Look for evidence of the criteria in the sample task(s) provided.
- Distribute Handout 6.38 and explain that we will now go over each of the steps in developing a CTS performance assessment task using an example created by a middle school teacher in Maine. Use the task on page 85 in the CTS parent book so participants can connect the steps to an actual task. Point out that the process begins by doing "CTS Groundwork" to clarify the learning goal(s) being assessed and teaching and learning considerations. After Part 1, the CTS Groundwork, is completed, the task development process begins. This is consistent with the

backwards-planning model that starts with the goal and works backwards rather than starting with a task and trying to match it to a goal.

- *Step 1*: Using the "Purchasing CDs" example, explain that the first step is to identify a disciplinary content learning goal from your state standards or local curriculum that you want to assess. Refer participants to the teacher notes on page 86 of the CTS parent book and ask them to find the content goal from the Maine standards that was selected for this example task. Participants should identify *Maine Learning Results G1: Patterns Relations and Functions* "Describe and represent relationships with tables, graphs and equations." (Note: We are only looking at the Algebra goal right now. The "Reasoning" goal will come later in the process.) State how that very broad and comprehensive goal would be unrealistic to assess in one task. Ask participants what part of the learning goal was selected for assessment. Participants should respond that the goal doesn't point out which type of relationships should be represented.

- *Step 2*: The next step is to select a CTS topic guide that can be used to study the goal. Ask which guide would be the best match for this goal. Response: Symbolic Representation. (Note: Some participants may also suggest a broad topic such as Patterns, Relations, and Functions or a more narrow topic such as Linear Relationships. By having already seen the end result, the "Purchasing CDs" assessment task, these would be appropriate responses.)

- *Step 3*: Explain how Section III of the CTS topic guide is used to clarify the learning goal, specifically looking for key ideas related to symbolic representation. Refer participants to the teacher notes on page 86 in the parent CTS book to examine the key ideas that were identified to match the learning goal being assessed. Point out the bullets that describe the related representation ideas from the national standards. Briefly have them discuss how those key ideas help to clarify the state standard that was selected for assessment.

- *Steps 4 and 5*: Refer to Sections II and IV on the "Purchasing CDs" teacher notes on page 86. These two sections are combined in this example. Ask participants why they think it is important to look at instructional implications and the research on learning before developing a task. Have participants look at the three bullets and ask them to think about and discuss how they think the middle school teacher used them to inform her thinking about the task described on page 84. (10 minutes)

- *Step 6*: (Note: This step was not included in the example provided on pp. 85–86.) Explain how CTS Section V, using the *Atlas of Science Literacy*, helps the task developer consider important prerequisite ideas that students should know and build from in order to understand the targeted learning goal. If you have the *Atlas*, Vol. 1 handy, refer them to the "Symbolic Representation" map on page 117. Ask participants to identify two to three prerequisite ideas that contribute to understanding ideas related to symbolic representation (refer to map strands "alternative representations," "symbols and equations," and "working with equations" and to ideas 3–5/2a/2 and 3–5/9B/1). Discuss why it would be important for a task developer to take into account these prerequisite ideas.

- Say that this now concludes the "disciplinary content goal" groundwork necessary to clarify the content and teaching and learning considerations prior to developing the task. It also helps to tightly align the learning goal to the task so that the task asks students to do what the learning goal intends. Remind participants that CTS is sometimes called the "up-front part of backwards design." In other words, it is important to study a learning goal before working backwards from the goal to align and design instruction or assessment. Mention that Template #1 is provided to record information from the Part 1 CTS Groundwork.

- Point out Part 2: Task Development on Handout 6.38 and explain that this phase of the process involves the actual development of the task. Mention that Template #2 is provided to record information and track progress as you go through the steps in developing the task.

- *Steps 7 and 8*: Explain how this process can be used to turn some mathematics activities into performance tasks, modify or strengthen existing performance tasks, or come up with an idea to develop a task from scratch. The developer of "Purchasing CDs" used the CTS Section III idea "Relationships among quantities can be extracted from tables and graphs and represented using equations." She decided to start with the creation of the graph looking at the CTS Section IV research and finding that students often are confused by use of symbols in equations and have difficulty moving from tables and graphs to equations. She also considered the cognitive demand of the task and chose it because it matched the cognitive level of the performance verb in her state standards. Ask participants to imagine what kinds of things the teacher was considering as she reviewed these criteria with an idea for the task in mind. Ask participants to share some of their thoughts about what the teacher may have been thinking. (15 minutes)

- *Step 9*: As Table 6.12 shows, CTS performance tasks also include one or more integrated ideas or process skills that connect to the disciplinary content and can be addressed in the task. Ask participants what integrated idea or process skill was identified (answer: *Use of justification*). Refer participants to the Purchasing CDs teacher notes to see where additional CTS groundwork was done to clarify the CTS Section VI learning goal on justification. Ask them what part of the learning goal was selected (answer: *Students should be able to develop arguments to support their reasoning*).

- *Step 10*: At this point the teacher then began drafting the task. She started with an engaging scenario about various CD clubs (although with changes in technology, today one might want to change this to "music download" clubs). This phase of development starts with a "hook" or background material students need to understand the task. Have them examine the first paragraph of the Purchasing CDs task on page 85 in the parent book and discuss why it is important to start off a performance task this way.

- Task developers often choose a role or audience. Ask participants to list some of the possible roles students can assume in performance tasks (e.g., mathematicians, journalists, fashion designers, etc.) and audiences (e.g., younger children, tourists, parents, etc.). In this case, the students are asked to present their findings to another classmate.

- Now it is time to clearly describe what the task involves, what students are specifically requested to do in order to complete the task (including scaffolding steps if needed), and what the final product or performance will be. Ask participants to examine the task and discuss what it is the teacher is asking the students to do. Point out that knowing the students, their limitations, and the kind of support they need should be considered when drafting the task.

- After the task is drafted, the teacher comes up with an engaging title for the task. In this case the title is "Purchasing CDs." Ask participants to practice coming up with a different engaging title for the task.

- *Step 11*: After the first draft of the task is written, it is reviewed for accuracy and alignment with the criteria described on Handout 6.39. Modifications are made and the task is shared with colleagues for feedback. Although we don't have a record of the feedback, further modifications were made after receiving feedback from the developer's colleagues.

Facilitator Note

Since different schools, assessment systems, or programs have their own methods and requirements for designing rubrics, this guide will not specify a particular format or way to develop scoring guides or rubrics. You are encouraged to use your own techniques and templates for scoring guide/rubric development.

- *Step 12*: Whether the task is used for formative or summative purposes, a scoring guide is developed which is used to provide feedback or assess the extent to which the student met the standard set for the learning goal(s). A scoring guide or rubric was not included with the Purchasing CDs example. Ask participants what guidelines they use in their schools to draft scoring guides or rubrics for performance assessment. Provide participants with Handout 6.40: Guidelines for Drafting Scoring Guides and Rubrics (changing the language to match the words your teachers use to describe levels of proficiency and adapting it to fit the assessment context you work in if necessary).

Give participants an opportunity to review the guidelines and ask any questions regarding scoring guide or rubric development.

- *Step 13:* The last step is to write up teacher notes that would help other teachers use and understand the task. Template #3 is provided as a guide to write the teacher notes. Point out that page 86 shows an example of what CTS performance assessment task teacher notes might look like. Discuss with participants the rationale for having teacher notes and how the different sections of the teacher notes provide useful information. Ask if there is other information teachers might add to the teacher notes.

After introducing the task development process, provide time for feedback and reflection. Questions to use might include the following:

- How is this process different from the way you typically develop performance assessments?
- What value does CTS add to the development of performance assessments?
- What other questions do you have about this process?

Developing Their Own Task

After participants are introduced to the CTS performance task development application, your professional development program might include time for participants to develop their own performance task. Tasks can be developed for a CTS topic that is the focus of your professional development or topics that individuals or teams of teachers can work on together. Distribute the templates and provide time and guidance for participants to develop a draft task using the steps described in the introduction. Depending on the experience of the teachers and whether they develop a task from scratch or adapt an existing activity, you will need a minimum of 3 hours to produce a first draft. Be sure to provide time for participants to give feedback on each other's tasks using a protocol of your choosing (e.g., tuning protocol, exchanging work and using sticky notes for feedback, etc.). A timely, structured peer review process helps task developers refine their designs and provides an additional opportunity to discuss the link between the CTS results, the task, and teaching and learning. Leaders should encourage participants to give specific, descriptive feedback guided by the criteria for quality performance tasks and results of the CTS findings.

Ideally, if participants are part of an ongoing professional development group or program, and will be meeting again, encourage them to administer their tasks in their classroom and bring back samples of student work to discuss in small groups at their next meeting. The professional learning can be further extended by having teams examine the student work and do one or all of the following: (1) make adjustments to the performance task or scoring guide/rubric that will improve the use of the assessment; (2) select anchor papers that represent each of the score points on the scoring guide or rubric used for evaluation that will give teachers and students clear examples of what different levels of proficiency look like; or (3) make interpretations that reveal knowledge about their students' learning as well as their teaching and identify further actions for improvement.

By using this CTS context application to design performance assessment tasks, teachers enhance their understanding of the content being assessed as well as the implications for standards- and research-based curriculum and instruction. They understand what it really means for students to demonstrate important ideas and skills in mathematics. Although the focus is on development of the performance task, the teachers' conversations and thoughts during the development process keep linking back to CTS. By incorporating CTS as an essential part of the assessment design process, the alignment between content, curriculum, instruction, and assessment becomes much clearer and is addressed more explicitly.

OTHER EXAMPLES OF CONTEXT APPLICATIONS OF CTS

This chapter addressed the content, curricular, instructional, and assessment contexts for applying CTS. There are other contexts described throughout the CTS parent book and this *Leader's Guide*. The remainder of Chapter 4 in the CTS parent book (pp. 85–91) describes how CTS is used in the context of preservice and novice teacher support, leadership development, and professional development strategies. The next chapter addresses these contexts by providing examples of the ways CTS can be embedded in preservice courses and inservice professional development designed to support mathematics educators at various stages of the teacher continuum ranging from preservice teachers to novice teachers to experienced teachers to teacher leaders and professional developers.

7

Embedding CTS Within Professional Development Strategies

WHY USE CTS WITHIN OTHER PROFESSIONAL DEVELOPMENT STRATEGIES?

A major theme of the preceding chapters is that curriculum topic study (CTS) is a professional development strategy that helps teachers develop their important professional knowledge base in mathematics and supports and helps focus learning on the standards and research to improve curriculum, instruction, and assessment. This last chapter addresses how CTS fits into and enhances many *other* professional development strategies that are used to improve mathematics teaching and learning. The chapter provides guidelines for using CTS as a component or activity within six other specific professional development strategies, including Application 1: Study Groups or Professional Learning Communities; Application 2: Collaborative Inquiry Into Examining Student Thinking; Application 3: Video Demonstration Lessons; Application 4: CTS and Case Discussion; Application 5: CTS Seminars; and Application 6: CTS Mentoring and Coaching.

We include these guidelines and designs for embedding the use of CTS into specific professional development strategies because they all involve teachers making judgments and decisions about what is quality mathematics instruction and learning. To do so effectively, teachers use CTS findings as evidence to inform their judgments and decisions. For example, if teachers are engaged in using the professional development strategy demonstration lessons, a teacher conducts or videotapes a classroom lesson that other teachers observe and later discuss. The observing teachers usually meet before they do the observation to discuss the goals and intent of the lesson they will observe and meet again following the observation to debrief the experience (Loucks-Horsley, Stiles, Mundry, Love, & Hewson, 2010). A critical element for the success of this strategy is that all of the teachers involved are prepared to observe for whether and how the important mathematics content knowledge is developed in the lesson and to judge the appropriateness of the activities or mathematics problems for the students in the classroom, so that they gain insights for their own classroom practice. Yet some groups using demonstration lessons have found it difficult to build a consensus of what to look for in the lessons and develop conclusions, lessons learned, and next steps for their own lessons. In these cases, observers may focus on and notice different things they are interested in (e.g., how the teacher is using groups, what is displayed on the classroom walls, who seems to be engaged or not engaged), rather than focus specifically on the mathematics in the lesson, how it is developed, what activities are chosen to show the mathematics and why they are chosen, and how the teacher elicits what students know and understand and addresses misconceptions. Embedding CTS in the process of planning for and debriefing demonstration lessons is an ideal way for the teachers to come to a shared understanding of what concepts or ideas the students should be learning from the lesson and the ways a teacher might probe for and address students' prior knowledge and misconceptions or difficulties to increase the chances that the students learn what is intended.

Likewise, a group of teachers using the professional development strategy examining student work and thinking may have the same challenge: What evidence of learning should they look for in the students' work? What are the most important mathematical concepts students should know? What do the students understand? Given what they understand, what would be a next step for the students in terms of their mathematics learning? Examining student work is a strategy for teacher learning and school improvement that is widely used in schools organized as professional learning communities, in schools that use student work as part of an intervention program, and in grade-level teams. The purpose is for teachers to increase their pedagogical content knowledge by examining students' work carefully and reflecting on what students understand, noting misconceptions or difficulties they have, and identifying what instructional strategies would support further learning (Loucks-Horsley et al., 2010). Productive examinations of student work or thinking requires teachers to clarify and understand the mathematics content students should know at their particular grade level and recognize common difficulties students face.

Examining the standards and research on learning through the CTS process before examining student work provides teachers with several advantages. When teachers use CTS as part of their strategy for examining student work, they often conduct a topic study even before they gather the student work. The results of the topic study inform the questions or assessment prompts they use to gather the student work. This ensures that the assessments they use directly address worthwhile mathematics ideas (according to the standards) and they can adequately probe for whether their students have any of the common misunderstandings discussed in the research. Later, as teachers examine student work, they can see what important mathematics content students understand as well as where they have difficulty. Furthermore, teachers can use CTS to consider the instructional implications cited in the standards and research for teaching the mathematics topic, which can then inform how they may modify or adapt their instruction to improve student understanding. Embedding CTS activities into any of these professional development designs will increase the focus on the mathematics content in the standards and research on how students learn mathematics.

CTS AND PROFESSIONAL LEARNING COMMUNITIES

Many of the professional development strategies included in this chapter are ones that are "job-embedded" or that take place in the course of teachers' regular work day as opposed to "pull-out" professional development where teachers attend courses or institutes on their own time and outside of school. Both types of professional development are important and serve different purposes. Increasingly, the more ongoing and "job-embedded" strategies are used in schools organized as "collaborative or professional learning communities." These types of organizational structures value and support ongoing teacher collaboration in the service of learning—for students *and* staff. Professional learning communities come in many shapes and sizes, with some focused on constant assessment and interventions in the classroom, others on intensive improvement of lessons, action research to collect evidence of learning in the classroom, and other strategies (Mundry & Stiles, 2009). One way to encourage the ongoing use of CTS in teachers' work, whether it be planning for the classroom or enhancing their professional knowledge base, is for the continued development of such professional cultures among teachers that use standards and research to inform practice. We have advocated for many years a halt to one-shot, one-size-fits-all professional development and a redirection of resources toward more ongoing teacher learning and organizational arrangements in schools that support teachers to collaborate on practice. Learning Forward (formerly the National Staff Development Council) and other key education groups now advocate for professional learning that is grounded in practice, builds professional community, and is sustained over time because evidence suggests that schools with strong culture, trust, and community are more successful (National Staff Development Council [NSDC], 2001; Wei, Darling-Hammond, Andree, Richardson, & Orphanos, 2009). We are heartened by the growing recognition and evidence that schools organized as learning communities can make substantial changes in practice and improve learning, and we see CTS as a tool that can make the work of these professional communities more grounded in learning content and studying research and the standards.

In the newly released standards for professional development, Learning Forward posits that "the most powerful forms of staff development occur in ongoing teams that meet on a regular basis, preferably several times a week, for the purposes of learning, joint lesson planning, and problem solving. These teams, often called learning communities or communities of practice, operate with a commitment to the norms of continuous improvement and experimentation and engage their members in improving their daily work to advance the achievement of school district and school goals for student learning" (Learning Forward, 2011, "Learning Communities").

DuFour, Eaker, and DuFour (2005) defined several characteristics of professional learning communities. The first is a *focus on learning* where faculty members are committed to meeting clearly defined student learning goals and continuously work to improve results. We contend that it is very difficult for faculty to develop a productive focus on learning unless they have a solid grounding in the standards and research and are able to draw upon their professional knowledge to inform their deliberations and practice. In settings that lack such a foundation, faculty may say they have a "focus on learning," but they may be focusing on the wrong learning goals or strategies. CTS is a basic tool used by professional learning communities to ensure that the faculty are consulting the standards and research to inform what the important content for their focus on learning should be and the research that describes students' commonly held ideas related to that content.

Another characteristic of professional learning communities is that they have a *collaborative culture focused on learning*. Teams plan instructional interventions, gather and examine evidence of student learning, and reflect on what they are learning. For these collaborations to yield the desired results, it is essential that faculty members are able to engage in productive dialogue, including speaking from the evidence that comes from examining the standards and research, not just from their own opinions. Topic studies provide teachers with ample practice using "CTS talk," where teachers use their CTS findings to support their claims about teaching and learning.

Staff in professional learning communities also engage in *collective inquiry*, where they routinely ask themselves how well their students are achieving the desired outcomes, and what teachers and students need to learn or do next to be more successful. CTS can be particularly helpful in informing those next steps. When groups of teachers see students struggle to solve problems or master mathematical ideas, CTS can help them to become aware of research showing the common difficulties that students may face or developmental issues related to learning mathematics, and get ideas for how to effectively move students from where they are in their conceptual and procedural understanding to where they need to be. They may also need to step back from the specific idea with which students are struggling and trace the development of that idea back through the grades to discover what it is that might be the missing knowledge in the students' mathematical understanding. These are just a few examples of how CTS can enrich the work, dialogue, and decisions of teachers who work in professional learning communities, opening up new doors into understanding their own teaching that they may never have encountered without access to the professional resources and process for using them provided through CTS.

This chapter provides guidelines and materials that can be very applicable to making the work of professional learning communities productive and results oriented. For example, they can apply the guidelines for using study groups to identify and tackle a student learning problem or work together to choose an area of mathematics content that the group wants to study together to strengthen. The group could also use the guidelines in this chapter for using video-demonstration lessons or case discussion to study and improve practice or use the design for collaboratively examining student thinking (CIEST) to inquire into student learning. Professional learning communities provide the vehicle through which many of these CTS professional development strategies can be implemented. Regardless of what your professional development structure is, CTS is a versatile process that can be embedded within most teacher professional development ranging from a simple one-day workshop or seminars to the long-range, ongoing work of professional learning communities. The following sections illustrate the ways you can use CTS within specific professional development applications. Table 7.1 lists the many professional development strategies that can be strengthened by embedding them with the CTS process. How you would use CTS within each of these strategies will vary depending on your purposes and the focus of your particular work. Therefore, the guidelines in this chapter also vary widely. For some of the professional development strategies, we provide actual session designs including a facilitator script, PowerPoint slides, and handouts to invite you to replicate what we have done with specific groups. For others, we provide a general discussion and guidelines for using CTS with a professional development strategy and offer tools and protocols that we have used for you to adapt for your own use. (See Chapter 7 folder on the CD-ROM at the back of this book.)

Table 7.1 Enhancing Professional Development Strategies With CTS

Professional Development Strategies (Loucks-Horsley et al., 2010)	Description	How CTS Enhances
Curriculum alignment and selection	Teams of teachers and administrators from appropriate grade levels analyze the content, student learning activities, instructional methods, and teacher background information and assessment strategies within their instructional materials to select what materials to use with their students and ensure that their materials are aligned with standards.	Teams of teachers and administrators use the CTS results to identify the accuracy of the content in their instructional materials as compared with the CTS resources; how well the materials reflect the learning goals for their grade level suggested in the standards; if the learning strategies in their materials are aligned with the instructional implications from the standards; and how well the assessment activities are designed to uncover students' prior knowledge and any misunderstandings.
Curriculum implementation	Teachers are oriented to new curriculum or instructional materials that they will use with students. They learn how concepts are developed and the math content within the materials by engaging in selected lessons themselves as learners. They examine how they will use the lessons in the classroom, including reflecting on how their students will learn through the activities; and they practice and get feedback on how to implement the activities in their own classrooms.	Teachers conduct a CTS on topics within their new curriculum to identify how the concepts develop from lesson to lesson and grade to grade and if there are gaps that need to be filled. They examine the units and the lessons within the curriculum to see how they align with the standards and research and identify any modifications needed. Teachers review the assessments to identify how well they uncover students' understanding of important mathematics and make adjustments as needed.
Partnerships with mathematicians or mathematics faculty from local colleges	Mathematicians or mathematics faculty and teachers collaborate to enhance content knowledge through research projects or immersion in a real-world mathematics application such as a statistical modeling.	CTS provides invaluable support for mathematics professionals who are working with teachers. The mathematicians can complete a CTS to develop understanding of the learning goals for K–12. This can help them support teachers to connect what they are learning to what they can bring back to their own teaching.

(Continued)

Table 7.1 (Continued)		
Professional Development Strategies (Loucks-Horsley et al., 2010)	*Description*	*How CTS Enhances*
Study groups	Study groups are collaborative groups of educators who convene regularly to examine specific problems or topics related to teaching and learning. Book study groups focus on reading a professional book and connecting its contents to their own practice.	CTS findings can guide study groups as they examine instructional tools and methods to improve student learning. The study groups can explore what research says are common difficulties or misconceptions students have in mathematics. Study groups can investigate which students in their schools are having similar difficulties or misunderstandings and develop strategies to address them.
Action research	Teachers conduct classroom-based research to investigate students' learning and the impact of particular instructional strategies through observation, data collection and analysis, and reflection on results.	Teachers conduct a curriculum topic study to inform their action research question, decide what data would constitute evidence of student learning, and interpret findings.
Case discussions	Groups of teachers review and discuss a case of teaching (written or video) designed to provoke discussion and reflection on practice.	Teachers conduct a CTS on the topic covered in the case to inform their analysis of the case. They explore the extent to which the case reflects the standards and research in the CTS findings and derive learning about what actions they can take in their own practice.
Examining student work and thinking	Groups of teachers examine student responses to prompts or test items to move beyond just knowing if students got the right answer to being able to identify what students know and understand and identify next steps to deepen understanding.	CTS findings provide a shared understanding of what to look for in student work, e.g., what key ideas and learning goals are most important for student to know. Teachers use CTS to assess whether students understand key ideas, hold misconceptions, or are lacking understanding of important precursor knowledge.

Professional Development Strategies (Loucks-Horsley et al., 2010)	Description	How CTS Enhances
Lesson study	Groups of teachers meet over long periods of time to develop, try out, and refine lessons. Teachers consult research and instructional materials, discuss effective practice, and observe the lessons to gather data on needed refinements.	Lesson study groups use CTS to enhance lessons so that they reflect the research on how students learn. Teachers conduct CTS on the topics of the lessons or unit and then make modifications to the lessons that reflect the research. They speak from the evidence found in the CTS to inform their lesson design. They use CTS findings to inform the observation of the lesson and suggest adjustments as needed.
Immersion in content and immersion in problem solving	Groups of teachers participate in multiple-day sessions led by mathematics content experts, to learn mathematics content for teaching at their own grade level or to develop their adult-level math knowledge.	CTS can clarify the learning targets for the adult learners in the session. The instructors can consult the topics the immersion will address to clarify what a 12th-grade graduate would be expected to know. They also can consult the sections on research to find the common confusions or misunderstandings that people encounter when learning the topic.
Coaching	A teacher and an instructional coach collaborate to enhance classroom practice through observation and feedback. Most coaching involves a pre- and postconference and classroom observation of a particular teaching technique, grouping strategies, student-teacher interaction, or other topics of interest to the teacher.	The coach and the teacher with whom the coach is working conduct a CTS on the topic of the lesson prior to planning the lesson. They incorporate CTS findings by ensuring that the key ideas and learning goals from the CTS are reflected in the lesson and that assessment strategies uncover any student misconceptions and ways of addressing them.

(Continued)

Table 7.1   (Continued)

Professional Development Strategies (Loucks-Horsley et al., 2010)	Description	How CTS Enhances
Demonstration lessons	A teacher conducts a classroom lesson that is videotaped or other teachers observe. The demonstrating and observing teachers meet before the observation to discuss the goals and intent of the lesson and again following the observation to debrief the experience.	The demonstrating and observing teachers conduct a CTS prior to the demonstration to gain a shared idea of what learning goals should be targeted in the lesson and what prior knowledge students need. They identify the instructional implications suggested in the standards and use these to inform their observations. As they debrief the lesson, they explore how the lesson did or did not reflect the standards and research found in the CTS and what can be done to enhance the lesson.
Mentoring	New teachers are assigned a more experienced teacher to provide them with support and guidance about the school, instructional strategies, and the content they teach.	Mentors teach the CTS process to their mentees so that whenever new teachers have a question about content, they can turn to the CTS resources to find answers. Mentors meet with the new teachers to discuss the CTS findings and how they apply to their instruction.
Developing professional developers/leaders	Staff developers and teacher leaders learn to facilitate professional development activities such as study groups, lesson study, and mentoring, to examine student work, or to lead specific institutes, courses, and workshops.	Teacher leaders and staff developers conduct a CTS on the topics they are covering in professional development. They use the findings to design their professional development activities and may include CTS introductory sessions in their work with teachers so the teachers can learn how to access the standards and research any time on their own.
Workshops, institutes, courses, and seminars	Teachers participate in structured sessions lasting from a half-day to weeks or months to learn mathematics content or instructional strategies.	Leaders conduct a CTS on the main topics of their workshops/courses prior to designing their sessions. They use the findings to build in activities and content that is aligned with standards and research. They lead CTS introductory sessions or full topic studies in their workshops or courses to develop teachers' understanding of the standards and research on the topics they teach.

CTS Professional Development Strategy Application 1
Study Groups and Professional Learning Communities

DESCRIPTION OF CTS STUDY GROUPS AND PROFESSIONAL LEARNING COMMUNITIES AS A CTS PROFESSIONAL DEVELOPMENT STRATEGY

Through the professional development strategy of study groups teachers engage in regular, structured, and collaborative interactions about topics identified by the study group of interest to them for improving student learning (Loucks-Horsley, Stiles, Mundry, Love, & Hewson, 2010). A key feature of study groups is that they provide opportunities to study research, gather information, examine resources, and decide how to apply what they learn through their study to classroom practice. Schools that are organized as professional learning communities (PLCs) often engage in collaborative work that is very similar to how a study group operates. For example, PLCs, like study groups, work together to research how students best learn specific content or investigate how to use new specific instructional approaches, or they may read and discuss professional books to inform practice. Murphy and Lick (2001) developed the model of whole-faculty study groups, where the purpose is to create study groups that are focused on student learning, which parallels how PLCs work. They defined the study group as "a small number of individuals joining together to increase their capacity through new learning for the direct benefit of students" (p. 10). Schools organized in PLCs are also very similar to study groups that focus on setting learning goals, tracking student progress, and intervening to ensure successful learning for all.

Study groups have been used to lead whole school improvement, to guide the implementation of new curriculum materials, or simply to read and discuss professional literature. In a CTS study group, each of these purposes is tied to studying a mathematics topic. CTS study groups can also form for the purpose of meeting on a regular basis to do curriculum studies on different curricular topics selected by the group. The following are more than a dozen ideas for applying CTS in a study group or PLC:

1. Find and share examples of lessons that address the instructional implication identified in CTS Section II.

2. Examine student work using a protocol such as the CTS CIEST (Collaborative Inquiry Into Examining Student Thinking). See Application 2 in this chapter on pages 206–215.

3. Use formative assessment probes observational data (from observing in each other's classrooms), interviews, audiotapes, and videotapes of student learning to examine students' thinking for commonly held ideas identified in CTS Section IV.

4. Clarify performance indicators or other learning goals from CTS Section VI to ensure consistency in targeted learning goals.

5. Engage in a full CTS or a partial study to examine whether instructional materials used or under consideration for purchase include the teaching of the important ideas reflected in the standards.

6. Share strategies used in the classroom to have students demonstrate their learning of key ideas identified in CTS Sections III, V, and VI.

7. Share and demonstrate elicitation strategies that can be used to uncover students' existing conceptions before instruction and compare students' ideas to those identified in the research from CTS Section IV.

8. Design a lesson or modify an existing one based on CTS findings and the instructional design suggestions described in Chapter 4 of the CTS parent book.

> See Keeley & Rose, 2011; Rose & Arline, 2009; Rose, Arline, & Minton, 2007; and Rose Tobey & Minton, 2011, for sources of probes and strategies for elicitation.

9. Design a common assessment to be used by the study group based on district assessment protocols and an analysis of the targeted student learning goal(s) from CTS Sections III, V, and VI.

10. Identify, discuss, and practice strategies that help develop students' abilities to develop and use mathematical ideas across the disciplines (e.g., mathematics and science).

11. Investigate ways to increase students' motivation and engagement in mathematics by examining key ideas using CTS Sections III, V, and VI and strategizing ways to make the content more accessible and relevant to students.

12. Video a lesson using the CTS Video Demonstration Lesson protocol and share and discuss with the group how to improve the lesson, based on CTS. See Application 3 in this chapter on pages 216–223.

13. Use CTS findings to inform a discussion of a case of mathematics teaching. Use published case studies that describe a decision point or dilemma faced in the classroom or address content that is rife with student difficulties or misconceptions (e.g., computation with fractions). See sources for print or video cases listed on pages 228–229. Teachers can also write their own "cases" of when they saw students struggle or run into difficulty learning a specific mathematical idea and what they did to address it.

14. View and discuss videos of teaching and student learning available through the Annenberg collection at www.learner.org or Success at the Core (www.successatthecore.com). Use CTS to look for evidence of how the lesson reflects standards and research on learning.

15. Gain a deeper knowledge of particular mathematics content by teaching each other, using Sections I and III of the CTS guides.

16. Use the *Atlas of Science Literacy*, Vol. 1 and Vol. 2, and CTS Section V to examine connections among mathematical ideas and plan for increased curriculum coherence.

17. Use data from formative student assessment to identify content students are having difficulty learning. Conduct a CTS on these topics and investigate how the findings from Section II instructional implications and Section V research on learning might inform changes in instructional practice.

GOALS OF A CTS STUDY GROUP OR PLC

The goals of a CTS study group or PLC are to

- engage teachers in accessing new information, resources, and research that address student learning needs,

- deepen teachers' understanding of research and standards related to the mathematics topic of interest to them or that their students have difficulty learning, and
- apply the CTS findings to identify an effective instructional method or material to address a student learning need.

AUDIENCE

Using the CTS study group or PLC design is appropriate for any grade level but is best for teachers who can focus on similar content and grade levels.

STRUCTURE OF THE CTS STUDY GROUP OR PLC

This CTS strategy uses a protocol consisting of eight steps summarized as follows. You can use these steps to facilitate a CTS study group or PLC. A scaffold (Handout 7.1.1) guides study group members through each of the steps. All handouts can be found on the CD-ROM in the Chapter 7 Study Groups folder.

Step 1: Review Group Norms

Clarify the standards of behavior that your study group or PLC will use and if you do not already have a norm to "speak from the evidence," add that norm to your list. (Consult tips for establishing other norms for your group in Chapter 3 of this *Leader's Guide*.)

> **Facilitator Note**
>
> This scaffold is based on the work of Murphy and Lick (2001), modified to focus on embedding CTS within an existing study group. For more information on establishing whole-faculty study groups, see Murphy and Lick.

Step 2: Identify Student Needs in Mathematics

As a group, set a goal for the area(s) of mathematics education in which you would like to make improvements in student learning. Existing PLC groups already have clear goals for what they expect students to learn and track student progress to know where students are experiencing difficulties. These can be the need areas the group focuses on. Or, if that information is not yet available to the group, use local or state assessment results to inform your selection of goals for improved mathematics learning. For example, if your study group is composed of teachers who teach the same grade level, identify a particular topic for your grade level for which you would like to learn more about ways to enhance learning. If you are a schoolwide team, you may wish to study a combination of topics to see what students should be learning across multiple grades. If you are a districtwide team examining end-of-course studies, you may be interested in better understanding what all 12th-grade graduates should know. Handout 7.1.2 is an example of a planning template that can be used by study group members to plan what they will do during their study, the CTS guides they will use, the local or state standards they will target, and the data sources they will examine to identify areas for improvement in learning (Murphy & Lick, 2001).

Step 3: Elicit Prior Knowledge

Provide time for the group members to surface their prior knowledge about the mathematics topic and what they know about effective teaching and learning and difficulties related to learning the topic. (You can use a tool such as the KWL or other elicitation strategies.) Use this knowledge as a base to build from as you explore the CTS findings or challenge prior assumptions about teaching and learning the topic(s).

Step 4: Study Research, Standards, and Other Information

Identify the CTS guide(s) most relevant for the goal(s) established in Step 2. If your group needs a primer on how to find the right study guide (or section if you are doing only partial studies), you can use the Introduction to CTS Scaffold activity in Module A1 in Chapter 4 to practice. (See Handout A1.5 in Module A1.) Use readings from the guides to do the following:

1. Clarify the adult content knowledge associated with this area for mathematics improvement (CTS Section I),

2. Clarify the learning targets (CTS Sections III and VI),

3. Examine the curricular and instructional implications (CTS Sections II and V), and

4. Identify the common student misconceptions or difficulties (CTS Section IV).

Handout 7.1.3 provides an example of a recording sheet you might use with a study group or PLC to record the findings from each CTS section and how they might be used to address the identified student-learning problem. Select at least one reading strategy and a report out strategy from Chapter 3 of this *Leader's Guide* for use by the study group.

Step 5: Investigate Effective Instructional Methods or Materials

In this step, based on what the group learned from the CTS, it will identify and select some new instructional method(s) or materials or modify ones already in use to address the student learning need. Examine the methods or materials and discuss (1) how they link to the CTS findings and (2) why you would use them with their students. Encourage participants to take time to reflect on the session—what they learned and what they will try out with students back in the classroom.

Step 6: Use New or Adapted Instructional Methods and Materials

Discuss how the group will use the new or adapted methods or materials in the classroom and what evidence of student learning you will look for to provide evidence the new methods are enhancing learning. Evidence can consist of student work, common assessment scores, observations, anecdotes from students, videos, or even observations made by group members who observed the other members teaching a lesson.

Step 7: Collect Evidence of Learning

Collect evidence to bring back to the study group to show how the new or adapted methods or materials worked with the students and what might need to be adjusted in order to be more effective.

Step 8: Reflect on Results and Decide Next Steps for New Topics to Study

Reflect on how CTS informed changes in teaching and learning, including how well the new or adapted methods or materials worked with students and what your next steps are to sustain new practices that are working. Discuss modifications one might make to further improve the instruction. Decide on new topics to investigate by returning to Step 2 of the protocol and repeating the cycle.

OTHER RESOURCE MATERIALS FOR STUDY GROUP LEADERS

CTS study group and PLC members may wish to take turns completing a log to document the work of their group. An example of a log is provided on Handout 7.1.4. Time to meet and lack of incentives can pose barriers to forming and sustaining study groups and PLCs. Handout 7.1.5 offers suggestions for finding time for groups to meet and incentives to encourage participation. Handout 7.1.6 provides procedural suggestions for setting up and maintaining a CTS study group or PLC.

To introduce the use of CTS in study groups or PLCs, facilitators may wish to set up a "Mock Study Group" by choosing a student learning problem in mathematics and using Handout 7.1.1, the CTS Study Group or PLC Scaffold, to guide participants through an imaginary study group meeting in which participants will engage in CTS and use the results of their study to plan for ways to address the identified learning problem.

CTS Professional Development Strategy Application 2
Collaborative Inquiry Into Examining Student Thinking (CIEST)

DESCRIPTION OF CIEST AS A CTS PROFESSIONAL DEVELOPMENT STRATEGY

CIEST is a collaborative process that combines three elements: CTS, student work from assessment probes, and a tool called data-driven dialogue (Lipton & Wellman, 2004). As shown in Figure 7.1, the overlap of these three elements results in a process that deeply engages teachers in constructing a deeper understanding of students' thinking for the purpose of improving students' opportunities to learn important ideas in mathematics.

CIEST differs from other strategies for looking at student work because the primary focus is not to examine student work for the extent to which students have achieved a learning goal and are scored on their proficiency. Instead, CIEST is designed to examine students' thinking for formative purposes, often before instruction even targets a learning goal. It uses assessment probes that uncover students' ideas before, throughout, or even years after instruction. The assessment probes are designed to reveal students' commonly held ideas noted in the research in CTS Section IV and related to specific ideas in the standards as described in CTS Section III. The process helps teachers think about the actions they can take in their classrooms or curricular contexts to address students' commonly held ideas related to a concept they teach. Teachers work collaboratively to construct meaning around the ideas students bring to their learning and analyze data in order to inform curricular and instructional decisions.

Figure 7.1　Three Elements of CIEST

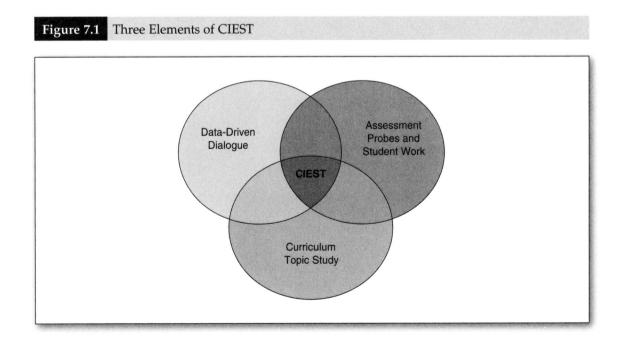

Schools are increasingly moving to use ongoing collaborative arrangements such as PLCs and study groups, where teachers learn together and make improvements in practice. Although research suggests these collegial arrangements can lead to improved outcomes (Lee, Smith, & Croninger, 1995; Marks, Louis, & Printy, 2000; McLaughlin & Talbert, 2001), we caution that success will depend on how well teachers build the norms, tools, and protocols to focus on learning. Collaborative inquiry is a powerful and increasingly popular way teachers are reflecting on their practice and student learning and making adjustments to improve outcomes. They use data and reflective dialogue to come to a shared understanding of student learning problems and agree on potential solutions to test out in the classroom (Love, Stiles, Mundry, & DiRanna, 2008). Although teachers certainly examine their own students' work and thinking quite often, the nature of collaborative inquiry changes the focus to also enhancing teacher learning, not just student learning. Teachers become very good at interpreting students' thinking and ideas and using what they learn to inform their instruction. This process uses an approach called data-driven dialogue (Lipton & Wellman, 2003; Love et al., 2008), which is a four-phase process in which (1) a team of teachers *predicts* what they will see in data; (2) then they *go visual* by looking at the raw data as a group; (3) they state facts that they *observe* in the data, sticking to just the facts; and (4) then they *infer* or *ask questions* of the data (see Figure 7.2). This process grounds everyone in the facts and data, before they jump to inferences.

GOALS OF A CIEST SESSION

The goals of this session are to

- learn about a CTS professional development strategy for collaboratively examining student thinking,
- practice using the CIEST protocol with a sample of student work, and
- consider how you might use the CIEST strategy and CTS developed probes to examine student thinking in your own work.

Figure 7.2	Data-Driven Dialogue

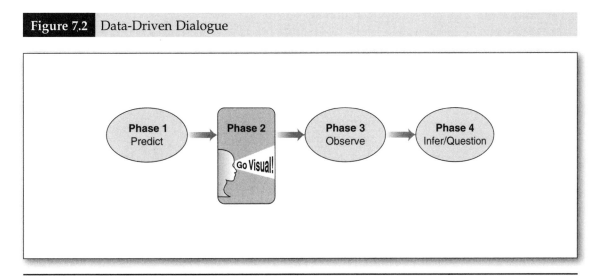

Source: Adapted from Lipton, L., & Wellman, B. (2003). *Data-Driven Dialogue: A Facilitator's Guide to Collaborative Inquiry.* Sherman, CT: MiraVia, LLC. In Love, N., Stiles, K. E., Mundry, S., and DiRanna, K. (2008). *The Data Coach's Guide to Improving Learning for All Students: Unleashing the Power of Collaborative Inquiry.* Thousand Oaks, CA: Corwin Press.

AUDIENCE

CIEST is appropriate for any grade level and can be conducted with mixed grade levels looking at samples of student work from different grade levels or with same-grade-level groups. This session uses a seventh-grade example of student work to introduce participants to the process, making it accessible to both elementary and high school teachers in the group, and is appropriate for introducing the process. Once the audience has learned the CIEST process, they can gather their own student work and use the process to focus on their own students.

STRUCTURE OF A CIEST SESSION

The CIEST session uses a protocol consisting of ten steps broken into four parts summarized below. A CIEST Scaffold (see Handout 7.2.1 in the Chapter 7 CIEST folder of the CD-ROM) guides participants through each of the steps.

CIEST PROTOCOL

Part One: Groundwork (Prior to Looking at Student Work)

- Establishing group norms
- Examining and completing the probe
- Clarifying the content
- Using CTS Sections III and VI to identify related ideas in the standards
- Sharing assumptions about how students might respond

Part Two: Examining Student Thinking

- Sorting and tallying Tier 1 responses
- Sorting and organizing students' reasoning
- Displaying the data (go visual)

Part Three: Analyzing the Data

- Analysis of data from student work
- Examining commonly held ideas from the research (CTS Section IV)
- Comparing research findings to data from student work
- Examining coherence (CTS Section V) and instructional implications (CTS Section II)

Part Four: Integrating Data From Student Work and CTS Findings

- Drawing inferences, making conclusions, and offering explanations
- Examining new understanding of students, student thinking, curriculum, and instruction
- Group and individual reflection

Time

A full introductory CIEST session requires approximately 3 hours.

MATERIALS AND PREPARATION

Materials Needed by Facilitator

CTS Parent Book

Mathematics Curriculum Topic Study: Bridging the Gap Between Standards and Practice (Keeley & Rose, 2006), or copies of the CTS guide "Probability" on page 182 of that book.

Resource Books

CTS selected resources or copies made of selected readings from CTS guide (include the *Atlas*, Vol. 1, map on Statistical Reasoning with a focus on the "Probability" strand, if available).

State or Local Curriculum Framework or Standards

If you are working with a group from the same district, copy sections of the local curriculum frameworks or standards that address probability for the CTS Section VI readings. Facilitators may wish to include the *Common Core State Standards for Mathematics* or the NCTM *Focal Points*.

PowerPoint Presentation

The PowerPoint presentation is located in the Chapter 7 CIEST folder on the CD-ROM. Review it and tailor it to your needs and audience as needed. Insert your date and location on Slide 1, add additional graphics as desired, and add your own contact information on the last slide. (Adapt slides and script described below if you are not using the "Gumballs in a Jar" probe.)

Supplies and Equipment

- Computer and LCD projector to show PowerPoint presentation
- Flipchart easel, pads, and markers (each table group will need at least one sheet of chart paper and one to two markers)
- Paper for participants to take notes
- Sticky notes for notes and marking charts

Wall Charts

- Prepare a bar graph wall chart of PowerPoint Slide 17 if whole group is using the Gumballs in a Jar probe. (Substitute your own visual if you are using a different probe for student work.)

Facilitator Preparation

- PowerPoint slides for CIEST (in Chapter 7 folder on CD-ROM). Insert your own graphics and additional information as desired. (Optional: Print out copies of the PowerPoint slides for participants.)
- Conduct your own "Probability" CTS prior to leading the session.
- Prepare an evaluation form to collect feedback from participants.

Materials Needed for Participants

(*Note:* All handouts can be found in the Chapter 7 folder CIEST on the CD-ROM.)

- Handout 7.2.1: CIEST Scaffold
- Handout 7.2.2: Gumballs in a Jar Assessment Probe (or substitute your own assessment probe)

Facilitator Note

You can substitute copies of your own student work from two-tiered assessment probes. (Go to www.corwin.com or www .uncoveringstudentideas.org for information on the *Uncovering Student Thinking in Mathematics* series, a source of CTS-developed assessment probes, or create your own probe using the assessment design process described in Chapter 4 of the CTS parent book or pp. 179–185 in this book.)

- Handout 7.2.3: Gumballs in a Jar Cards (cut and placed in plastic bags or envelopes for each small group of three to four participants)
- Handout 7.2.4 Gumballs in a Jar Explanation

DIRECTIONS FOR FACILITATING CIEST

The following directions describe how to lead an introductory CIEST session for first-timers using the *Gumballs in a Jar* (Grade 7) example. If you use a different probe, substitute your probe in the directions and make modifications to Slides 12, 14, 15, 17, 18, and 21.

Introducing CIEST (10 minutes)

Show Slides 1 and 2. Welcome the participants and explain that this session will introduce them to a CTS professional development strategy called CIEST—Collaborative Inquiry Into Examining Student Thinking. This process will engage them in using CTS to enhance inquiry into student ideas and thinking. Review the goals on Slide 2.

Show Slide 3. Describe how CIEST is used to examine student thinking for the purpose of informing curriculum and instruction. It differs from other ways of looking at student work since the assessments used are often not summative in nature and the emphasis is on examining thinking rather than determining proficiency and scoring the student work.

Show Slide 4 and suggest that there is great benefit to working with others to share insights and engage in collaborative inquiry. Point out that one tool that supports collaborative inquiry is the use of a protocol. Show Slide 5 and give participants a few minutes to activate their prior knowledge about protocols and discuss their use. Show Slides 6 and 7, explaining what a protocol is and why we use protocols in professional development.

Facilitator Note

The assessment probes in these books were developed using the CTS process. However, you can also develop and use your own CTS probes. The process for developing them is described in Chapter 4 of the CTS parent book (facilitators may also want to use the process described in this book on pp. 179–185).

Show Slide 8 and describe how the CIEST protocol combines three elements: CTS, assessment probes and student work, and data-driven dialogue. Data-driven dialogue allows us to move away from our opinions and inferences and speak from the student data and CTS findings. We use assessment probes to generate examples of student thinking that often match findings from cognitive research. We use CTS to make our analysis of student work research- and standards-based. Show Slide 9 to describe the resources and tools we will be using. Explain that the *Gumballs in a Jar* assessment probe we will use in this session comes from *Uncovering Student Thinking in Mathematics* (Rose, Arline, & Minton, 2007) (point to the book on the slide or hold up a copy if you have one).

Refer everyone to Handout 7.2.1—CIEST Scaffold. Say this will be our step-by-step process for engaging in collaborative inquiry to examine student thinking. Give everyone a minute to look it over.

Step 1: Establish Norms (5 minutes)

Show Slide 10. Say we will start at Step 1 by developing norms for our group. Ask the group to take 1 minute to brainstorm norms they would like to guide their work together.

Have a cofacilitator or volunteer write the norms on chart paper as they are offered. Then ask the group if there are any additions. Add one more, "sticking to the protocol," if it isn't already there, and discuss ways the group can monitor to make sure they stay on track. Post the norms where everyone can see them throughout the session. Remind everyone to take responsibility for "enforcing" the norms in their small group work.

Facilitator Note

If anyone seems confused, offer an example of a norm such as "avoid vague terms and clarify meaning" or "begin and end on time." Ask for one suggestion from each table (going around the room quickly).

Step 2: Examine and Complete the Probe (10 minutes)

Show Slide 11 and move to Step 2 of the protocol. Pass out Handout 7.2.2: Gumballs in a Jar Assessment Probe. Ask everyone to complete the probe and jot down the notes requested on the slide. In case you have a mixed group with some participants who may not be comfortable with the mathematics content, let them know they will not need to make their answers public. Show the probe on Slide 12 and be sure everyone understands the task. Allow 5 minutes to work on the probe, using the questions on Slide 11.

Facilitator Note

The facilitator will have to pay close attention to whether the participants follow the steps of the protocol. Ask them to stick to the scaffold and refrain from sharing stories about their own students or making suggestions for how to fix the problem. Remind everyone there will be time for that later, but for now, they should stick to the protocol!

Step 3: Probe Clarification and Standards Groundwork (15 minutes)

Show Slide 13. In table groups of two to three people, ask participants to discuss the first three questions on the slide. Depending on the grade levels and background of participants, they may be unsure of the correct answer or how to explain it. Tell participants that it is essential for them to understand the topic before they examine students' ideas about the topic. Distribute Handout 7.2.4: Gumballs in a Jar Explanation and allow time to review. Ask if there are any questions about the mathematics content in the probe. Ask for a volunteer to summarize the mathematics explanation. (As an alternative to this step you can do a quick mathematics talk on the topic to give the mathematics explanation or ask a "mathematician" in the group to explain. See Facilitator Note.)

Facilitator Note

If you or one of your partner facilitators is a mathematics specialist or mathematician, you can opt to do a short lecture to explain the probability ideas in the probe and provide the teachers with the correct answer and the explanation.

Refer everyone to the last two points on the slide. Ask them which CTS guide would be helpful for this probe (response: "Probability" is the most specific guide). Tell them they will now use CTS Section III to find out the specific ideas in the standards related to the probe. Show Slide 14. Tell them to look at the grade span of the students who responded (Grades 6–8) as well as the grade span that comes before (Grades 3–5). Explain that the latter is important because often students miss precursor ideas when they move from one grade span to the next, leaving gaps in their understanding. If they have their local or state frameworks or standards available, ask them to identify their related standards. You can also have them look at the *Common Core State Standards for Mathematics (CCSM)* or the NCTM *Focal Points*. Check to make sure they indicate the following specific ideas in the following box (and add *CCSM* or *Focal Points* if used). You might wish to post these on a wall chart.

SPECIFIC IDEAS ABOUT PROBABILITY

Benchmarks Grades 3–5

- Events can be described in terms of being more or less likely, impossible, or certain.

Benchmarks Grades 6–8

- How probability is estimated depends on what is known about the situation. Estimates can be based on data from similar conditions in the past or on the assumption that all the possibilities are known.
- Probabilities are ratios and can be expressed as fractions, decimals, percentages, or odds.

NCTM Principles and Standards Grades 3–5

By the end of Grade 5, all students should
- describe events as likely or unlikely and discuss the degree of likelihood using such words as *certain, equally likely,* and *impossible;*
- predict the probability of outcomes of simple experiments and test the predictions; and
- understand that the measure of the likelihood of an event can be represented by a number from 0 to 1.

NCTM Principles and Standards Grades 6–8

By the end of Grade 8, all students should
- use proportionality and a basic understanding of probability to make and test conjectures about the results of experiments and simulations; and
- compute probabilities for simple compound events, using such methods as organized lists, tree diagrams, and area models.

Spend a few minutes discussing the meaning and intent of each learning goal. Point out how each learning goal addresses ideas related to the transfer of heat.

Step 4: Anticipate Student Thinking (5 minutes)

Show Slide 15. Based on the teachers' knowledge of their own students, and the expectations of the learning goals described in the standards, ask them to share at their tables some assumptions they have about how seventh-graders would respond to this probe. Have each table share one assumption they discussed as a small group.

Facilitator Note

Put out bags of student response cards (Handout 7.2.3) during the break.

Break (10 minutes)

Step 5: Organizing Data (35 minutes)

Refer to Step 5 of the scaffold and Slide 16. Say we will now analyze the student responses. Point out the bags of student responses that you made from cutting up all the student responses on Handout 7.2.3: *Gumballs in a Jar* Cards. Explain that these are real student responses copied word for word from actual student work. Tell participants to clear a space on their tables where they can all read and sort the student work. Ask them to quickly scan through the work samples and sort them by selected response (A, B, or C). Direct the teachers to follow the prompts on the slide. Ask the table groups to first tally the tier one responses (How many students answered with responses A, B, or C?). Then show the bar graph of student responses on Slide 17.

Remind the groups we are still working on Step 5 and are not drawing any conclusions yet—they are just sticking to the facts they see in the student work. Show Slide 18 and ask them to examine the reasoning used by the students in their tier two responses. Ask them to look at the student work and see if they can identify different categories of reasoning. For example, a student may use thinking such as "there are more black marbles." Let them come up with their own categories of reasoning. Then each group should "go visual" and create a chart that visually shows the different types of reasoning they saw in the student responses.

> **Facilitator Note**
>
> If you are using the *Gumballs in a Jar* probe with the whole group, they do not need to make a graph since all the graphs would look the same. At this point you can post the wall chart graph made in advance and show Slide 17 to illustrate what their graphs would look like. After participants have been through this introduction to CIEST session, they will be able to make their own graphs when they analyze their own student work. The point of this session is to introduce the CIEST process so they can go through the steps on their own later with their own sets of student work.

> **Facilitator Note**
>
> There is no one right answer to the categorization exercise. It is possible for each group to come up with different ways of categorizing students' explanations based on the data they have.

Step 6: Analyze the Data (20 minutes)

Show Slide 19. Ask participants to examine and analyze their data display. Have groups state facts that are evident from the data on their charts. Look for trends or patterns. Note interesting or surprising findings. Examine correct responses for evidence of the specific idea(s) identified in the CTS groundwork (Step 3). Remind everyone to remember the group norms and also refrain from making inferences, drawing conclusions, or suggesting ways to address the problem at this stage. Engage participants in a "fact-based" discussion. Remind them of the old Jack Webb quote from Dragnet: "Just the facts ma'am, just the facts."

Ask everyone to post their charts of the student responses on one long wall and invite everyone to visit each chart for a few minutes. After everyone has had a few minutes to look at the charts, gather everyone around and ask participants to report out on what they noticed. You might ask them what was interesting or surprising. For example, some participants might say, "A number of students chose C but gave more black marbles as the explanation." You might ask them to look at the extent to which students used qualitative, subjective, or ratio reasoning. Refer to the questions on Slide 19 to guide the analysis and discussion. Stop people from making any inferences—reminding them we are still just looking at the facts. We will draw inferences and conclusions later.

Step 7: Examine Cognitive Research (20 minutes)

Ask participants to return to their seats to move on to Step 7 of the scaffold (Handout 7.2.1). Show Slide 20. Ask everyone to work with a partner and read the selected CTS readings for Section IV and examine the research notes for Section V if the *Atlas* is available.

Ask them to jot down notes or highlight sections of the research that are related to students' thinking in the work they analyzed. After about 10 minutes, ask them to share their findings at their tables. Allow 10 minutes for table discussions and then ask for a few people to respond to the question on Slide 21: "How did CTS Section IV, Research on Student Learning, help you understand the seventh graders' thinking about probability in the Gumballs probe?"

Step 8: Examine K–12 Learning Goals and Instructional Implications (10–15 minutes)

Have participants examine the *Atlas* map in CTS Section V, focusing on the probability strand, to see what a coherent progression of learning might look like that leads up to and connects with the learning goal(s) targeted by the Gumballs in a Jar probe. Focus on the Grades 3–5 and 6–8 bands. Ask participants to also examine CTS Section II to get a sense of the types of instructional experiences that may help students in Grades 3–8 understand the ideas on the map. If you have a group from the same district and have their local or state standards available, examine the learning goals for this topic. Show Slide 22, and provide time for discussion of questions on the slide.

Step 9: Integrate the Data (10 minutes)

Bring the group back together for Step 9. Show Slide 23. Have the table groups create a list of the inferences, explanations, or conclusions they can draw from the data. What additional data would they like to collect? How has their understanding of students, student thinking, curriculum, or instruction changed as a result of the CIEST?

Step 10: Next Steps and Reflection (15 minutes)

Show Slide 24. Ask table groups to discuss what they will do as a result of what they learned. What actions would they like to take as a group? What are the implications of their findings for ensuring all students in their school have opportunities to learn the ideas necessary for mathematical literacy?

Ask participants to step back from the collaborative inquiry they have just experienced to think about implications for them as individuals. Ask them to stand up and make eye contact with someone who they haven't worked with today. Ask them to pair up with that person and discuss the questions on Slide 25. Remind them to share their talk time so that each one can share a few ideas and reflections.

Wrap-Up and Evaluation (10 minutes)

Bring the group back together and with everyone still standing ask for three to four people to share one reflection and then ask them to return to their seats. Show Slide 26 explaining that CIEST is powerful because it brings the classroom directly into professional development, thereby increasing its potential impact on practice. Using Slide 27, point out the professional development value of CIEST and invite participants to think more about how they can use the CIEST protocol in their own work. Thank everyone for their participation and ask them to complete an evaluation form of your own choosing, if applicable.

Optional Extension to Make This a Full-Day Session

Once participants learn to use the ten-step scaffold for CIEST they will benefit greatly from examining their own students' work and using CIEST to explore mathematics topics they teach. You can use the above session design to introduce CIEST using a common set of student work from Gumballs in a Jar. After participants have experienced the introduction as a group, they can break into small groups conducting their own CIEST with student work from their own students. (Note: they will have to choose an assessment probe ahead of time, administer the probe to their students, and select student work samples to bring to the session.) An optional poster session, sharing each group's analysis and findings, can be included. There is also an advantage to having teachers go through the process looking at anonymous work from an unknown class or school first, since it helps them learn to use the process and stick to the protocol in a safe and comfortable way, before using it to analyze their own students' work.

CTS Professional Development Strategy Application 3
CTS Video Demonstration Lesson (VDL)

DESCRIPTION OF VIDEO DEMONSTRATION LESSON (VDL) AS A CTS PROFESSIONAL DEVELOPMENT STRATEGY

A CTS Video Demonstration Lesson (VDL) provides a structured opportunity for teachers to collaboratively examine and discuss classroom practice related to specific mathematics content and teaching goals. VDL consists of three elements: (1) CTS, (2) a discussion protocol, and (3) a diagnostic classroom observation tool on the content of a lesson (Saginor, 2008). Combined, these elements guide teachers to identify and discuss evidence of accurate content being taught, see the connections to standards and research on learning, and explore teaching practices that support learning the content. VDL provides an opportunity for teachers to view and discuss a typical example of teaching (not an exemplar), viewed through the lens of the standards and findings from a CTS. The strategy's effectiveness lies in its ability to promote and support a cycle of discussion based on evidence—evidence that provides participants with an understanding of the criterion through which the lesson will be examined prior to viewing and discussing the lesson.

As outlined in the beginning of this chapter, demonstration lessons are one of several professional development strategies that focus squarely on the practice of teaching. They involve teachers preparing and teaching lessons in the classroom while other teachers observe (or they are videoed for later viewing). Teachers who will observe meet ahead of time to discuss the goals and intent of the observation and then observe the lesson and debrief the experience to derive learning and connections to their own teaching. It is important to stress that demonstration lessons are usually not exemplars or the perfect lesson; rather they should be thought of as examples of practice that can be sources of learning for other teachers (Loucks-Horsley, Love, Stiles, Mundry, & Hewson, 2003).

Demonstration lessons have been widely used as a professional development strategy because they provide a direct window into the classroom and give teachers opportunities to examine instruction carefully. The strategy is often used when teachers are learning to use new instructional strategies and also for beginning teachers who may benefit from seeing more experienced teachers teach a lesson. While demonstration lessons are often done "live" with a few teachers visiting the demonstrating teacher's classroom, VDLs are easier to use for professional development because they can be viewed anytime. They can also be used more than once, and the school can build its own video library of lessons. Video allows teachers to stop and rewind a section of the lesson to inform their discussion, and they can view over and over from different perspectives or focus areas. For example, one might view the video in its entirety the first time to just get a sense of the whole lesson, how it flowed, what the instructional strategies were, and what students were doing. Then one might revisit parts of the video to analyze how well the lesson aligned with the learning goals and standards for the lesson.

The CTS VDL differs from other types of video lesson analysis in that it focuses primarily on the mathematics content of a lesson and utilizes findings from a topic study to guide participants to examine how the lesson reflected related standards and research.

GOALS OF A VDL

The overarching goal of a VDL is to provide an opportunity for teachers to improve their content and pedagogical content knowledge by examining teaching. The box on this page describes some of the reasons for using videotaped lessons.

WHY USE VIDEO-RECORDED MATHEMATICS LESSONS

- Creates norms and routines for teachers to collaborate and learn together.
- Moves teaching from a solitary act to a shared practice.
- Encourages teachers to shift from an evaluative focus on the teacher to one in which practices and student learning are examined, rather than the individual teacher.
- Promotes teacher reflection on practice—their own and that of their colleagues.
- Increases teachers' awareness of different instructional practices and their impact on student learning.
- Opens the door to others' classrooms that are otherwise difficult to visit during the day.
- Fosters a sense of professional community and camaraderie.
- Provides opportunities for teachers to get feedback from their peers on their use of new practices.
- Deepens content understanding—teachers work hard to understand at a deep level the "issues" around teaching particular mathematics content.
- Levels the "playing field"—all teachers, experienced or novice, are seen as having something others can learn from.

As a result of participating in a VDL, teachers will

- become familiar with viewing ethics and a protocol for watching, discussing, and providing feedback on a colleague's (or other teacher's) video-recorded lesson;
- use CTS to improve their understanding of effective teaching and learning as it relates to the content of a lesson; and
- recognize the value and importance of making teaching public.

AUDIENCE

CTS VDL is appropriate for teachers at all levels of the teacher professional continuum, from novice to experienced. The VDL was originally developed for use with mentor teachers and novices in the Northern New England Co-Mentoring Network (an NSF-funded project of the Maine Mathematics and Science Alliance) as a way to collaboratively view and safely discuss teaching practice in a learning community made up of coaches and mentor teachers and novices.

COMPONENTS OF VDL

VDLs require the following components:

- Videos of classroom lessons (teachers make videos of a complete lesson or a segment of a lesson or choose commercial videos of classroom lessons)
- Curriculum topic study (teachers complete a CTS of the topic of the lesson in the video)

- Norms (teachers establish and follow viewing ethics and norms)
- Content and instructional indicators to guide viewing
- General indicators for other factors such as student engagement
- Discussion
- Reflection
- VDL protocol

STRUCTURE OF A CTS VDL

CTS VDL is structured around the use of a protocol with six parts described as follows and shown in Table 7.2.

VDL PROTOCOL

Step 1: Review of Related CTS

Prior to the observation, participants conduct and discuss the grade-level specific CTS on the topic or subtopic of the lesson they will observe (Option A) or participants review and discuss a summary of the CTS topic that the demonstration lesson teacher or the facilitator prepared on the specific topic of the lesson (Option B).

Step 2: Teacher Introduction to the VDL

The VDL teacher sets the stage for viewing the video by describing the classroom context (grade, discipline, grouping, topic, curriculum materials used, etc.). The teacher will briefly describe what the purpose of the lesson is, what students will be doing, and what students did prior to this lesson. The VDL teachers provide an observation sheet for the lesson with key ideas identified and indicators that describe what they are particularly interested in having the viewers look for in the video segment.

Step 3: Viewing of the Video

Participants observe the VDL, noting specific evidence that the lesson addresses the key ideas from the standards and the instructional indicators on the observation sheet.

Step 4: Small Group Discussions of the VDL

Small groups discuss their observations and point out the evidence that the lesson addressed the indicators. Each small group generates one to three comments or "I wonder" questions to report out to the large group.

Step 5: Group Share: Observations and Comments

One by one the facilitator will ask the small groups to share their findings with the large group. At this point, it is the role of the VDL teacher to listen and take notes, but not respond to any comments.

Facilitator Note

Doing the CTS beforehand helps develop a shared understanding among participants of the content of the lesson, connection to grade-level standards, implications for teaching, possible misconceptions and misunderstandings, and difficulties students may encounter.

Facilitator Note

If you have a small number of participants such as a grade-level team, you may only have one group.

Facilitator Note

The VDL teacher may respond to questions for clarifications as needed, but keep this very brief so that the focus is on the observers sharing what they observed.

Facilitator Note

The VDL professional development strategy is most useful when the videos come from the participants' classrooms. However, it is possible to modify this strategy by using commercially available videos of teaching. If these videos are used, the facilitator takes on the role of "speaking for" the teacher in the video, omitting the personal comments and reflection that come at the end and summarizing and responding to comments from the facilitator's perspective instead.

Table 7.2	Structure of a CTS Video Demonstration Lesson

Time	*The VDL Protocol*
15–40 minutes	Review of related CTS (see Options A and B)
5 minutes	Teacher introduction to the VDL
20–30 minutes	Viewing of the video
15 minutes	Small group discussions of the video
5–10 minutes	Group share: observations and comments
5–10 minutes	Demonstration teacher comments and reflection

Step 6: Demonstration Teacher Comments and Reflection

Following the discussion, the VDL teacher clarifies or comments on the points made during the large group discussion referring to the notes taken. The teacher will summarize what he or she has gained from the process and share any personal reflections on how this will benefit his or her teaching.

Time

The CTS VDL takes about 90 minutes if the CTS is done in advance. If the CTS readings are done during the VDL session, build in an additional 30 to 40 minutes.

GUIDELINES FOR INTRODUCING AND LEADING VDLS

Materials Needed by Facilitator and for Participants

- *Mathematics Curriculum Topic Study: Bridging the Gap Between Standards and Practice* (Keeley & Rose, 2006)
- Access to all CTS resource books used with Sections I–VI of the CTS guides
- Optional: CTS summary developed ahead of time by the facilitator
- 20–30 minute segment of a videotaped lesson
- TV/VCR, TV/DVD or LCD/DVD and speakers
- Handouts (all handouts are in the Chapter 7 VDL folder on the CD-ROM):

  - Handout 7.3.1: VDL Protocol
  - Handout 7.3.2: VDL Viewing Ethics and Professional Courtesies
  - Handout 7.3.3: VDL Technical Tips
  - Handout 7.3.4: VDL Content of the Lesson Indicators
  - Handout 7.3.5: VDL Observation Worksheet (blank)
  - Handout 7.3.6: Example Observation Sheet—"The Largest Container" Lesson (Optional)
  - Handout 7.3.7: CTS Summary for "The Largest Container" Lesson (Optional)

Facilitator Preparation

- Collect CTS books and resources for the group to use or have them bring their own if they have them. One set of books per five people is sufficient if they are doing the CTS in a meeting prior to observing the lesson. If there are not enough books, copy the study guide you will be using and the readings from the resource books that go with the study guide or prepare a CTS summary of the topic (see Facilitator Note on p. 221).

- Identify teachers to video a 20- to 30-minute segment of their classrooms to model the VDL process, offer to video it for them so you can use it in the CTS VDL sessions, or select a commercial video from the Annenberg collection at www.learner.org (purchased or streaming) or other videos. Some teachers may already have videotaped lessons they are willing to share, such as lessons they may have prepared for certification, Presidential Award applications, or graduate study, or to gain national board certification. You might tap these teachers to see if they would provide some video you can use to get the group started.
- If a teacher-made video is used and the process is modeled by the teacher, the facilitator works with the teacher to create the VDL Observation Worksheet that will be used for introducing the VDL. The VDL teacher and the facilitator will review the video in advance and select one or two key ideas and one to three indicators of the content of the lesson (from Handout 7.3.4) to focus on and one general indicator of their choice. Include these on the Observation Worksheet (see Handout 7.3.5), and fill in the rest of the information needed to view the lesson. (See example on Handout 7.3.6 from a middle school geometry lesson, "The Largest Container.")
- If a commercial video is used, the facilitator can represent the teacher in the video to model the process for the teachers who will later be videotaped and become the VDL teachers themselves. In this case, the facilitator will create the Observation Worksheet based on what was observed while watching the video.
- If participants do not have their own copies of the CTS parent book, make copies of the topic study guide from Chapter 5 that they will need. Option: The facilitator can complete the CTS on the topic of the lesson and make a CTS summary that is grade-level specific for the topic of the VDL. Participants will read the summary in advance of viewing the lesson instead of doing the CTS themselves. (See Handout 7.3.6 for an example of a CTS summary using the "2D and 3D Geometry" CTS guide for a middle school "The Largest Container" geometry lesson in the Chapter 7 folder on the CD-ROM.)
- Make a set of all handouts for the session.

DIRECTIONS FOR INTRODUCING CTS VDL

Introducing VDL (5 minutes)

The first time you do this with your group, introduce VDL as a professional development strategy that uses examples from real classrooms as the subject for teacher learning. Ask your group to suggest what they might gain from viewing and discussing video demonstration lessons. Describe how this introduction will use a prepared video (explain that it is from one of the teachers in your VDL group who volunteered, or say you will be using a commercially available video to introduce the process and that in the future you will ask for some volunteers to video a lesson).

Setting Norms: Review of Video Ethics and Professional Courtesies (5 minutes)

Point out that it is essential to create a safe environment for discussion so everyone is comfortable engaging in honest, professional dialogue about teaching and learning. Acknowledge that watching a videotape of one's practice can be uncomfortable and share the importance of establishing norms for viewing and discussing teaching practice. Review Handout 7.3.2: Video Viewing Ethics and Professional Courtesies and discussion norms. Clarify any questions and allow for discussion of the norms the group wants to use. Add any additional norms that the group suggests. Ask the group to agree to follow the guidelines, and during the session, remind everyone to keep the norms in mind. Ask one or two people to monitor and remind the group when the norms are not being followed.

Introduce the Protocol and Observation Worksheet (5–10 minutes)

Introduce Handout 7.3.1: VDL Protocol. Briefly explain the flow and the purpose of each section of the protocol. Clarify questions.

Distribute Handout 7.3.5: VDL Observation Worksheet, which you prepared in advance by inserting the material specific to the lesson, to address the video you will view. The VDL Observation Worksheet contains the key idea(s) from the lesson, content-based instructional indicators, and a general instructional indicator.

Explain how the VDL Observation Worksheet has been created specifically for the VDL lesson that will be viewed. Introduce the worksheet and explain each of the components, including how the facilitator and the VDL teacher prepared the worksheet in advance. Provide Handout 7.3.4: Content of the Lesson Indicators so participants can see the indicators that the VDL teacher selected from and the evidence to look for that supports each of the indicators.

Explain that the group will use the VDL Observation Worksheet to record specific evidence they find as they watch the video demonstration lesson. Divide the group into three smaller groups and assign each group one of the three components on the worksheet. Ask the small groups to focus on and collect evidence on their assigned component throughout the lesson. For example, in a small group of six, two people would look for evidence of key ideas, two people would divide up the content of the lesson indicators, and two people would look for evidence of the general indicator. Everyone should be observing for specific evidence of how the CTS findings are reflected in the demonstration lesson.

Review of the Related CTS (15–40 minutes, depending on whether summaries are used)

Explain how a partial CTS (i.e., reading just Sections II, III, IV, V, and VI for the specific grade level of the lesson only) is done by the group prior to viewing the lesson, or a CTS summary is prepared by the VDL teacher or facilitator and reviewed by the group in advance of viewing the lesson.

Have participants conduct the CTS or spend a few quiet minutes reviewing the CTS summary for this lesson. Pose the following question for small group discussion:

> **Facilitator Note**
>
> If using CTS summaries, two to three VDLs can be viewed in a half-day session. If the teachers will be doing the CTS readings themselves in the session before the VDL, plan on just one VDL for a half-day session.

Based on your review of the CTS information, what do you think you might look for or find in the lesson in terms of learning goals, specific content, instructional approaches, or research-identified misconceptions or student difficulties?

After small groups have discussed their ideas, have each report out one or two predictions based on a summary of their findings from the CTS.

Teacher Introduction to Video Lesson (5 minutes)

Introduce the teacher featured in the VDL. The VDL teacher sets the stage for viewing the videotaped lesson by briefly describing the classroom (grade, discipline, grouping, topic, and any relevant context issues), explaining what learning experiences have come prior to the segment to be viewed, the key idea(s) (learning goals) of the lesson, and a brief description of the lesson. The teacher may choose to provide the group with a one-page written summary of these details. The teacher also shares what he or

> **Facilitator Note**
>
> If using a commercially available video to introduce VDL, the facilitator will stand in for the teacher in the video and provide similar information on the lesson that will be viewed.

she is particularly interested in the audience looking for in the demonstration lesson, referring to the indicators he or she selected on the VDL Observation Worksheet.

Viewing of Video (20–30 minutes)

Allow time for small groups to determine who will be observing for evidence of each component on the worksheet. Provide time for participants to familiarize themselves with the indicators and descriptors of evidence assigned to them. Remind participants to use the VDL Observation Worksheet to note specific evidence that supports their observations. Remind everyone to record any connections they see to the CTS findings.

Small Group Discussion of Video (15–20 minutes)

Prompt groups to discuss the observations made during the video. Remind participants to base their discussion on the evidence collected. Ask each table group to generate one to three comments or questions to report out to the larger group. The group may choose to summarize their findings or ask clarifying questions.

Group Sharing of Observations and Comments (5–10 minutes)

Invite the small groups to take turns sharing the comments and questions each group generated about the lesson. During this time, the VDL teacher is not directly addressed, but listens to the group and takes notes regarding comments made or questions posed. The VDL teacher does not respond at this point—he or she only listens. The role of the facilitator at this time is to act as a "sounding board," keeping the group's comments and questions focused on evidence.

Teacher Comments, Reflection, and Wrap-Up (5–10 minutes)

Invite the VDL teacher to address any of the comments or questions raised during the large group discussion and then wrap up the VDL by publicly reflecting on what he or she has learned from the process.

After the VDL teacher shares his or her reflection with the group, ask all participants to write a short reflection on what they learned during the process. Ask them to focus on what they learned about the mathematics topic and mathematics teaching and learning by observing the lesson and summarizing the CTS. Ask them to also reflect on the process of collaborating with other teachers to examine practice. Bring the group back together and ask, "How might this type of work be useful to the teachers in the future?" Ask for a few people to share their reflections. If it does not come up in the teachers' reflections, point out that VDLs can help redefine the solitary view of teaching, moving it toward a more collaborative, open view of teaching, a professional activity open to collective observation, study, and improvement, and grounded in standards and research on learning.

Be sure to publicly acknowledge, thank, and celebrate the VDL teacher(s) for making their teaching public to the group.

Next Steps

After this introduction to VDL, solicit volunteers to become the VDL teachers for future meetings. VDLs can be used in the context of professional learning communities where teachers use common planning time to do curriculum topic studies and share and learn from their video recorded lessons with their colleagues.

DESCRIPTION OF CASE DISCUSSION AS A CTS PROFESSIONAL DEVELOPMENT STRATEGY

A CTS Case Discussion provides a structured opportunity for teachers to collaboratively examine and discuss classroom practice related to specific mathematics content and teaching goals. Case discussions are among several professional development strategies that focus squarely on the practice of teaching. Such strategies involve teachers in learning mathematics and pedagogy *in* and *through* practice (Nikula, Goldsmith, Blasi, & Seago, 2006).

Cases allow teacher to look through the "window" of someone else's practice to consider the issues of a situation, and at the same time, serve as a "mirror" as they provide opportunities for teachers to reflect on their own practice (Miller & Kantrov, 1998). Both written cases and video cases offer practice-based learning experiences that can provide transformative growth opportunities for teachers. Reading written cases and studying videos of others can provide a degree of distance from the personal attachments to the instructional situation, allowing greater objectivity of analysis. It is important to stress that the cases ought not be portrayed as exemplars or as "perfect" lessons; rather, they should be thought of as examples of practice that can be sources of learning for teachers (Loucks-Horsley, Stiles, Mundry, Love, & Hewson, 2010; Seago, Mumme, & Branca, 2004; Smith, 2001).

CTS case discussions consist of four elements: (1) CTS, (2) engagement in a mathematics activity related to what teachers will read or view in the case, (3) a set of focused questions to guide reading or viewing of the case as well as the ensuing discussion, and (4) opportunities for application of ideas from the case to teachers' own classroom practice. Combined, these elements guide teachers to identify and discuss evidence of what they see in terms of the content being taught and connections to standards and research on learning. They also allow for the exploration of teaching practices that support student learning of the content. The case discussion provides an opportunity for teachers to view and discuss a typical example of teaching (not as a model or exemplar), considered through the lens of national and local standards as well as findings from a CTS. The strategy's effectiveness lies in its ability to promote and support a cycle of discussion based on evidence—evidence that provides participants with a common understanding to ground the viewing or reading and discussion of the case.

Cases have been widely used as a mathematics professional development strategy because they are sited directly in the classroom and give teachers opportunities to enhance their practice. Cases can be used to deepen teachers' mathematics content knowledge, specifically the specialized knowledge needed for teaching mathematics (Ball, Thames, & Phelps, 2008). Cases can support teachers in learning to use new instructional strategies and are also useful for beginning teachers who may benefit from seeing and analyzing lessons of more experienced teachers (Merseth, 1996).

Cases are ideal for use in professional development because they can be read or viewed anytime, and they can be used multiple times. In using cases, teachers can stop and look back at the narrative or rewind the video to inform their discussion, and they can consider the case over and over from different perspectives or focus areas. For example, one might view/read the first time just to get a sense of the mathematics content, how the lesson flowed, what the instructional strategies were, and what the teacher and students were doing. Then one might revisit the case to analyze any one of these areas in depth. (See list at end of this strategy for commercially available case curricula for mathematics professional development.)

The CTS case discussion is distinctive in that it connects research to practice. Whether focusing primarily on the mathematics content of the lesson, instructional moves, or what students seem to understand or not understand, the CTS case discussion utilizes findings from a topic study to guide participants in analyzing the lesson and examining how it reflects what they have read in the research.

GOALS OF A CTS CASE DISCUSSION

The overarching goal of a case discussion is to provide an opportunity for teachers to improve their mathematics content and pedagogical content knowledge by examining teaching.

As a result of participating in a case discussion, teachers will

- become familiar with a process for engaging as a collaborative learning community in watching or reading, discussing, and analyzing a case;
- use CTS to improve their understanding of the important relationship between mathematical content understanding and effective teaching and learning; and
- recognize the value and importance of making teaching public as a way of supporting teacher learning in and through practice.

AUDIENCE

CTS case discussions are appropriate for teachers at all levels of the teacher professional continuum, from novice to experienced. Cases serve as a means through which teachers collaboratively engage with the written or video artifacts of classroom practice and safely discuss teaching practice within a supportive learning community.

COMPONENTS OF CTS CASE DISCUSSIONS

Cases discussions require the following components:

- Artifacts of classroom practice (i.e., written cases, videotapes of mathematics lessons) to use as an object of inquiry
- CTS (teachers complete a CTS of the topic of the lesson in the artifact)
- Engagement in mathematics task they will see in the case
- Focus questions to guide viewing/reading and discussion of the case
- Reflection and application to practice

STRUCTURE OF A CTS CASE DISCUSSION

The CTS case discussion is structured to include an overview in which the norms for working together as a collaborative learning community are shared, four steps of the case discussion process, and a wrap-up/reflection on the case experience. The following constitute the four steps of the case discussion process:

Step 1: Review of Related CTS

The specific section(s) of the CTS guide that are reviewed will vary from case to case, depending on the particular content and/or pedagogical focus of the case the leader wishes to have participants pursue. Prior to embarking on the case, participants are engaged in CTS in one of two ways:

Option A: Participants conduct and discuss the grade-level specific CTS on the topic or subtopic of the video they will view.

Option B: Participants review and discuss a summary of the CTS topic prepared in advance by the session facilitator.

Once the CTS is completed in this step, participants can be invited and encouraged to refer back to the appropriate sections as they work their way through the case discussion and the application to practice.

> **Facilitator Note**
>
> Doing the CTS before engaging in the case helps develop a shared understanding among participants of the mathematics content, how the topic connects to grade-level standards, implications for teaching, and possible misconceptions or difficulties students may encounter.

Step 2: Preparing to Engage in the Case Discussion—Doing the Mathematics

Participants engage in the exploration of the same mathematical tasks as those portrayed in the video or narrative case. The purpose is to develop an understanding of the mathematical demands of the task in order to be able to interpret students' thinking and teacher decisions. This engagement supports participants in deepening their own mathematical understandings. Building on the CTS study, these explorations attempt to build teachers' understanding of the mathematics from the perspective of the work of teaching and how students might approach the task.

Step 3: Reading/Viewing, Analyzing, and Discussing the Case

This is at the heart of the session, but it cannot stand alone. The experience with the narrative or video case is intended to engage teachers in thinking and reasoning about mathematics teaching and learning. The facilitator sets the stage for the case by describing the classroom context (grade, discipline, grouping, topic, curriculum materials used, etc.). Participants read the narrative or view the video clip, noting specific evidence of what is going on. They may be asked to pay specific attention to what is happening mathematically, what they see as teacher moves, and/or what students seem to understand or not understand. In an iterative process of both small and whole group discussions, participants exchange ideas based on their observations, drawing on evidence from the case to support their analysis. After the first round of discussion, it is often helpful to go back to the case a second time, asking participants to consider specific ideas and issues or to try to understand differences of interpretation that have arisen in the discussion.

Step 4: Application to Practice

These activities bridge the gap between the learning that takes place within the session and teachers' own practice. The linking to practice activities provide participants with opportunities to apply their new ideas to their own teaching situation. The application to practice may include planning to use a task with one's own class, examining samples of student work from the case, or other practice-based activities.

GUIDELINES FOR INTRODUCING AND LEADING CASE DISCUSSIONS

Materials Needed by Facilitator and Participants

- *Mathematics Curriculum Topic Study: Bridging the Gap Between Standards and Practice* (Keeley & Rose, 2006)
- Access to all CTS resource books used with Sections I–VI of the CTS guides
- Copies of the CTS guide that has been selected to accompany the case
- Materials identified for use with the selected narrative case or video case

- PowerPoint Slides: Math Cases (this is a collection of five slides that can be incorporated into existing case discussion slides)
- Computer, LCD projector, and speakers (if using a video case)

Time

The CTS Case Discussion takes 2.5 to 3 hours if the CTS is completed by the facilitator in advance and reviewed by participants in the session. Build in an additional 30 to 40 minutes if participants are to complete the CTS readings during the session.

Time	Activity
10–15 minutes	Introduction/Overview; Norms for Working With Cases
15–40 minutes	Review of Related CTS
35–40 minutes	Preparing to Engage in the Case Discussion—Doing the Mathematics
45–60 minutes	Viewing/Reading, Analyzing, and Discussing the Case
15–20 minutes	Application to Practice
10 minutes	Wrap-Up/Reflection

Advance Preparation for Introducing the CTS Case Discussion

- Collect CTS books and resources for the group to use or have them bring their own if they have them. One set of books per five people is sufficient if they are doing the CTS together prior to the case. If there are not enough books, copy the CTS study guide you will be using and the readings from the resource books that go with the study guide or prepare a CTS summary of the topic related to the case.
- Option: If time is an issue, the facilitator can complete the CTS on the topic of the lesson in the case and make a CTS summary that is grade-level specific. In the session, participants then read the summary in advance of engaging in the case discussion instead of doing the CTS themselves.
- Make copies of all handouts needed for the particular case that is being discussed during the session. (Facilitator Note: There are no handouts provided in this *Leader's Guide* as the handouts depend on the Case and CTS topic selected for the session.)

DIRECTIONS FOR INTRODUCING CTS CASE DISCUSSION

Introducing the Case Discussion and Setting Norms (10–15 minutes)

Case discussion is a professional development strategy that uses examples from real classrooms as the subject for teacher learning. In introducing this strategy, ask the group to suggest what they might gain from engaging with such artifacts of actual classroom practice.

Point out that it is essential to create a safe environment for discussion so everyone is comfortable engaging in honest, professional dialogue about teaching and learning. A learning community involves everyone in the group taking responsibility for engaging with important ideas. Negotiating group norms will be essential for productive professional learning. These shared expectations for the ways people interact in the group evolve over time and are rarely shared uniformly by all group members.

Some preestablished groups have a well-established set of norms that might either help or hinder the inquiry process. Even new groups come with certain expectations about what it means to work in a group. Depending on your group, the time it takes to establish productive norms will vary. This initial focus on norms can serve as a reference point for supporting the productive work of the group throughout the case discussions.

Review of the Related CTS (15–40 minutes)

Explain how the group will prepare for the case discussion by engaging in either a partial CTS (i.e., reading just a subset of the section of the guide for the specific grade level of the lesson only) or a review of the CTS summary that has been prepared by the facilitator. (Note: The time depends on whether you use a pre-prepared CTS summary or have participants complete their own CTS related to the case.)

Have participants conduct the CTS or spend a few quiet minutes reviewing the CTS summary for this lesson. Pose the following question for small group discussion:

Based on your review of the CTS information, what do you think you might look for or find in this case in terms of the lesson's learning goals, specific content, instructional approaches, or research-identified misconceptions or student difficulties?

After small groups have discussed their ideas, have each report out one or two points that summarize their findings from the CTS. Remind participants that they now have this resource (CTS findings) to which they can refer back at any time during the case discussion.

Engaging in the Mathematics Task From the Case (30–40 minutes)

Have participants work together on the task on which the lesson in the case is based (this will depend on what case you select). As they begin working, remind them to pay attention to the group norms and to how they are making sure that all their members have access to the mathematics and the discussion. In completing the task, participants will generate potential solutions, anticipate student challenges, and consider what important mathematical ideas the task might help students learn. The ensuing discussion provides teachers an opportunity to share their approaches, solutions, and challenges with their colleagues before moving into the case itself.

Reading/Viewing and Discussing the Case (45–60 minutes)

This segment of the session will vary greatly depending on whether the case is written or video. Although the commercially available case curricula each have their own particular structure, we offer here a few comments to summarize this phase, first for a video case discussion, then for a narrative case discussion.

Video case discussion: Teachers typically watch and discuss a video clip two times and engage in an iterative discussion process. In the first viewing, the focus is on the mathematics. Following this viewing, participants consider what students are saying and doing mathematically and how that might connect with their own experience with the task. Having grounded themselves in the mathematics of the lesson and the CTS, participants then watch the video a second time, this time focusing on the work of the teachers and/or what students are doing with the task. In this phase of the discussion, participants note key teacher moves and discuss why they consider the moves significant and how the moves seem to impact what is happening mathematically. They use findings from CTS to support their discussion. For example, if the research from CTS Section IV indicates a common overgeneralization students tend to make, this may be pointed out in a spot in the video where the students are struggling with a concept. The discussion might include instructional strategies from CTS Section II that are supported by the teacher's moves or that could be suggestions that would help the teacher move the students' thinking forward.

Narrative case discussion: Depending on the length and complexity of the written case, participants may be asked to read the entire case and follow that with small and whole group discussions, or they may engage in an iterative process of reading and discussing smaller segments of the case. In either case, focus questions generally provide guidance for participants' reading and then help focus the direction of the case discussions. As is true with video cases also, participants pay attention to teacher moves and student contributions and use their CTS findings to support their discussion.

Application to Practice (15–20 minutes)

These activities are designed to connect the work within the session and teachers' own practice. They provide participants with opportunities to apply their new ideas from CTS and the case to their own teaching situation. Participants may plan for trying out a line of questions they've seen in the case, engaging their students in the mathematics task from the case, or applying some other aspect of the case experience in their own classroom. They can work with a partner in this phase, and then come back and share their experiences and reflections in a future session.

Wrap-Up and Reflection (10 minutes)

Provide a few minutes for reflective writing and then ask for volunteers to share some of their ideas. Ask participants to think of how they might draw on some aspect of this CTS case discussion experience in their classroom teaching.

Conclude the session by sharing any next steps such as how participants might employ CTS case discussions at their school sites.

Collect written feedback on the session using your own evaluation form.

Next Steps

Cases can be used in the context of professional learning communities where teachers use common planning time to do CTS and share and learn from their videotaped lessons or written cases with their colleagues. Over time, participants may choose to use some of the mathematics tasks with their students and revisit the CTS and the case in conjunction with student work from their own enactment of the lesson.

SELECTED CASE-BASED RESOURCES TO USE FOR CTS CASE DISCUSSIONS

Barnett, C., Goldstein, D., & Jackson, B. (Eds.). (1994). *Mathematics teaching cases: Fractions, decimals, ratios, and percents: Hard to teach and hard to learn?* Portsmouth, NH: Heinemann.

Barnett-Clarke, C., & Ramirez, A. (Eds.). (2003). *Number sense and operations in the primary grades: Hard to teach and hard to learn?* Portsmouth, NH: Heinemann.

Barnett, C., Goldstein, D., & Jackson, B. (Eds.). (1994). *Mathematics teaching cases: Fractions, decimals, ratios, and percents: Hard to teach and hard to learn? Facilitator's discussion guide.* Portsmouth, NH: Heinemann.

Boaler, J., & Humphreys, C. (2005). *Connecting mathematical ideas: Middle school video cases to support teaching and learning.* Portsmouth, NH: Heinemann.

Merseth, K. (2003). *Windows on teaching math: Case discussions of middle and secondary classrooms and facilitator's guide.* New York: Columbia University Press.

Schifter, D., Bastable, V., & Russell, S. J. (1999). *Developing mathematical ideas: Building a system of tens.* Parsippany, NJ: Dale Seymour.

Schifter, D., Bastable, V., & Russell, S. J. (1999). *Developing mathematical ideas: Making meaning for operations.* Parsippany, NJ: Dale Seymour.

Schifter, D., Bastable, V., Russell, S. J., & Monk, G. S. (2008). *Developing mathematical ideas: Patterns, functions, and change.* Parsippany, NJ: Dale Seymour.

Schifter, D., Bastable, V., Russell, S. J., & Monk, G. S. (2008). *Developing mathematical ideas: Reasoning algebraically about operations.* Parsippany, NJ: Dale Seymour.

Seago, N., Mumme, J., & Branca, N. (2004). *Learning and teaching linear functions.* Portsmouth, NH: Heinemann.

Smith, M. S., Silver, E. A., & Stein, M. K. (2005). *Using cases to transform mathematics teaching and learning, Volume 1: Improving instruction in rational numbers and proportionality.* New York: Teachers College Press.

Smith, M. S., Silver, E. A., & Stein, M. K. (2005). *Using cases to transform mathematics teaching and learning, Volume 2: Improving instruction in algebra.* New York: Teachers College Press.

Smith, M. S., Silver, E. A., & Stein, M. K. (2005). *Using cases to transform mathematics teaching and learning, Volume 3: Improving instruction in geometry and measurement.* New York: Teachers College Press.

Stein, M. K., Smith, M. S., Henningsen, M. A., & Silver, E. A. (2009). *Implementing standards-based mathematical instruction: A casebook for professional development* (2nd ed.). New York: Teachers College Press.

A variety of videotapes to use for cases can be accessed free through streaming video at learner.org or purchased through the Annenberg collection (purchasing information is provided on the learner.org website.

CTS Professional Development
Strategy Application 5
CTS Seminars

DESCRIPTION OF SEMINARS AS A
CTS PROFESSIONAL DEVELOPMENT STRATEGY

CTS seminars are content-focused seminars in which small groups of teachers engage in discussion and dialogue of readings from a CTS. The seminar provides a structured format for small groups of teachers to discuss their CTS readings, which are read previous to attending the seminar. It is a way for teaching professionals to raise questions and discuss important content-related ideas, rejuvenate themselves, and come together as a learning community.

CTS seminars enable teachers to engage in intellectual text-based conversations that build the learning capacity of a group. These are not freewheeling discussions; they incorporate a type of Socratic seminar structure that supports inquiry into a curricular topic. The close examination and discussion of the findings that result from a topic study not only contribute to teachers' content and pedagogical knowledge of the concepts and skills in the mathematics topics they teach, but also contribute to building the knowledge base of the group and their schools. Through the seminar format, a CTS learning community focuses on developing and strengthening the skills and dispositions of analytical professional reading, use of common professional language, careful listening, citing evidence from text, disagreeing respectfully, being open-minded about new ideas, and connecting theory from the text of standards and research to practice.

The adult learning skills teachers draw upon during a CTS seminar parallel the K–12 critical skills teachers want students to acquire and use when discussing expository text. These skills include oral discourse, use of academic language, respectful discussion, healthy skepticism, critical thinking and reasoning, constructing meaning from reading, and applying learning from text to real-life situations.

GOALS OF A CTS SEMINAR

The goals of a CTS seminar are to

- provide a structured opportunity for teachers to have content-focused intellectual discussions about topics they teach,
- deepen teachers' content knowledge and understanding of pedagogical implications that surface from doing a curriculum topic study, and
- surface awareness of one's own ideas and ideas of others as they relate to the topic studied.

AUDIENCE

It is suggested that a CTS seminar include no fewer than five participants and no more than twelve. Readings, questions, and conversations will differ according to the audience's grade level, school context, familiarity with CTS, and content backgrounds of the teachers.

KEY COMPONENTS OF A CTS SEMINAR

CTS Text Readings

Choose a mathematics topic that is relevant to the group attending the seminar. CTS seminar discussions revolve around the text-based readings from CTS. Topics and their associated text readings are chosen based on the needs of the group to learn more about a particular mathematics curricular topic. The CTS text readings anchor the discussion in the important content of the topic and provide an opportunity for teachers to cite and use findings from CTS to discuss implications for teaching and learning. Supplementary readings, which may include content readings, primary research articles from journals, or technical professional literature, offer an opportunity for teachers to collaboratively tackle more difficult readings than they might read on their own.

Questions

Once the topic is selected, the seminar leader prepares questions to facilitate discussion of the CTS findings from the text resources. Even though you might not get to all the questions during a seminar, it is important to plan questions ahead of time to help participants collaboratively construct a deeper understanding of the text readings. Use the questions on pages 39–41 of the CTS parent book to focus on specific sections of the CTS guide or develop your own. It is also important to include a few open-ended, thought-provoking questions that teachers may not be able to answer quickly from their text notes, but may need to think about before responding. Questions should be clear and succinct and not open to a wide array of interpretations.

Seminar Leader

The CTS seminar leader has several tasks. These tasks include the following:

- *Preparation:* The seminar leader is responsible for making sure participants have books or copies of the readings and know what the assigned readings are, developing the questions for the seminar, and planning for after-seminar follow-up where necessary (Handouts 7.5.1, 7.5.2, and 7.5.3 can be used to prepare to lead CTS seminars).
- *Participation:* The primary role of the seminar leader during the seminar is to listen, think, and question. Seminar leaders participate to some extent, but it is important that their voice is not the most frequently heard one in the room. Their role is to help participants get deeply into the text readings and elicit and surface ideas for all to engage with.
- *Maintaining an engaging, respectful, professional environment:* The seminar leader keeps participants engaged, makes sure all ideas are listened to and participants are not interrupted or ignored, keeps the group on task and away from tangential storytelling, and encourages the skills of group dialogue and discussion. Seminar leaders should continually encourage participants to explain where their ideas come from so that they learn to develop the skill of citing CTS evidence during the discussion. The seminar leader also establishes and posts norms that all participants agree to during the seminars. If the seminar leader decides to provide a written summary after the seminar has taken place, then the seminar leader will also take notes during the seminar.

Reflection

Reflection is a critical component that links the knowledge gained from CTS findings, the discussion among participants, and thoughts about what could be done as a result to improve teaching and learning. Every seminar builds in time for shared reflections at the close of the seminar to examine how the group met its group goal(s). Reflection should also include time to examine the extent to which teachers' personal goals were met.

STRUCTURE OF A CTS SEMINAR

The CTS seminar structure includes three parts: (1) preseminar activities, (2) seminar questions and discussion, and (3) postseminar activities.

Preseminar Activities

The preseminar activities take place prior to and right before the seminar. Prior to the seminar, participants read the CTS sections, make notes in preparation for the discussion, and choose a personal learning goal related to the topic. Activities that happen right before the seminar begins include establishing or reviewing the seminar norms and setting two group goals for the seminar—one content and one process goal. Individuals may also set their own personal goals related to these.

The Seminar

The seminar itself includes three phases: the opening, the core, and the closing. The opening should begin with a question that requires participants to refer to their CTS text readings in order to set the stage for practicing "text-based" discussions. It should be broad enough to allow everyone to have an entry point into the CTS readings and stimulate conversation. The core forms the bulk of the seminar. Core questions focus on specific aspects of the CTS readings and are designed to get participants to delve deeply into the CTS findings. The closing question helps participants connect the group's discussion to their own practice. The closing is an opportunity for participants to contextualize and personalize their CTS findings.

Postseminar Reflection

The postseminar reflection happens at the very end of the seminar. Participants consider the content and process goal(s) they established for the group and reflect on how well the seminar helped them reach the goal(s). Participants also reflect on their individual goals. Attention to this part of the seminar structure is critical, as reflection is often shortchanged for the sake of time. It is through reflection that participants can improve upon the social and intellectual skills that are part of the seminar experience.

GUIDELINES FOR LEADING CTS SEMINARS

Materials Needed by Seminar Leader

CTS Parent Book

- *Mathematics Curriculum Topic Study: Bridging the Gap Between Standards and Practice* (Keeley & Rose, 2006)

Resources

- All CTS resource books that the group uses or copies made of selected readings
- Discussion questions prepared in advance

- Handout 7.5.1: Seminar Norms
- Handout 7.5.2: Seminar Leader Checklist
- Handout 7.5.3: Resource Checklist

Materials Needed by Participants

- CTS guide with selected seminar readings identified
- CTS selected resource books or copies made of selected readings
- Notes made by participants on readings to bring to the seminar

Time

Seminars range from 1 to 1.5 hours, depending on topics, lengths of readings, and number of questions selected. They are usually held after school or during the school day.

Participants' Responsibility

Participants have three main tasks in any CTS seminar: (1) preparation—by doing the readings in advance and highlighting, annotating, or taking notes; (2) participation—by active listening and thinking, speaking, and referring to the text and not their own personal opinions and stories; and (3) respect—acknowledging differences, honoring the process, and being aware of "air time" so that everyone has a chance to participate.

> **Facilitator Note**
>
> The best way to introduce teachers to this strategy is to model a CTS seminar using the following directions. Because it is a seminar, there are no PowerPoint slides and few handouts. The materials come primarily from the CTS book and CTS readings. The questions used depend on what direction the discussion takes.

DIRECTIONS FOR LEADING THE SEMINAR

Welcome (5–10 minutes)

Welcome participants, review group norms if necessary (refer to Handout 7.5.1), and generate two goals on chart paper, one for content and one for group process. For example, two group goals for a middle school CTS seminar on ratio and proportion might include the following:

1. Understand why students have difficulty with ratios and proportions (content goal).

2. Improve our ability to practice wait time after someone speaks (process goal).

Post the goals on a chart for all participants to see. Also provide time for participants to share one personal goal that describes what they hope to gain from the seminar with a partner or triad. If the seminar group is small, have participants go around and briefly share their goals with the group.

Opening Question (5–10 minutes)

The opening question is broad and allows everyone an entry point into the conversation. Try to encourage all participants to respond to the opening question. Why is ratio and proportion an important middle school topic?

The Core (30–45 minutes)

The seminar leader poses the prepared questions in an order that fits with the flow of the conversation and may pose additional questions as needed. The seminar leader guides the conversation and at times may interject with probes and extenders such as the following:

"Can you tell us more about that?"
"Can you show us where you found that in the CTS references?"
"Would anyone like to add anything?"

During the core discussion, the seminar leader keeps the group focused on the findings that emerge from the text and redirects when personal stories or opinions draw the discussion away from the CTS readings. When the discussion of one question appears to be exhausted, the seminar leader raises a new question. The seminar leader makes sure participants see the link between the discussion questions and the CTS text. Here are some example questions a seminar leader might use during the core for a seminar focused on the topic of ratio and proportion:

1. What does CTS reveal are the specific ideas students need to know in order to understand ratio and proportion?

2. What misconceptions or common errors related to ratios and proportions do we need to be aware of that may pose barriers to students' learning?

3. What are suggested instructional approaches for helping students to understand proportional relationships?

4. What type of contexts help students see the value of real-life applications of ratios and proportions?

5. What does the *Atlas* map reveal about prerequisite ideas we need to pay attention to? Does it appear that we have any gaps in our district curriculum that may affect our students' understanding of ratios and proportions?

The Closing (15–20 minutes)

The closing allows participants to connect their discussion about the readings to their own practice. The closing may consist of one or two questions posed by the seminar leader that relate directly to the participants' context and the nature of the discussion during the seminar. Seminar leaders may use a question developed prior to the seminar or may pose a new one based on major points from the readings that participants were most interested in discussing. Examples using the ratio and proportion topic might include the following:

- Considering what we just discussed, how well do the CTS findings describe the way our students currently learn about ratios and proportions?
- What are you thinking about doing differently, and why, based on what we discussed today?

The Reflection (15–20 minutes)

The seminar leader transitions from closing to reflection by referring participants to the chart that lists group goals. Ask participants to comment on the extent to which they felt the seminar met the group's goals. Also provide time for reflection on their own personal goals, asking if people would like to share what they learned from the seminar that helped them meet those goals.

Next Steps (5 minutes)

If the seminar is a continuing series, take a few minutes for the group to identify the next topic, date, location, and seminar leader.

Optional

Seminar leaders or a designee may wish to write a summary of the seminar to share with participants or disseminate at the next seminar meeting.

CTS Professional Development Strategy Application 6
CTS Mentoring and Coaching

DESCRIPTION OF MENTORING AND COACHING AS A CTS PROFESSIONAL DEVELOPMENT STRATEGY

Mentoring and coaching are teacher-to-teacher professional development strategies that provide one-on-one opportunities for teachers to improve their practice with the help of their experienced colleagues. Mentoring usually involves an experienced teacher working with a new or novice teacher. Dunne and Villani (2007) identified four of the most important roles played by mentors. These are as follows: (1) a collegial guide, orienting new teachers to the culture of a school; (2) a consultant, working with new teachers to resolve difficulties and adopt strategies for addressing problems; (3) a seasoned teacher, offering professional insights based on extensive experience in the classroom; and (4) a coach, leading new teachers through collaborative inquiry into practice and to expand their instructional repertoire. We focus here on the fourth aspect of a mentor's role, that of instructional coach.

Beyond the induction phase, a coaching relationship can continue to be an important support for teacher development throughout one's teaching career. Such coaching involves two experienced teachers working together, with one teacher having more expertise in a certain area that can be used to support and guide the less experienced teacher. Over the years, different forms of coaching have emerged with different purposes and correspondingly different techniques. Many traditional forms incorporate a supervisory model focused on observations and use a preconference/observation/postconference cycle. More recently, coaching has shifted to focus less on a supervisory model and more on collaborative learning and provision of support to teachers who are making changes in their instructional practice at all stages of their careers (Loucks-Horsley, Stiles, Mundry, Love, & Hewson, 2010). Coaches frequently work one-on-one with a teacher directly in the classroom and meet with the teacher before or after a lesson. They also often work with small groups of teachers in planning and reflecting on lessons.

Instructional coaches may be called upon to lead groups of other teachers as they examine student work, to organize demonstration lessons, to assist with curriculum planning, and to take other actions that help teachers reach high levels of performance and use of effective practice. For example, sometimes coaches are used to support implementation of new instructional materials. They might demonstrate use of the materials in the classroom, observe and provide feedback to teachers new to the materials, and meet with the new users to reflect on student work derived from the new instructional materials.

CTS coaching addresses the recognized need for a specific focus on mathematics content knowledge for teaching and mathematics-specific pedagogy (Ball, Thames, & Phelps, 2008; West & Staub, 2003). At the elementary level in particular, new teachers are sometimes assigned mentors whose content focus is not mathematics. Although these experienced mentors can help teachers acclimate to the school and provide general instructional techniques, they are limited in how they can help with mathematics content or coach a new teacher of mathematics in effectively planning lessons that target key mathematical ideas. Likewise, general instructional coaches don't always have sufficient grounding in the mathematics content or mathematics-specific pedagogy to help their colleagues implement new instructional materials or approaches that are specific to the discipline of mathematics. Thus, rather than being a specific "model" of coaching, CTS coaching addresses the subject-specific needs of mathematics teachers. Its intent is to enhance existing coaching models to add the content specificity coaches need to support mathematics teachers to improve their practice.

CTS coaching is based on a special form of coaching called content-focused coaching (Hansen, 2009; West & Staub, 2003), in which the tools of CTS are used to support individuals or groups of teachers in designing, implementing, and reflecting on mathematics standards and developing content-rich, research-based lessons.

GOALS OF CTS COACHING

The goals of CTS coaching are

- to increase the capacity of coaches to address standards and research on learning in their work,
- to familiarize mathematics teachers with the CTS tools and resources, and
- to provide "experts at teachers' fingertips" when they have questions about mathematics content and pedagogy.

AUDIENCE

CTS coaching is designed for K–12 coaches who have been through (or are currently engaged in) professional training to become a coach and are now interested in using CTS to enhance the focus on content in their coaching work. It is also designed for people who provide training for coaches who are interested in embedding the CTS tools into their coaches' professional development programs.

STRUCTURE OF CTS COACHING

CTS coaching is guided by the Framework for CTS Instructional Coaching shown in Figure 7.3. This framework consists of

- identifying the topic of a lesson and the content one needs to know to teach it (CTS topic guide and Section I);
- an examination of the key ideas and concepts identified by the standards that are learning targets to be aligned with the lesson (CTS Sections III and VI);
- examining instructional contexts, effective strategies, relevant phenomena, connections to other ideas, and a coherent sequence of learning (CTS Sections II and V);
- learning about the research on learning in order to understand the commonly held ideas students bring to the lesson, research-identified difficulties students might have, and developmental considerations (CTS Section IV);
- examining one's own beliefs about teaching and learning;
- knowledge of one's own students' prior experiences, learning styles, preconceptions, and learning difficulties; and
- using all of the above to collaboratively plan a lesson.

The Framework for CTS Instructional Coaching is designed to be embedded into the existing coaching structure used in any school or district.

| **Figure 7.3** | CTS Instructional Coaching Framework for Mentors and Coaches |

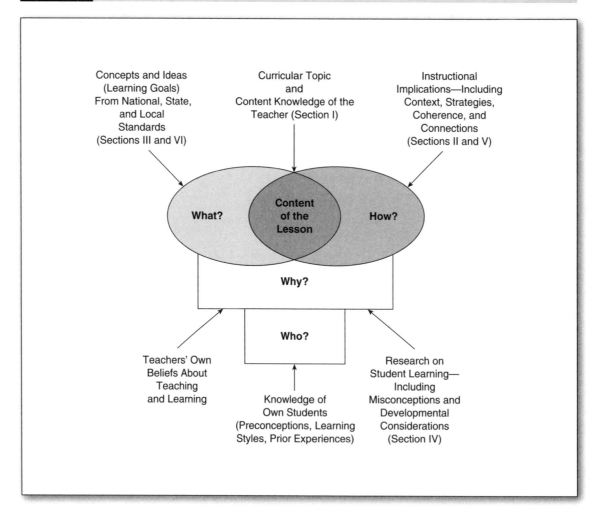

GUIDELINES FOR INTRODUCING CTS COACHING

Introducing the Use of CTS in a Coaching Context, Including the Use of the Framework for CTS Instructional Coaching

Facilitators use the session to introduce the Framework for CTS Instructional Coaching and provide coaches with an experience of applying CTS in mathematics coaching situations.

Time

Depending on participants' familiarity with CTS, this introductory session can take anywhere from 2 to 2.5 hours.

Time	Activity
5–10 minutes	Slides 1–3. Introduction/Overview
15–20 minutes	Slides 4–10. CTS Content-Focused Coaching: Characteristics, Rationale, Context
35–40 minutes	Slides 11–13. Framework for CTS Instructional Coaching and applications to coaching work
45–60 minutes	Slides 14–15. Coaching Scenario
15–20 minutes	Slide 16. Wrap-Up/Reflection

Materials Needed

- *Mathematics Curriculum Topic Study: Bridging the Gap Between Standards and Practice* (Keeley & Rose, 2006), or copies of the CTS guide "Fractions, Decimals, and Percents," page 122
- Resource books for CTS or use copies of all readings from resource books for the CTS guide "Fractions, Decimals, and Percents"
- Handout 7.6.1: Framework for CTS Instructional Coaching
- Handout 7.6.2: Instructional Coaching Questions
- Handout 7.6.3: Mathematics Coaching Scenario
- Optional: Copy of PowerPoint presentation: CTS Mathematics Coaching

DIRECTIONS FOR INTRODUCING THE USE OF CTS IN A COACHING CONTEXT

Show Slide 1 and welcome participants.

Show Slide 2 and review the goals for this session.

Show Slide 3 and explain that there are a variety of forms of coaching. Explain that these forms of coaching each serve different purposes. This session will focus on how CTS can enhance the last one of these—content-focused coaching.

Show Slide 4 and explain that CTS coaching is designed to improve teaching and promote student learning by having a coach and a teacher seeking assistance work collaboratively using the tools of CTS. Review the characteristics of CTS coaching listed on the slide. Ask if anyone has used a similar coaching model. Share examples (if any). Ask participants why content-focused coaching is needed in mathematics as opposed to, or in addition to, more generic forms of coaching. Accept responses and add to the discussion as needed, drawing on points raised under the introduction to this application, "Description of Coaching as a CTS Professional Development Strategy."

Show Slide 5 and explain that although we are calling this a "model," the CTS coaching approach is really designed to be embedded within an existing coaching model in schools and districts. Point out how the bulleted characteristics are unique to the way CTS is used in coaching. For example, coaches have access to a "tool kit" of content-specific resources used in CTS.

Show Slide 6. Explain that although this session will focus just on using the instructional planning aspect of coaching work, coaches who are familiar with CTS and the designs in this book can also lead other professional learning strategies that build community among their colleagues. Inclusion of these strategies can be thought of as a type of enhanced coaching that they might want to consider.

Show Slide 7. Reinforce the idea that "content talk" is at the core of the approach we use in CTS. Specifically, CTS provides teachers an opportunity to draw on enhanced content understanding to link learning goals for their students to research on student learning.

Show Slides 8 and 9. Point participants to the core resources used in the CTS coaching approach. Hold up a copy of each book if there are some participants who may not be familiar with them, or invite participants to take a few minutes looking through the books. Facilitator Note: If using the Common Core Mathematics Standards or the NCTM Focal Points, add these to the slides.

Show Slide 10. Discuss potential value of CTS for enhancing coaching. Ask participants who have had previous experience with CTS why they think it is so useful in working with new and experienced teachers.

Show Slide 11 and comment that a major focus of CTS coaching is on instructional planning. The Framework for CTS Instructional Coaching is designed to guide coaches in using CTS-informed instructional planning in their collaborative relationships. It shows how the sections of CTS are used along with the teachers' knowledge of their own students to plan effective lessons. Point out the framework on the slide or have everyone refer to Handout 7.6.1: Framework for CTS Instructional Coaching and review the parts of the framework and the sections of CTS that relate to each, including the following:

1. *Content of the Lesson*: Identifying the topic of a lesson and the content one needs to know to teach it (CTS guide and Section I).

2. *What Content to Teach*: An examination of the key ideas and concepts identified by the standards that are learning targets to be aligned with the lesson (CTS Sections III and VI).

3. *How to Teach Content Effectively*: Examining instructional contexts, effective strategies, relevant phenomena, connections to other ideas, and a coherent sequence of learning (CTS Sections II and V).

4. *Why Students Have Different Ideas or Learning Difficulties*: Learning about the research on learning in order to understand the commonly held ideas students bring to the lesson, research-identified difficulties students might have, and developmental considerations (CTS Section IV).

5. *Why Our Own Beliefs Can Affect How We Teach*: Examining one's own beliefs about teaching and learning (drawing on our own knowledge).

6. *Knowing Who Our Students Are as Learners*: Recognition of diversity and knowledge of one's own students' prior experiences, learning styles, preconceptions, and learning difficulties (drawing on our own knowledge or gathering additional data).

7. Using all of the above to collaboratively plan a lesson.

Show Slide 12. CTS and the Framework for CTS Instructional Coaching help coaches do these things more effectively. Distribute Handout 7.6.2: Instructional Coaching Questions and explain that these questions are based on the framework and can be used to guide coaches and their colleagues through CTS-focused instructional planning. Suggest that participants review the questions, making connections back to the framework. Ask for comments and thoughts on the framework and its applicability to their coaching work.

Slide 13. Invite participants to pause and reflect on what they have learned thus far. Ask them to summarize what the framework and instructional coaching questions provide and identify questions that need to be addressed before they practice using the framework. After 5 minutes, take time to answer questions from participants. Tell participants they will now have a chance to practice using the framework.

Show Slide 14. Distribute Handout 7.6.3: Coaching Scenario. Set the stage by reviewing the scenario and asking participants to work in pairs to use sections of CTS to plan for the lesson in the scenario. One participant will pretend to be the coach and the other the "coached." Review Handout 7.6.2: Instructional Coaching Questions, and encourage the coach to use it to guide his or her work.

Let participants know that their goal is not to come up with a fully designed lesson, but rather to engage in the steps of the lesson planning process and consult the CTS readings to gather enough information to describe what the lesson might involve. For example, when they turn to the questions related to the content of the lesson, they will look at CTS Section III or VI and ask, "What do these learning goals suggest about the content of the lesson?"

Listen in on the groups as they work. If participants are stuck, guide them in finding the right CTS section and reading or respond to their questions, as needed. Remind participants to use the questions on Handout 7.6.2 Instructional Coaching Questions to guide their planning process.

Show Slide 15. Participants reflect on their experience of using CTS as a coaching tool. Ask each pair to spend 5 to 10 minutes reflecting on their work together. Then ask several pairs to briefly share their planning with the rest of the group, using the questions to highlight how CTS informed their lesson planning, and what they found helpful.

Show Slide 16. Invite participants to consider how they might use CTS coaching in their own practice as an instructional coach or mentor. Provide a few minutes for reflective writing and then ask for volunteers to share some of their ideas.

Conclude the session by sharing any next steps such as how participants can get access to all the CTS resources so they can use the framework and the instructional coaching questions in their buildings. (Note: Point out the CTS website and show where they can access most of the CTS resources online.) Ask participants to think of how they will introduce some aspect of the CTS tools to the teachers with whom they are working.

Collect written feedback on the session using your own evaluation form.

A FINAL WORD

This chapter—and, in fact, the whole book—has many "moving parts." Detailed background information is included to share as much as we could about our own experiences with CTS. Scripts are provided for many of our designs so that facilitators will have as much guidance as we had when we field-tested the CTS designs and applications. Hundreds of handouts, examples, and facilitator resources are included on the CD-ROM. We encourage you to use any and all of these materials to the extent that they work for you and to adapt them to your own style, interest, and audience. Our ultimate goal is not that the particular materials are used exactly as we have suggested, but rather that leaders have many varied designs, tools, and resources to help teachers develop and use the specialized professional knowledge of mathematics content and pedagogy. Through the many activities in this book, we think that is quite possible. Please let us know what you discover as you use CTS and this guide and share any new ideas and designs with us by visiting the website www.curriculumtopicstudy.org.

References

Achieve, Inc. (2010). *Comparing the common core state standards in mathematics and NCTM's focal points.* Retrieved from http://www.achieve.org/CCSSandFocalPoints

Allen, J. (2007). *Inside words: Tools for teaching academic vocabulary, Grades 4–12.* York, ME: Stenhouse Publishers.

American Association for the Advancement of Science. (1989). *Science for all Americans.* New York: Oxford University Press.

American Association for the Advancement of Science. (1993). *Benchmarks for science literacy.* New York: Oxford University Press.

American Association for the Advancement of Science. (2001). *Designs for science literacy.* New York: Oxford University Press.

American Association for the Advancement of Science. (2001–2007). *Atlas of science literacy* (Vols. 1–2). New York: Oxford University Press.

American Association for the Advancement of Science. (2009). *Benchmarks online.* Retrieved from http://www.project2061.org/publications/bsl/default.htm

Ball, D. L., Thames, M. H., & Phelps, G. (2008). Content knowledge for teaching: What makes it special? *Journal of Teacher Education, 59,* 389–407.

Beane, J. (Ed.). (1995). *Toward a coherent curriculum.* Alexandria, VA: Association for Supervision and Curriculum Development.

Birman, B., Desimone, L., Garet, M., & Porter, A. (2000). Designing professional development that works. *Educational Leadership, 57*(8), 28–33.

Bransford, J., Brown, A., & Cocking, R. (2000). *How people learn.* Washington, DC: National Academies Press.

Brown, C., Smith, M., & Stein, M. (1996, April). *Linking teacher support to enhanced classroom instruction.* Paper presented at the annual meeting of the American Educational Research Association, New York, NY.

Carroll, C., & Mumme, J. (2007). *Learning to lead mathematics professional development.* Thousand Oaks, CA: Corwin.

Cohen, D., & Hill, H. (1998). *Instructional policy and classroom performance: The mathematics reform in California.* Philadelphia: Consortium for Policy Research in Education.

Cohen, M., & Hill, H. (2000). Instructional policy and classroom performance: The mathematics reform in California. *Teachers College Record, 102*(2), 294–343.

Danielson, C. (1996). *Enhancing professional practice: A framework for teaching.* Alexandria, VA: Association for Supervision and Curriculum Development.

Darling-Hammond, L. (2000). Teacher quality and student achievement: A review of state policy evidence. *Education Policy Archives, 8.* Retrieved from http://epaa.asu.edu/epaa/v8n1

Donovan, M. S., & Bransford, J. D. (Eds.). (2005). *How students learn: Mathematics in the classroom.* Washington, DC: National Academies Press.

DuFour, R., & Eaker, R. (1998). *Professional learning communities at work.* Bloomington, IN: National Educational Service.

DuFour, R., Eaker, R., & DuFour, R. (Eds.). (2005). *On common ground: The power of professional learning communities.* Bloomington, IN: National Educational Service.

Dunne, K., & Villani, S. (2007). *Mentoring new teachers through collaborative coaching: Linking teacher and student learning.* San Francisco: WestEd.

Eaker, R., DuFour, R., & Burnette, R. (2002). *Getting started: Reculturing schools to become professional learning communities.* Bloomington, IN: National Educational Service.

Erickson, L. (1998). *Concept-based curriculum and instruction.* Thousand Oaks, CA: Corwin.

Feger, S., & Arruda, E. (2008). *Professional learning communities: Key themes from the literature.* Providence, RI: Brown University. Retrieved from www.alliance.brown.edu/db/ea_catalog .php

Fosnot, C., & Dolk, M. (2001). *Young mathematicians at work: Constructing number sense, addition, and subtraction.* Portsmouth, NH: Heinemann.

Fosnot, C., & Dolk, M. (2002). *Young mathematicians at work: Constructing fractions, decimals, and percents.* Portsmouth, NH: Heinemann.

Fosnot, C., & Dolk, M. (2004). *Fostering children's mathematical development.* Portsmouth, NH: Heinemann.

Fosnot, C., & Dolk, M. (2006). *Fostering children's mathematical development K–8.* Portsmouth, NH: Heinemann.

Fosnot, C. T., Dolk, M., Cameron, A., & Hersch, S. (2004–2006). *Young mathematicians at work: Professional development materials* (15 CDROM Learning environments and Facilitator Guides). Portsmouth, N.H.: Heinemann Press.

Frayer, D. A., Frederick, W. C., & Klausmeier, H. J. (1969). A schema for testing the level of concept mastery. *Technical Report No. 16.* Madison: University of Wisconsin Research and Development Center for Cognitive Learning.

Garmston, R. J., & Wellman, B. M. (2008). *The adaptive school: A sourcebook for developing collaborative groups* (2nd ed. with CD-ROM). Norwood, MA: Christopher-Gordon.

Goldhaber, D. D., & Brewer, D. J. (2000). Does teacher certification matter? High school teacher certification status and student achievement. *Educational Evaluation and Policy Analysis, 22*(2), 129–146.

Griffin, P., & Madgwick, S. (2005). *Multiplication makes bigger and other mathematical myths.* Sowton, UK: DCS Publications.

Hansen, P. (2009). *Mathematics coaching handbook: Working with teachers to improve instruction.* Larchmont, NY: Eye On Education.

Hord, S. M. (1997). *Professional learning communities: Communities of continuous inquiry and improvement.* Austin, TX: Southwest Educational Development Laboratory.

Hord, S. M., & Sommers, W. A. (2008). *Leading professional learning communities: Voices from research and practice.* Thousand Oaks, CA: Corwin.

Jacobs, H. H. (2004). *Getting results with curriculum mapping.* Alexandria, VA: Association for Supervision and Curriculum Development.

Jolly, A. (2007). *Building professional learning communities.* Retrieved from http://www .edweek.org/chat/transcript_11_19_2007.html

Keeley, P. (2005). *Science curriculum topic study: Bridging the gap between standards and practice.* Thousand Oaks, CA: Corwin.

Keeley, P. (2007). *Science formative assessment: 75 practical strategies for linking assessment, instruction, and learning.* Thousand Oaks, CA: Corwin.

Keeley, P., & Rose, C. M. (2006). *Mathematics curriculum topic study: Bridging the gap between standards and practice.* Thousand Oaks, CA: Corwin.

Keeley, P., & Rose Tobey, C. (2011). *Mathematics formative assessment: 75 practical strategies for linking assessment, instruction, and learning.* Thousand Oaks, CA: Corwin.

Kennedy, M. (1999). Form and substance in mathematics and science professional development. *NISE Brief, 3*(2), 1–7.

Learning Forward. (2011). *Standards for professional learning.* Retrieved from http://www .learningforward.org/standards/learningcommunities/index.cfm

Lee, V. E., Smith, J. B., & Croninger, R. G. (1995). *Another look at high school restructuring: Issues in restructuring schools.* Madison: Center on Organization and Restructuring of Schools, School of Education, University of Wisconsin–Madison.

Lipton, L., & Wellman, B. (2003). *Data-driven dialogue: A facilitator's guide to collaborative inquiry.* Sherman, CT: MiraVia.

Lipton, L., & Wellman, B. (2004). *Pathways to understanding: Patterns and practices in the learning-focused classroom* (3rd ed.). Sherman, CT: MiraVia.

Loucks-Horsley, S., Hewson, P. W., Love, N., & Stiles, K. E. (2010). *Designing professional development for teachers of science and mathematics* (3rd ed.). Thousand Oaks, CA: Corwin.

Loucks-Horsley, S., Love, N., Stiles, K. E., Mundry, S., & Hewson, P. W. (2003). *Designing professional development for teachers of science and mathematics* (2nd ed.). Thousand Oaks, CA: Corwin.

Loucks-Horsley, S., Stiles, K. E., Mundry, S., Love, N., & Hewson, P. (2010). *Designing professional development for teachers of science and mathematics* (3rd ed.). Thousand Oaks, CA: Corwin.

Love, N., Stiles, K. E., Mundry, S., & DiRanna, K. (2008). *The data coach's guide to improving learning for all students: Unleashing the power of collaborative inquiry.* Thousand Oaks, CA: Corwin.

Marks, H. M., Louis, K. S., & Printy, S. M. (2000). The capacity for organizational learning: Implications for pedagogical quality and student achievement. In K. Leithwood (Ed.), *Understanding schools as intelligent systems* (pp. 239–265). Stamford, CT: Jai Press.

Marzano, R., Pickering, D., & Pollock, J. (2001). *Classroom instruction that works: Research-based strategies for increasing student achievement.* Alexandria, VA: Association for Supervision and Curriculum Development.

McLaughlin, M. W., & Talbert, J. (2001). *Professional communities and the work of high school teaching.* Chicago: University of Chicago Press.

Merseth, K. (1996). Cases and case methods in teacher education. In J. Sikula (Ed.), *Handbook of research on teacher education* (2nd ed., pp. 722–744). New York: Simon & Schuster Macmillan.

Miller, B., & Kantrov, I. (1998). *A guide to facilitating cases in education.* Porstmouth, NH: Heinemann.

Monk, D. H. (1994). Subject area preparation of secondary mathematics and science teachers and student achievement. *Economics of Education Review, 13,* 125–145.

Mundry, S., Keeley, P., & Landel, C. (2010). *A leader's guide to science curriculum topic study.* Thousand Oaks, CA: Corwin.

Mundry, S., & Stiles, K. E. (Eds.). (2009). *Professional learning communities for science teaching: Lessons from research and practice.* Arlington, VA: NSTA Press.

Murphy, C. U., & Lick, D. W. (2001). *Whole-faculty study groups: Creating student-based professional development.* Thousand Oaks, CA: Corwin.

National Council of Teachers of Mathematics. (2000). *Principles and standards for school mathematics.* Reston, VA: Author.

National Council of Teachers of Mathematics. (2003). *Research companion to principles and standards for school mathematics.* Reston, VA: Author.

National Council of Teachers of Mathematics. (2006). *Curriculum focal points for prekindergarten through Grade 8 mathematics.* Reston, VA: Author.

National Governors Association Center for Best Practices, Council of Chief State School Officers. (2010). Common core state standards for mathematics. Washington, DC: National Governors Association Center for Best Practices, Council of Chief State School Officers. Retrieved from http://corestandards.org

National Research Council. (1996). *National Science Education Standards.* Washington, DC: National Academy Press.

National Research Council. (2002). *Investigating the influence of standards.* Washington, DC: National Academy Press.

National Research Council. (2007). *Taking science to school: Learning and teaching science in Grades K–8.* Washington, DC: National Academies Press.

National Staff Development Council. (2001). *Standards for staff development.* Oxford, OH: Author.

Nikula, J., Goldsmith, L., Blasi, Z., & Seago, N. (2006). A framework for the strategic use of classroom artifacts in mathematics professional development. *NCSM Journal of Mathematics Education Leadership, 9*(1), 57–64.

Organization for Economic Cooperation and Development. (2003). *Glossary of statistical terms.* Retrieved from http://stats.oecd.org/glossary/index.htm

Paulos, J. (1992). *Beyond numeracy.* New York: Vintage.

Rose, C., & Arline, C. (2009). *Uncovering student thinking in mathematics, grades 6–12: 30 formative assessment probes for the secondary classroom.* Thousand Oaks, CA: Corwin.

Rose, C., Arline, C., & Minton, L. (2007). *Uncovering student thinking in mathematics: 25 formative assessment probes.* Thousand Oaks, CA: Corwin.

Rose Tobey, C., & Minton, L. (2011). *Uncovering student thinking in mathematics, K–5: 25 formative assessment probes for the elementary classroom.* Thousand Oaks, CA: Corwin.

Saginor, N. (2008). *Diagnostic classroom observation: Moving beyond best practice.* Thousand Oaks, CA: Corwin.

Schmoker, M. (2004). Tipping point: From feckless reform to substantive instructional improvement. *Phi Delta Kappan, 85*(6), 424–432.

Seago, N., Mumme, J., & Branca, N. (2004). *Learning and teaching linear functions.* Portsmouth, NH: Heinemann.

Shulman, L. S. (1986). Those who understand: Knowledge growth in teaching. *Educational Researcher, 15*(2), 4–14.

Smith, M. S. (2001). *Practice-based professional development for teachers of mathematics.* Reston, VA: The National Council of Teachers of Mathematics.

Sparks, D. (2002). *Designing powerful professional development for teachers and principals.* Oxford, OH: National Staff Development Council.

Wei, R. C., Darling-Hammond, L., Andree, A., Richardson, N., & Orphanos, S. (2009). *Professional learning in the learning profession: A status report on teacher development in the United States and abroad.* Dallas, TX: National Staff Development Council.

Weiss, I. R., Gellatly, G. B., Montgomery, D. L., Ridgeway, C. J., Templeton, C. D., & Whittington, D. (1999). *Executive summary of the local Systemic Change Through Teacher Enhancement Year Four cross-site report.* Chapel Hill, NC: Horizon Research.

Weiss, I. R., Pasley, J. D., Smith, P. S., Banilower, E. R., & Heck, D. J. (2003). *Looking inside the classroom: A study of K–12 mathematics and science education in the United States.* Chapel Hill, NC: Horizon Research.

West, L., & Staub, F. (2003). *Content-focused coaching: Transforming mathematics lessons.* Portsmouth, ME: Heinemann.

Wiggins, G., & McTighe, J. (2005). *Understanding by design* (2nd ed.). Alexandria, VA: Association for Supervision and Curriculum Development.

Wiley, D., & Yoon, B. (1995). Teacher reports on opportunity to learn: Analyses of the 1993 California learning assessment systems. *Educational Evaluation and Policy Analysis, 17,* 355–370.

Yetkin, E. (2003). *Student difficulties in learning mathematics* (ERIC Document No. ED482727). Retrieved from http://www.ericdigests.org/2004-3/learning.html

Index

CORWIN
A SAGE Company

The Corwin logo—a raven striding across an open book—represents the union of courage and learning. Corwin is committed to improving education for all learners by publishing books and other professional development resources for those serving the field of PreK–12 education. By providing practical, hands-on materials, Corwin continues to carry out the promise of its motto: **"Helping Educators Do Their Work Better."**

WestEd, a national nonpartisan, nonprofit research, development, and service agency, works with education and other communities to promote excellence, achieve equity, and improve learning for children, youth, and adults. WestEd has 16 offices nationwide, from Washington and Boston to Arizona and California. Its corporate headquarters are in San Francisco. More information about WestEd is available at WestEd.org.

- **Vision**: The Maine Mathematics and Science Alliance endeavors to enhance science, technology, engineering, and mathematics education to elevate student aspirations and achievement, so all students will meet or exceed state and national standards.
- **Mission**: The MMSA will provide and conduct research, development, and implementation strategies, and form active partnerships to support excellence in STEM curriculum, instruction, and assessment in schools and districts for educators at all stages of their careers.
- **Beliefs**: All activities of the Maine Mathematics and Science Alliance (MMSA) are based on five core beliefs. They are:
  - Strong mathematics and science content knowledge and the skills of inquiry and problem solving.
  - Data-informed planning and decision-making.
  - Research based instructional practice and professional development.
  - Equity of opportunity.
  - Rigorous alignment with state and national standards.